MINGULAY

MINGULAY

An Island and Its People

Ben Buxton

BIRLINN

To Caroline

This edition published in 2016 by
Birlinn Limited
West Newington House
10 Newington Road
Edinburgh
EH9 1QS

www.birlinn.co.uk

ISBN 978 1 78027 304 4

British Library Cataloguing-in-Publication Data
A catalogue record for this book is available from the British Library

Typeset by Initial Typesetting Services, Edinburgh
Printed and bound by Grafica Veneta, Italy

Contents

List of Illustrations & Maps

List of Maps

'Deserted Village on Mingulay'
From a photograph by Margaret Fay Shaw Campbell

Not far had men's hands to raise from the stony ground
Blocks the ice and rain had hewn.
The dry-stone walls of the houses of Mingulay still stand
Long after the sheltering roof is gone.
Not far had the heather thatch to blow back to the moor.

Children were born here, women sang
Their songs in an ancient intricate mode
As they spun the wool of sheep on the hill
By a bog turf fire hot on the swept hearth-stone.
Earth's breast that nourished and warmed was near
As cow-byre and lazy-bed
Made fertile with sea-wrack carried up from the shore
In creels of withies cut in a little glen,
Near as shelter of hill-side, fragrance of clover-scented air.

Not far had the dead to go on their way of return,
Not far had the circle of the old burial-ground
Whose low wall sets its bound to encroaching wild
That never has put on pride of human form,
Worn face of maiden or fisherman, mother or son.
Never far the washer of shrouds, the hag with grey hair;
Yet those who here lived close to the mother of all
Found, it may be, in her averted face, little enough to fear.

Kathleen Raine

Notes to readers
To minimise referencing, reference numbers are not generally given
where the source, if in published form, is quoted in the text; the
reader can refer direct to the bibliography. If no source is given
for details of the islands' histories, the information has been ob-
tained verbally from the people of Barra and Vatersay listed in the
Acknowledgements.

The forms of Gaelic place names used, if found on the Ordnance
Survey maps, are those given on the maps.

Preface to the new edition

This revision incorporates some of the remarkable discoveries resulting from archaeological fieldwork, and from research in newly available documentary material, since 1995. In that time the internet revolution has transformed historical research, and some of the new material is online. The main revisions have been to the historical chapters, 2, 4, 13 and 14, and to chapters 15 and 16, Berneray and Pabbay. The most important new sources are as follows.

Study of the physical remains of the human past through archaeological fieldwork has transformed our knowledge of the human history, of all periods, of the three islands. The archive of the antiquary and folklore collector Alexander Carmichael is now accessible online, and the notes he made on ancient sites and the historical traditions about them he recorded in the 1860s and '70s are published here for the first time. The records of the Barra Head Lighthouse not only document the lighthouse, with insights into the lives of the resident population, but are also the only source for the evictions of the people of all three islands in the 1830s; this is the first publication to make use of this material. Old newspapers are now not only online but searchable too, and they have provided details of incidents and court cases for which no other evidence has so far been found.

I have made use of the published research of Professor Keith Branigan on General Roderick MacNeil, his chemical factory, and emigration from the islands in the early nineteenth century. I have revised chapter 13 in the light of my own research for *The Vatersay Raiders*. In that book I covered Sandray in more detail, in places, than I did in the first edition of *Mingulay*, and for that reason, and because historically Sandray was more closely associated with Vatersay, I have dropped it from this edition. I welcome the publication of *Muinntir Mhiughalaigh* by Lisa Storey on the culture and oral tradition of the Mingulay people, her ancestors.

There is more interest in the islands from the outside world than ever. This is partly due to their purchase, in 2000, by the National Trust for Scotland, a recognition of the islands' exceptional cultural and natural heritage. The Trust has initiated research into the heritage, which is now safeguarded for the future.

Ben Buxton, 2016

Acknowledgements

I would like to thank Mary Kate MacKinnon for her help in the preparation of this revision, and I am also grateful to the following: Susan Bain, Professor Ewen Cameron, Professor Hugh Cheape, Dr Barbara Crawford, Piers Dixon, George Geddes, Jonathan Grant, Dr Alex Hale, Jill Harden, Andrew Kerr, Father Michael MacDonald, Calum MacNeil, Professor Andrew Newby, Dr Daniel Rhodes, Ian Riches, Magdalena Sagarzazu, Dr Anke-Beate Stahl, Dr Andrew Wiseman. I am of course responsible for any errors. I am grateful to Lesley McClymont for making available to me the research material gathered by her late husband, John MacInnes, on Berneray, the island of his ancestors. I would like to thank Hugh Andrew and Andrew Simmons of Birlinn for providing the opportunity to revise this book.

Ben Buxton, 2016

Photograph Credits:
Plates 3, 5, 6, 7, 8, 9, 10, 11, 12, 13, 14, 15 and 19 are by Robert M. Adam; plates 23, 24, 25, 26 and 27 are by R.M.R. Milne; plate 1 is by William Norrie (published in Harvie-Brown and Buckley 1888); plate 18 is by Margaret Fay Shaw; plate 31 is by Erskine Beveridge; the remainder are by Ben Buxton.

For permission to reproduce material I am grateful to the following: Comunn Eachdraidh Bharraigh agus Bhatarsaigh (plate 24 and Appendix 5); Edinburgh University (quotations from the Carmichael Watson Archive); HarperCollins Publishers Limited and the estate of Dr Kathleen Raine (the poem 'Deserted Village on Mingulay'); Historic Environment Scotland (plate 31); the Keeper of the Records of Scotland (material in the National Records of Scotland); the estate of Teresa MacNeil (Neil MacPhee's letters and song); the Trustees of the National Library of Scotland (plate 20, and Hector MacLean's letters); the Trustees of the National Museums of Scotland and Alasdair MacRae (letters of John Finlayson and Morag Campbell Finlayson); National Trust for Scotland (plates 23, 25, 26, 27); Roberton Publications ('Mingulay Boat Song'); St Andrews University (Robert M. Adam photographs); School of Scottish Studies, Edinburgh University (tape recordings of Mingulay people and quotations from Tocher); Scots' College, Rome (letters of Fr N. MacDonald).

Preface to the 1995 edition

My interest in Mingulay goes back to 1975 when, aged sixteen, I stayed there during one of many summers spent wandering in the Outer Hebrides. In 1980 I carried out an archaeological survey of the village area for a student dissertation, and some years later I embarked on what has become this book, focusing on the more recent history. Despite the remarkable amount of information which has emerged, I am aware that the book is still only a beginning, for research of this kind, using written sources, oral history and fieldwork, can never end. Being a non-Gael has been a handicap as regards my understanding of a distinct culture, and I have been unable to make full use of the potential of oral history.

This book is in fact about four islands: it includes, more briefly, the three other formerly inhabited islands south of Barra – Berneray, Pabbay and Sandray. These islands were closely associated with Mingulay, but very much less is recorded of, or known about, their histories.

Over the years, I have received help from a huge number of people, too many for me to mention them all by name. They have helped in various ways, including providing information and advice about the islands, and places and people connected with them; suggesting sources; making material available; advising on, and translating, Gaelic; and commenting on drafts of text. I am particularly indebted to the following: Dr Alan Bruford and Ian Fraser, School of Scottish Studies; Dr John Lorne Campbell, Canna; Hugh Cheape, National Museums of Scotland; Patrick Foster, University of Sheffield;

Andrew Kerr, Barra; and Ian MacDonald, Gaelic Books
Council.

I am indebted also to the people of Barra and Vatersay for
sharing their heritage with me, an outsider with no island
connections. Without their marvellous support this book
would be much the poorer, but I hope they will forgive what
will be, for them, its inevitable shortcomings. Special mention
must be made of Mary Kate MacKinnon, Glen, and I am
also grateful to the following: Peggy Ann Campbell, Vatersay
Village; Donald Ferguson, Borve; Morag MacAulay and
the late Calum MacAulay, Castlebay; Ishabel MacDougall,
Glen; Morag MacDougall, Caolis; the late Nan MacKinnon,
Vatersay Village; Archie MacLean, Skallary; Donald Mac-
Lean, Eoligarry; the late Jonathan and Marion MacLean,
Uidh, both formerly of Mingulay; Mary MacLean, Eoligarry;
Calum MacNeil, Nask; Catriona MacNeil, Vatersay, formerly
of Mingulay; Catriona MacNeil, formerly of Kentangaval;
John MacNeil, Nask; John Alan MacNeil, Castlebay; Mary
Ann MacNeil, Vatersay; Morag MacNeil, Garrygall; Neil
MacNeil, Castlebay; Teresa MacNeil, Bruernish; Roderick
MacNeil, Kinloch; Margaret Nixon, Uidh; the late Donald
Sinclair, Garrygall; and Lisa Storey, formerly of Vatersay.
I would also like to thank Mary Sinclair, Registrar, Father
Donald MacKay, Roman Catholic priest, and Rev. Dr Donald
Greer, Church of Scotland minister. I am grateful to Richard
Langhorne of Museum nan Eilean, Stornoway, and Mary
Kate MacKinnon for enabling me to work on an exhibition
about Mingulay as part of a student project in 1991, when
some of my work in Barra was undertaken.

I would also like to thank: Colin Archer, Lisbon; Eve
Beadle, Bruton; Derek Cooper, Richmond; Trevor Cowie,
National Museums of Scotland; Rev. Dr Mark Dilworth and
Dr Christine Johnson, respectively former and present Keepers
of the Scottish Catholic Archives; Professor Alexander Fenton,
Dr Margaret MacKay, and Donald Archie MacDonald, School
of Scottish Studies; Lesley Ferguson, RCAHMS; Noel Fojut,

Historic Scotland; Angie Foster, Barra; Fiona Gorman, Arran; Eleanor Hunter, Glasgow; Bill Lawson, Genealogy Research Service for the Western Isles; Rev. Alan Macarthur, Lochcarron; Dugald MacArthur, Connel; Dr Martin MacGregor, Museum Sgoil Lionacleit; Ian Maciver, National Library of Scotland; Fiona MacLeod and Robert Steward, Highland Regional Archives, and their predecessors at Inverness Public Library; Alasdair MacRae, Dunblane; Helen Murchison, Achintraid; Joan Murray, Scottish Natural Heritage; Rev. Douglas Nicol, Church of Scotland, Edinburgh; Robert Smart, St Andrews University; and Francis Thompson, Stornoway. To the staff of various other collections of material, and to other individuals who have helped, I extend my thanks.

Finally, I must thank my parents, for always supporting my Hebridean ventures. Above all, I must thank my wife, Caroline, with whom I have shared many happy times in the islands, for her support, ideas on innumerable drafts of text, and for giving me time off from family responsibilities.

1

'The Nearer St Kilda'

Away beyond Skye, and seen from it in misty outline
on the edge of the ocean, stretches a series of islands
from the Butt of the Lews to Barra Head . . . As seen
on the map the group looks like a stranded ichthyo-
saurus of geological times, the Lews forming its skull,
the Uists its chest, and the Barra Isles the detached
vertebrae of its lower spine.

At the very point of the saurian tail rises the rocky
islet of Bernera, terminated by the grand cliff, where
gleams the lighthouse of Barra Head. Immediately to
the north of this island there hides a larger island called
Minglay. It bears a population of interesting people
having the least possible intercourse with the outer
world, to which it is almost unknown even by name.
The other islands between Barra Head and Barra are
tenanted only by the lightkeeper and his family, and
by sheep and cattle and their few attendants. Minglay
thus forms an isolated colony in the Atlantic, in all respects a nearer St. Kilda, as remarkable for sea scenery,
solitariness, self-containedness, and the peculiarities
thence arising, as the more popular place of pilgrimage.

With these stirring words William Jolly introduced his article
'The Nearer St Kilda: Impressions of the Island of Minglay',

published in 1883. It is fitting to quote this introduction to the first and only comprehensive description of the island when it was inhabited. Mingulay is indeed comparable to St Kilda, one of the best known and most written-about of Scotland's islands, 64 kilometres (40 miles) west of the Outer Hebrides.

Mingulay is the last but one of the chain of small islands forming the southern end of the Outer Hebrides (also known as the Western Isles and, in the past, the Long Island) which form the northwesterly bastion of Scotland (map 1). In size, 4 kilometres (2½ miles) long, north to south, and 3 kilometres (1¾ miles) wide, it is the second largest of the five principal islands south of Barra: Vatersay, Sandray, Pabbay, Mingulay and Berneray. From the sea, however, it appears to be the biggest, as Vatersay, though having a larger surface area, looks like two small islands, having a low and narrow middle; and Mingulay is much the highest of the five islands, rising to 273 metres (891 feet). This accounts for the probable origin of the name Mingulay (Mhiùghlaigh in Gaelic) – 'Big Isle' in Old Norse. Mingulay, Berneray and Pabbay have most in common with each other in terms of remoteness, physical features and recent human history, and they have been owned by the National Trust for Scotland since 2000. Sandray is different in many ways and, being nearer to Vatersay and Barra, was more influenced by those islands historically.

The islands are part of Barra Parish, described in 1847 as 'composed of a cluster of islands surrounded by a boisterous sea, making the passage from one island to another a matter of very considerable hazard'.[1] There is another group of small islands off the northeast coast of Barra which, being close to Barra and sheltered by it from the Atlantic, have a different character from the southern isles. The whole group is known as the Barra Isles. All five of the southern islands were inhabited into the twentieth century, Mingulay latterly having by far the largest population; but since 1912, when Mingulay was finally abandoned, only Vatersay has had a permanent population. Several of the islands off the northeast of Barra

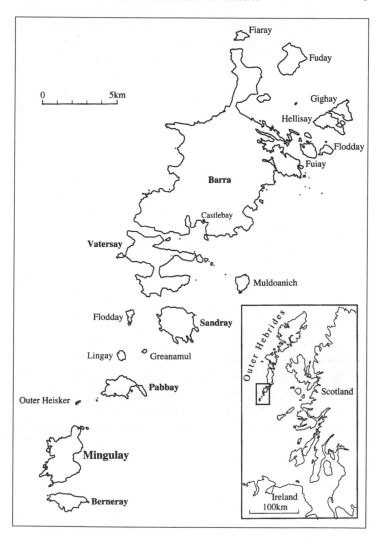

Map 1. The Barra Isles

were also inhabited, though none continuously in the eighteenth and nineteenth centuries. The 'capital' of the parish, since the later nineteenth century, has been Castlebay, where the castle of the MacNeils of Barra commands an islet in one of the best natural harbours in the Hebrides.

Mingulay's shape was likened by Jolly to a 'rude figure eight written with a shaky pen' (map 2). The broad eastern indentation is Mingulay Bay (Gaelic, Bàgh Mhiùghlaigh), called Church Bay by Jolly; at its head is a fine sandy beach, and above that, and now partially buried in it, the remains of the village. Lush green pasture, the former fields of the inhabitants, extends inland into a broad glen enclosed by an amphitheatre of barren hills. Starting at the southeast of this arc, they are Hecla (Shecla), a pleasing cone, rounded Càrnan, the highest at 273 metres (891 feet), joined by a ridge to rugged MacPhee's Hill (Cnoc Mhic a Phi) on the north. North of MacPhee's Hill a narrow bulge (the 'Ard') forms the northern point of the island, and a fourth hill, though much lower, is Tom a' Reithean. The southern and eastern slopes of the hills descend fairly gently to the sea, and a small valley, Skipisdale (Sgiobasdail), opens onto the south coast. Most of the western and northern slopes, by contrast, are truncated abruptly by tremendous sea cliffs, eaten away by the incessant pounding of the Atlantic.

The cliffs are Mingulay's most notable feature, first described in awesome terms in 1840.[2] The highest of these, Biulacraig or Aoineig (also called Eagle Cliff),[3] reaches 229 metres (753 feet), and as late as 1878 was thought to be the highest sea cliff in Scotland.[4] It is exceeded in western Scotland only by those of St Kilda. The cliff features on the crest of the MacNeils of Barra, and 'Biulacraig' formed the rallying cry of the clan.[5] The top of it can be seen from Barra, including parts of Castlebay. Jolly described it thus:

> It rises from the Atlantic in an unbroken wall facing the north . . . It consists of layer upon layer of thick bedded gneiss, traversed by numerous veins of red felspar and by a broad basaltic dike which has thrust itself through the strata with volcanic power. In

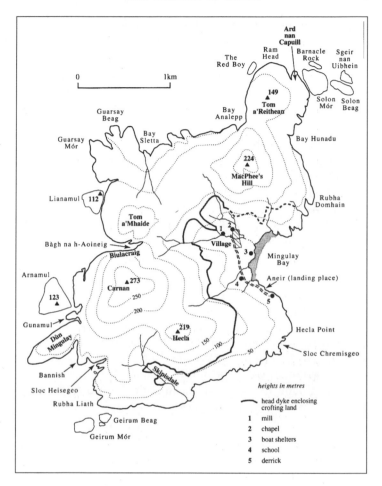

Map 2. Mingulay at the time of its desertion

front of it and running parallel to it, a lower cape
juts out into the ocean, separated from the Aonig by
a narrow ravine, into which the sea rolls hundreds
of feet below. This cape forms an admirable point
for seeing the rock ... There the mighty vertical
precipice towers right in front of you, revealed from

base to summit, ledge above ledge, in inexpressible grandeur.

The narrow ravine or chasm mentioned by Jolly, between the cliff and Tom a' Mhaide, was jumped by the principal character in a local story, one Iain Og. He was the son of one of the MacNeils of Barra. The site of this feat was known as Leum Iain Oig, 'Young John's Leap'. [6]

While the cliffs may not be the highest in Scotland, the cliff scenery rivals any. 'It is hardly possible to point out a scene more worthy of being visited for grandeur and variety than that of these rocks, particularly during the months of June and July', wrote Alexander Nicolson, minister of Barra, in 1840, referring to the 'innumerable tribes of aquatic fowls' with which they are festooned in the summer. A feature of the cliff-bound coastline is the number of deep chasms with which it is riven, and the interplay of chasms, promontories, and precipitous sea stacks provides an endless variety of dramatic vistas. This is especially so at the southwest end where the peninsula of Dun Mingulay (Dùn Mhiùghlaigh) and the stack of Arnamuil enclose an inlet into which a precipitous peninsula, Gunamuil, protrudes.

Through the neck of this headland, the sea had, wrote J. Wedderspoon after a visit early last century:

> cut a winding tunnel about 60 to 70 feet in height, and 50 yards in length. The mouth of the tunnel looked black and forbidding, strange noises issued from it magnified by countless echoes; sea-birds in myriads poured from the opening, their clamour barely heard in the babel of sounds. The sea chafed and churned with the strife of conflicting currents in the narrow channel, and as the boatmen half shipped their oars under the gloomy archway, the warning injunction on 'Dante's Inferno' occurred to my mind. Fending the boat off the opposing rock

with the oars, we glided into the unknown. The
black walls rose perpendicular from the depths
below, and disappeared into the impenetrable darkness overhead . . . with a sigh of relief we emerged
from that battlefield of titanic forces . . .

According to Jolly, the caves and arches 'are called by the
natives *cailleach,* or "old woman". When the sea rushes into
one of them, it causes a concussion of air and water which
results in a kind of deep hollow snort and upward rush of
spray, which is picturesquely described by the natives as "the
old woman taking snuff!"'

The cliffs of Mingulay and Berneray are among the most important breeding grounds for seabirds in the west of Scotland,
ranking with the outliers of the main Outer Hebridean chain
such as St Kilda, North Rona, the Flannans, and others. Fifteen
species of seabirds breed on the islands. The most numerous
are as follows, with breeding numbers recorded on Mingulay
in 2015: razorbill, 11,336; common guillemot, 16,474;
northern fulmar, 6,315; black-legged kittiwake, 1,627; and
Atlantic puffin, 855. Mingulay and Berneray together have
the largest colony of razorbills in the British Isles, about 15
per cent of the European population; the majority of these are
on Berneray. In addition to these five, ten other species of seabirds breed on the islands: storm petrel, common and arctic
terns, great skua, black guillemot, European shag, and four
species of gull: common, herring, greater and lesser black-
backed.[7] Since 2011 a few pairs of gannets have nested on
Berneray and raised chicks. The nearest colony is St Kilda, so
presumably they came from there. Manx shearwaters, which
the people had caught for food and used for paying the rent,
inhabited the summit of the stack of Liànamuil (123 metres,
368 feet) until the late eighteenth century, when they were
driven away by puffins. 'The natives, in revenge,' wrote the
naturalist Harvie-Brown in 1887, 'have extirpated them on
the larger stack of Arnamul, in order to preserve the grazing

for about a score of sheep.' Birds are attracted not only by
the cliffs and coastal rocks and caves for nesting sites, but by
the rich fish supply in the area, where the currents of the Sea
of the Hebrides and the Atlantic meet.[8] As in St Kilda, the
birds and their eggs were an important source of food for the
islanders, who also sold their feathers for cash.

The stacks attracted attention much earlier than the cliffs
of the main island. One of them is presumed to be the 'Scarpa
Vervecum, i.e. of wethers' referred to by Buchanan in 1592;
the name is Latin meaning 'green stack' or 'green scarp', the
'wethers' meaning the sheep which grazed their summits.
Martin Martin, about 1695, described fowling operations
on Liànamuil, and in 1794 MacQueen wrote: 'Close by the
island of Mingalay is a high rock, with very luxuriant grass
growing on the top of it. The inhabitants of this island climb
to the top at the risk of their lives, and by means of a rope
carry up their wedders to fatten.'

Harvie-Brown considered Liànamuil

> the most densely packed guillemot station he had ever
> seen, owing to the unsurpassed suitability, regularity,
> depth and number of the breeding ledges, along many
> of which two men could crawl abreast on hands and
> knees, with a roof of solid rock above . . . the top of
> the stack is tunnelled and honeycombed by puffins
> . . . and over their heads waves a dense crop of red-
> seeding sorrell in summer. Later in the year the whole
> surface is one sticky compound of mud and dung,
> feathers, bad eggs, and defunct young puffins ankle
> deep or deeper [a wonderful fertiliser, if only it were
> accessible]. Formerly [continued Harvie-Brown] the
> stack was reached by a suspended rope-bridge from
> the mainland across the great chasm, but for many
> years back it has been reached at a landing place, and
> by a severe climb, only in exceptionally fine weather,
> from the seaward side, near the southern extremity.

This 'rope-bridge' may in fact have been a rope of horse-hair tied to the mainland, by which, tradition has it, one could swing out over the abyss onto the stack. The rope was secured to the top of the cliff, and by climbing down to a lower level, one swung over to a place on the rock wall opposite.

The cliffs are not only striking visually: the roar of the sea, the cacophony of the birds, wheeling about or sitting on the ledges, and the smell of their guano, are all part of the experience. It was Alexander Carmichael's opinion that 'There is probably no more interesting island in Britain than this Island of Miuley [an anglicised spelling of Mingulay's Gaelic name, Mhiùghlaigh], with its wonderful precipices, long narrow sea galleries, several hundred feet high in the perpendicular sides, and marine arcades, winding their gloomy subterraneous ways under the precipitous island. To boat through these galleries and arcades needs a calm sea, a good crew, and a steady nerve.' Writing in 1883, he claimed to be 'the first to discover, and the first and last to go through much the longest, largest, and gloomiest of these wonderful sinuous sea arcades'.

According to local tradition, French gold intended for Prince Charles's army in the Highland uprising of 1745 is supposed to have been hidden in a sea cave on the west coast. This provides the basis for Neil Munro's novel *Children of Tempest*, the climax of which involves an imaginary climb on the cliffs.

Mingulay's name has been given to a remarkable cold-water coral reef complex in a wide trench in the seabed to the east, the nearest point being 13 kilometres (eight miles) from Mingulay. During a seabed-mapping programme in 2003, huge mounds up to 150 metres (500 feet) high were discovered, at depths of between 100 and 250 metres (330–800 feet). Further investigation showed that they were made up of the coral *Lophelia pertusa*. It is the only such reef complex in UK inshore waters, and it was designated as the East Mingulay Special Area of Conservation in 2013.[9]

Mingulay's appeal was, and is, due not only to its intrinsic attractions, but also to its remoteness and inaccessibility. It was described in 1897 as 'an island so remote that it is easier to reach America than to get there'.[10] To do so from Barra, 19 kilometres (12 miles) distant, one has to contend with the fierce tide races between the islands, as well as with the often unpredictable and rapidly changing state of the Atlantic and of the weather. In the days of the oar and the sail these were major considerations. But that is not all. There is no sheltered landing place on the island. Mingulay Bay, where the landing places are, is exposed to the wind and the swell from most directions except the west, and getting ashore was, and still is, a matter of jumping onto rocks; the inhabitants had to land their boats on the beach. They were often cut off for weeks on end, and even today, though motorboats make getting there easier, a landing is still dependent on the state of the swell.

The young naturalist Theodore Walker described his journey south from Barra (along the west side of the intervening islands, it being more usual to keep to their east) in the lighthouse mail boat, in June 1869:

> We have passed Pabba's precipices and are in the Sound of Mingalay, where the billows of the Atlantic, meeting the waves and tide of the Minch, the tide running like a mill-race, the huge waves are humbled, and in rage and despair are leaping, foaming, tumbling and whirling us close under a reef of rocks . . . The foam is dashed in our faces, as, encased in waterproofs from head to feet, I clench my teeth and grasp the tiller.
>
> Rory says it is impossible to reach Barra Head today, as wind and tide are against us, and as we have manfully battled with wind and tide for six long cold hours, we are unwilling to turn back. Rory says he can land us on Mingalay; there are two men there who can speak English, and we can get shelter, and cross over the Sound of Bernera to Barra Head if the

weather moderates ... A quarter of an hour's cold wet sail, with the salt foam in our faces – an indistinct black mass rises, seemingly pressed down by the weight of clouds; it is the beetling cliffs of Mingalay. A white gleam of sand in a sheltered nook, on which the ground swell is heavily breaking, a few battered boats drawn up, a black amphitheatre of hills, and we catch a dim outline of a group of huts as we sail past. Into a sheltered cove Rory glides, and as the boat is lifted on the wave we spring out, catching and dragging out our gun-cases and impedimenta. A parting cheer to Rory, and here are we on a barren island, on which no strangers have landed for more than a year.

While Mingulay Bay can provide shelter from westerly gales for boats at sea, landing on the beach is another matter. Under the heading 'Ship's boat swamped, with melancholy loss of life', the *Scotsman* reported on 6 March 1839:

On the 16th of February, the *Herriot Rockwall* of Portsmouth, New Hampshire, from Liverpool to Boston, of 450 tons, with a general cargo on board, was seen from Barrahead Lighthouse with her sails spent, and American colours reversed, in token of distress. Signals were made from the lighthouse, and the vessel was brought to an anchor between the Island of Barrahead and Mingalay. The ship's boat was immediately put out, when Mr Jewett the commander, the second mate and four of the crew attempted a landing at Mingalay. There is not one upon that island who can speak English, and the master of the Rockwall, mistaking the signals of the natives, directed the boat upon a sandy beach instead of toward a small creek, where a safe landing might have been effected. The consequence was that the boat swamped, and was turned over and over by the

heavy swell, when all on board unfortunately per-
ished. One man, after a severe struggle, got so near
the shore that the inhabitants, joining hands, formed
a line through part of the surf, and had nearly got
hold of him when a heavy rolling sea carried him
off for ever . . . Mr Reid, the principal lighthouse
keeper, mustered such assistance for a crew among
the islanders, and got the sails so repaired, as enabled the mate to carry the ship to Tobermory.

An idea of the violence of the sea and wind in the area is
gained by the fact that the cliff tops of Mingulay and Berneray
are drenched with salt spray in times of storm, and in about
1868 a huge wave washed right over the islet of Gearuim Mòr,
51 metres (167 feet) high, between Mingulay and Berneray,
taking sheep with it. During a storm in 1836 a block of rock,
estimated to be 504 cubic feet (142 cubic metres) in volume
and 42 tons (42,672 kg) in weight, was moved by the sea
5 feet (1.5 metres) from where it lay on the coast of Berneray.[11]

In terms of its size, cliffy bird-inhabited coastline, eastward
facing glen, bay and village, formerly-inhabited secondary
valley, and inaccessibility, Mingulay was and is a 'nearer St
Kilda', or rather, a nearer Hirta, the principal island in the
group. The rather austere and forbidding grandeur of Village
Bay, Hirta, however, finds no parallel in Mingulay, which is
altogether more welcoming if less impressive. There were sim-
ilarities in some aspects of the way of life of the islanders too,
which was part of the lure for visitors to both islands. Visitors
often compared the two, as we have seen; Harvie-Brown found
Mingulay 'of fresher interest, and much more primitive than St
Kilda, especially as regards the cottars' and crofters' houses'.

Geologically, the Outer Hebrides are composed of Lewisian
gneiss, a hard, acidic, metamorphic rock which represents the
roots of a mountain chain once extending through Greenland
and North America before being split up by continental drift in
more recent geological times. The rock is the oldest in Britain,

and amongst the oldest in the world, around three thousand million years old. The banded and twisted gneiss bears witness to its tortuous history of deep burial in the earth's crust and metamorphosis by tremendous temperatures and pressures. In places the gneiss has developed into so-called 'flinty crush rock' associated with a major fault running east of the islands, and actually running through the east side of Sandray giving that side its distinctive appearance. In Mingulay, Berneray and Pabbay the layered gneiss tilts from west to east, which partly accounts for the islands' distinctive profiles. Lines of weakness in the rock caused by joints are exploited by marine erosion to form deep chasms, promontories and, ultimately, stacks (precipitous islets) where the line of weaker rock has been eroded away completely. Vertical intrusions of softer igneous rocks (dykes) are likewise eroded out. The peninsulas of Gunamuil and Dun Mingulay owe their existence partly to a dyke, forming their necks, and in time they too will become stacks.

During the Ice Age (the last phase of which ended about 10,000 years ago) the islands were scoured and smoothed by ice sheets moving west from the Scottish Highlands, and south and east from the Outer Hebridean ice cap. Existing east–west valleys and other lines of weakness were gouged out and deepened, and when sea level rose after the Ice Age – a process continuing to this day – the deeper valleys were flooded to form the present-day sounds. The ice deposited boulder clay on the islands, and this survives in the area around Mingulay Bay, and southwards to Skipisdale, and on the north coast of Berneray. The boulder clay contains mainland rocks, and this accounts for the presence of 'alien' material, including large blocks, on the islands.[12]

The rock and the wet climate together are responsible for the barren aspect of the islands, typical of the Outer Hebrides as a whole. The gneiss is impermeable and weathers to form a thin acidic infertile soil which accumulates in depressions leaving a good deal of rock bare. However, much of Mingulay is covered in peat. This has formed from decaying vegetation which, because of the impermeability of the rock and the heavy rainfall, does not decompose but gradually builds up to depths of up to two metres. The peat was cut as fuel by the islanders. The main features of the islands' climate are rain and wind. Rainfall, while not as high as on the mainland, is spread fairly evenly throughout the year; winds are predominantly southwesterly and frequently blow as gales, especially in winter. Summer and winter temperature variations are not great, and snow and frosts are not common.

The peat supports the maritime grassland and heath characteristic of the Outer Hebrides – composed of heather, sphagnum moss, sedges and grasses. There are no trees, the only representative of that class on Mingulay being a species of poplar (aspen) growing to about half a metre (2 feet) in height on a cliff above the beach. This, and ivy, rose and wood horsetail also found there in 1938, were thought to be survivals of formerly more extensive woodland; none of them were recorded in 1985. Other notable plants are the sea holly, which is very rare in the Outer Hebrides, and was noted as early as 1883 by Jolly; and the sea milkwort, which is normally found at sea level, but grows on the high cliff-tops because of the spray and seagull manure. Since 1938 heather, which was formerly rare, and bracken, have increased, while weeds associated with cultivation have decreased or disappeared.[13]

Around Mingulay Bay the heathland gives way to the greenery of the former croftlands of the inhabitants. Here the soil is based on boulder clay and shell sand blown from the beach, and some of it was fertilised and cultivated for generations. The inland margins of the area, defined by the head dyke, are returning to a heathland state in places. This process has accelerated since 1998, when the sheep, which maintained the grassland, were removed.

The varied summer flowers are a delight. The green pastures around the bay are spangled with buttercups, daisies, birdsfoot trefoil, ragged robin, silverweed and yellow flag (iris); while on the heathland are marsh orchids, scabious and sundew.

Mingulay and Berneray together were created a Site of Special Scientific Interest in 1983.[14] It is a grade 2 site (on a scale of two) of national importance on account of its maritime and paramaritime vegetation, rocky shore and cliff habitats, and the seabirds. The islands are the only ones in the main Outer Hebridean chain to be described as 'oceanic' in ecological terms, and to be designated in this way; they are thus comparable to the outliers of the main chain such as St Kilda and others mentioned above.[15] Their designation in 1994 as a Special Protection Area, on account of the seabird colony, tightens planning controls further and restricts the kinds of activities permitted on the islands. The SPA was extended in 2009 to include two kilometres of the adjacent marine environment to better protect the seabirds at sea.

An interesting feature of the bay is the accumulation of sand and its penetration inland. Above the high water mark of the beach there is a large area of sand rarely, if ever, covered by the sea. The Ordnance Survey maps of 1878 and 1901 show the high water mark in the same position as it is now (map 3), yet the photograph of 1887 (plate 1) shows the sea lapping the edge of the village, while showing a ridge of sand where the map marks high water mark. Today the stream drifts over this dry part after heavy rain, and the sea occasionally forms small pools where the stream has lowered the surface. This part of the beach is bounded to its north by a system of dunes, and the sandy area continues inland to the west for some distance, up to a height of about 30 metres (100 feet). The high proportion of sand in the soils inland show that sand has been blown inland over a long period, and this is also shown by the fact that a midden of Iron Age date, approximately 2,000 years old, rests on sand. There has been appreciable change since 1912 in two respects. The lower parts of the village have been overwhelmed by up to a metre and a half (5 feet) of sand; there is no sign of sand in the photographs of 1887 and 1905, but by 1922 the advance had begun. The movement of sand in the village had ceased by the 1970s, and vegetation

has stabilised it. The other change has been the development
of sand dunes on the north side of the beach, partly on areas
of sloping land surface, partly on the dry part of the beach.
These dunes developed dramatically in the 1950s and 60s,
and have now been largely stabilised by marram grass. There
has been similar accumulation of sand on the east coasts of
Pabbay and Sandray, and there are beaches on the east coast
of Vatersay. This contrasts with the main islands of the Outer
Hebrides from Barra northward, where most of the sandy
beaches are on the west coasts.

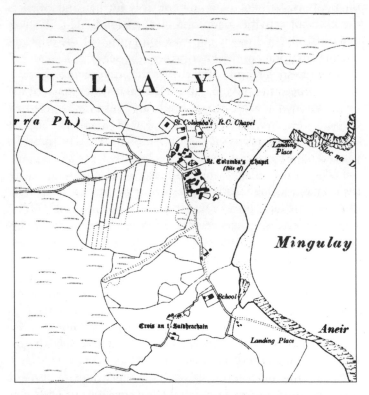

Map 3. Mingulay Village and its environs in 1901 (reproduced to
scale from the 6 inch to 1 mile Ordnance Survey map. The name
Crois an t-Suideachain refers to the three symbols 1cm to the east.)

This is the scene on which the human story of the island is set, a story that began perhaps 5,000 years ago. What is the evidence for this story?

Until Mingulay appears in the historical record in the sixteenth century, much of the evidence is archaeological. Thereafter, there is a remarkable amount of documentation for such a small and relatively insignificant island, making Mingulay amongst the best documented of those islands in the Outer Hebrides which have been inhabited in recent times. It is this, as much as the story of the island itself (which in many respects was representative of the Barra Isles as a whole), which makes Mingulay remarkable. In this respect, too, Mingulay is comparable to St Kilda; the amount of documentation, however, is very much smaller than for St Kilda, which was much better known and easier to get to by the later nineteenth century. St Kilda has many detailed contemporary accounts written both by visitors, some of whom stayed for long periods, and by resident incomers; and there is more information recorded by or from the islanders, who were evacuated in 1930.[16]

From 1549, when it was first mentioned, until the mid nineteenth century, little is recorded for individual islands, and most of what there is is ecclesiastical. One well-known contemporary account is that of Martin Martin, about 1695. He was a native of Skye, and as such one of the few native writers about the Hebrides. He has a good deal to say about Berneray or Mingulay, perhaps both, clearly derived from hearsay and much of it of dubious reliability; there are enough indications to make it very likely that Mingulay was intended, but one can't be sure. It is a pity he did not visit the islands personally as his own descriptions of other islands are apparently much more reliable.

During the nineteenth century the fingers of state bureaucracy began to penetrate the remotest corners of the British Isles, and interest of a scientific nature was awakening. Communications were improving, breaking down the barriers of isolation, and the opening of the Barra Head lighthouse on Berneray in 1833 drew attention to the area and made travel south of Barra easier. The result was an explosion of information relating to Mingulay; there are visitors' accounts of Berneray as well, but not for Pabbay or Sandray, and much less in the way of other records, folklore, and oral tradition. The bulk of this book, therefore, covers the last fifty or so years of the Mingulay community's life.

There are three main types of evidence: records of government and other organisations, visitors' and other contemporary accounts, and local sources. The first state-initiated records of the smaller islands are the detailed censuses which began nationally in 1841, and were taken every ten years subsequently; they record details of individuals as well as housing. National registration of births, marriages and deaths began in 1855, though there are church registers from 1805; and the first Ordnance Survey was conducted in 1878. By the end of the century there are records and accounts relating to education, the church, crofting, fishing, health, and the Barra Head lighthouse; and, in the twentieth century, records of the desertion.

The scenery, natural history, and archaeology of the Outer Hebrides, and the way of life of the inhabitants, which had remained backward in the material sense compared to the mainland, began to attract travellers during the nineteenth century. The Mingulay visitors we know about – those who wrote about their experiences – were a varied and sometimes colourful lot, all sharing a determination to get there against all odds.

The seabirds on the cliffs attracted natural historians from the 1860s. Captain Elwes visited in 1868, the young Walker brothers in 1869, and J.A. Harvie-Brown in 1870 and again in 1887, gathering material for his book on the fauna of the Outer Hebrides. In the latter year he brought his own photographer, William Norrie of Fraserburgh, who took the earliest known photograph on the island (plate 1). Harvie-Brown made friends with Mingulay's schoolteacher, John Finlayson, with whom he later corresponded. Robert Adam, the botanist and celebrated photographer of the Scottish scene, spent a week in Mingulay in June 1905 with his brother James and a friend, Charlie Watt. At first they camped, but when the weather deteriorated they moved in with John MacLean (Barnaidh; Iain Chaluim Iain) and his family.[17] Adam's main interest was in the flora and fauna, but he also took the marvellous photographs of human interest illustrating this book, the only ones known of the island when it was inhabited, apart from Norrie's and those taken by Milne in August 1909.[18] Adam's photographs are a great tribute to his skill and determination. He was only nineteen at the time, and the apparatus – heavy box camera, tripod, and hundreds of glass plates – was heavy and cumbersome. Getting photographs of people who were no doubt apprehensive and suspicious was a great achieve-ment, as was the photographing of seabirds in perilous places on the cliffs, with no telephoto lens to help him. Adam paid a second visit in 1922 when only ruins remained.

The folklore of the Outer Hebrideans was the subject of much interest from the 1850s, when it was realised that they had retained much more than people on the mainland, whose knowledge of traditional lore was fast dying out. A collector for John Francis Campbell of Islay visited Mingulay in 1860, and Campbell himself visited later. Alexander Carmichael was the first outsider to take an interest not only in the folklore but also in the history and antiquities of the island. He vis-ited on numerous occasions from 1865 onwards. T.S. Muir, the antiquary, visited very briefly in 1866, and was the first visitor to publish an account of the contemporary inhabitants and the island's antiquities. Father Allan McDonald of South Uist and later Eriskay was also interested in the folklore and antiquities, and visited on a number of occasions between 1884 and his death in 1905.

Another visitor with an ostensible interest in folklore was Ada Goodrich-Freer. She visited in 1898 and wrote an account quoting a number of historical stories. She was in

fact on a secret mission to seek evidence of 'second sight' in
the Hebrides, on behalf of the Society for Psychical Research.
She also purported to be a medium and a clairvoyant, but
she was eventually exposed as a fraud and had to flee from
England in 1901. Many years later, it was discovered that she
was a fraud in another sense – much of the material she published as her own had been pirated from other collectors.[19]
Her Uist and Barra material was collected mainly by Father
Allan McDonald, of whose assistance and good faith she
took advantage. The Mingulay stories she quotes were almost
certainly recorded by him, perhaps at the time of her visit;
she had no Gaelic and did not reveal in her book that Father
Allan accompanied her on her visit to Mingulay.

Several supporters of Mingulay's Free Church school visited it in the 1860s, and William Jolly visited in 1878 and
1879, and possibly later, in his capacity as school inspector.
Mrs Frances Murray, her husband and daughters were early
examples of tourists, landing from their schooner in 1888.

Most of the contemporary accounts of the way of life of the
islanders, while being important sources of detail, suffer from
their being based on only very brief visits, and being coloured
by the romanticism, prejudices and ignorance of their authors.
Most of the visitors were non-Gaels writing for geographi-
cally, and culturally, distant readers, or, in Murray's case, an
actual audience – her account was written as a lecture. Hers
and Jolly's accounts in particular are aimed at portraying the
islanders in ways to suit their purposes. In some cases, details
can be shown to be wrong, where there are other sources of
evidence. It is not only the outsiders' accounts that cannot
be relied on absolutely; all the sources of evidence need to be
considered in the context in which they were produced.

Local sources should be the best in any study of local history. There are few contemporary native sources, but we are
fortunate in that tape recordings of several Mingulay people
talking about life there were made in 1960 in Vatersay. They
were made by Lisa Sinclair of Vatersay whose father, Duncan

Sinclair, was one of the first of the 'Vatersay raiders' from Mingulay. She was then working at the School of Scottish Studies in Edinburgh, and spent a holiday at home recording people who had left Mingulay in their youth fifty years before (see Appendix 4). She wanted information of a general nature about the way of life of the islanders, and in this she was in advance of her time, for in those days interest in oral tradition in Scotland still concentrated on folklore, stories, songs and music. It was only nine years since the School of Scottish Studies had been established to collect and study such material. Her interest in her people's heritage was also unusual for this period.

The tape recordings relate to the last decade or two of the community's life, and in some cases they refer back to the informants' grandparents' generation. Although details are sometimes contradictory, they are almost our only native source, without which our knowledge would be much poorer. They are, of course, in Gaelic, and many terms, some used in a way unique to Mingulay, have thus been preserved. The recordings were the first, and for many years the last, attempt to record something of a vanished community and way of life. The last person who knew Mingulay as a resident, Flora Gillies, died in 1999. She was born in Mingulay in 1901 and left in 1908 when her family moved to Sandray and later to Vatersay. There remains a great deal of knowledge among the people of Barra and Vatersay, many of whom are of Mingulay descent. Other local sources include the letters of Neil MacPhee, letters written by, or rather on behalf of, other islanders at the time of the desertion; the petition for landing facilities; and the letters of the schoolteacher John Finlayson. As mentioned above, there are also the historical traditions, stories, songs, and other folklore recorded from Mingulay people. The oral history, whether recorded directly from Mingulay people or by an intermediary, is as interesting for what it includes as for what it does not. For instance, there is no reference to the clearance of the people of Mingulay and its neighbours in the 1830s, or of known events such as the drowning of six sailors trying to land in 1839.

In the early 1980s a local history society, Comunn Each-draidh Bharraigh, was formed in Barra, a result of the growing collective interest of the islanders in their heritage; the annual Gaelic festival, the Fèis, another expression of the revival of interest in the heritage, started at about the same time.[20] This was part of a movement in the Outer Hebrides in general, and further afield. The society mounted an exhibition on the history of Mingulay in 1992, and has held events and exhibitions since then. Dualchas, the heritage centre in Castle Bay, opened in 1996. The National Trust for Scotland has encouraged interest in the heritage of the islands since it bought them in 2000.

From these various sources, and from what is known of the islands in general, we learn something of the Mingulay community in its last few centuries, and particularly in its last few decades. Until the nineteenth century it was basically self-sufficient, but dependence on the outside world steadily increased, particularly when the population rose after the is-land was resettled following the evictions of 1835. The people lived by fishing, raising crops and animals, and fowling. They had a rich oral culture, and were devout Roman Catholics. A school was established by the Free Church in 1859, and this was succeeded by a state school. In the later nineteenth century fishing became an important industry, but the fish-ermen were handicapped by their isolation and the lack of an adequate landing place. Pressure on the land grew with the rising population, which reached a peak of over 160 in the 1880s, and the village became overcrowded and insanitary. Conditions deteriorated, and in 1907 desperate Mingulay men took the law into their own hands and followed Barra men in grabbing land on Vatersay. For this they were tried and imprisoned, but they won the land and settled there. By 1912 Mingulay was deserted. The story is in many respects unique, but it is also an example of life in the Barra Isles as a whole; and in a broader sense, it illustrates many themes of Highland and Island history and society.

2

Early Times

> The antiquities of these islands are really interesting
> and the more they are investigated the more inter-
> esting they become.

These words, written by Alexander Carmichael, folklorist
and antiquarian, of the Outer Hebrides in 1867, are as true
now as they were then.[1] Our knowledge of the cultural heritage of Mingulay, in terms of physical remains, has been
transformed by the archaeological surveys carried out by
the University of Sheffield in the 1990s and by the Royal
Commission on the Ancient and Historical Monuments of
Scotland (RCAHMS) in the 2000s.[2] There remains much to
learn however. Prior to these surveys, the Ordnance Survey
in 1878, and the RCAHMS in 1915, noted three ancient
sites: Dun Mingulay, the site of St Columba's Chapel, and
the enigmatic Crois an t-Suidheachain. The Ordnance Survey
carried out further brief surveys in the 1960s and 70s. The
present writer surveyed the settlement evidence, of all periods,
in the area around Mingulay Bay in 1980. Before the Sheffield
work there had been no archaeological excavation, although
a prehistoric stone object was found during a soil survey in
1975, and Iron Age pottery was found by a party of students
digging into a midden in 1971.

The recent surveys have revealed that Mingulay has over 400 sites, the highest density of all the southern islands, ranging in date from prehistoric up to the early twentieth century. However, from surface inspection alone, it is often difficult or impossible to identify or date man-made structures, because stones from early structures have been reused over time on the same sites, or removed to be reused nearby. In some cases therefore, sites have been interpreted or classified differently by different investigators. For instance, some of the structures on the high ground on the west of the island were identified by Sheffield surveyors as a distinct type of Bronze Age burial monument but as relatively recent platforms for peat stacks by the RCAHMS. In formerly cultivated areas, piles of stones may be just that: field clearance cairns rather than remains of actual constructions. The widespread development of peat since the second millennium BC has obscured many inland sites and formerly cultivated areas, and looking further back, earlier prehistoric coastal sites have disappeared due to rises in sea level.

Despite these problems, however, it is possible, from evidence from the island and from what is known of the prehistory of the Outer Hebrides as a whole, to hazard guesses about Mingulay's early inhabitants. Mingulay must always have been attractive to settlement, with its variety of food resources – fish, shellfish, seabirds – land for grazing and cultivation, and a beach for landing on. Although it is now regarded as relatively remote and inaccessible this was not so in the past, when the sea was a highway rather than the barrier it was to become in more recent times.

Somebody was the first person ever to set foot on the island. Who was it? The earliest signs of possible human activity in the Outer Hebrides date to the later Mesolithic period, about 6,500 BC, in South Uist. Here there is botanical evidence of clearance of the scrubby woodland covering the islands at that time, which is presumed to have been by human agency, creating clearings to attract red deer. These islanders were not necessarily the first, for there is evidence of earlier occupation of some of the Inner Hebridean islands: Islay and Tiree about 10,000 BC and Rum around 8,000 BC. They were hunter-gatherers who probably moved seasonally according to the availability of food, such as shellfish, or the resources of the woodland inland. In the Inner Hebrides many shell middens – rubbish dumps composed mostly of shells, the live parts of which had been eaten – of Mesolithic culture survive on coastal sites, because there relative sea level has fallen; but in the outer islands coastal sites would have been lost due to the rise in sea level since the last Ice Age. The rise could have been by up to five metres (16 feet) since 3,000 BC.

Agriculture, animal domestication and the more settled lifestyle characteristic of the Neolithic period reached the outer islands around 4,000 BC. The earliest evidence of human occupation of Barra is shortly after that date, at Allt Easdal. The best known legacy of the Neolithic, the megalithic or chambered tomb, is well represented in Barra.[3] These tombs originally consisted of a chamber or passage of (sometimes massive) upright blocks of stone, roofed with transverse blocks, covered with a mound of stone or earth. They were communal burial chambers serving families or groups of families. No definite tombs have been identified on Mingulay, although two or three sites incorporate massive stones which may be the remains of such tombs.[4] Berneray has a possible chambered tomb.

Possible evidence of early cultivators on Mingulay was found during a soil survey of the area around the bay in 1975.[5] In many of the survey pits charcoal was found, all well below the present surface. The charcoal was of heather, rank grasses and dwarf willow – similar, with the exception of the dwarf willow, to the present-day vegetation higher up the valley sides. The low level above bedrock of these charcoal layers, and the presence of layers of large stones above them, may suggest that the charcoal resulted from heath fires – on those sites or higher up – perhaps started by human agency

to improve grazing, or to clear vegetation in advance of cultivation. The stony layers may result from the breaking up
of the soil by early cultivators, and its movement downhill
over time; or they may be the natural results of erosion of soil
exposed by the removal of the vegetation.

Deep down in one of these pits, in the flat floor of the
main valley, an exciting find was made: a fragment of worked
stone. The stone is a portion of an originally lozenge-shaped,
flattened beach pebble of local stone, 11 centimetres (4 inches)
wide. A conical depression was sunk into the opposing flat
sides, such that they almost meet in the middle. The stone appears to have broken during the making of these depressions,
which were intended to join up to make a hole through it. The
stone belongs to an enigmatic class of object known as pebble
hammers. They are not closely datable, and examples found
over northern Britain date from as early as the Mesolithic
down to the Bronze Age. Some complete specimens were
clearly hafted and shaped to be used as axes, but it is hard
to imagine the intended function of the Mingulay stone.
The pebble hammer was found at a depth of 60 centimetres
(2 feet), 20 centimetres above bedrock. Immediately above
bedrock was a layer of coarse stones and some charcoal.
Above this was a finer layer in which the stone was found;
above this was another coarse stony layer, and then the main
depth of sandy soil. The land where the stone was found is
slightly elevated within the valley floor, so that downward
movement of material from the valley sides would not affect
it. Possibly the stone and its context are associated with the
introduction of agriculture.

The introduction of new religious and social practices,
as well as new material culture, marks the beginning of the
Bronze Age around 2,500 BC. Communal burial in chambered
tombs was replaced by single burials in stone cists, often
under cairns. A Bronze Age cairn has been identified north of
Hecla Point near the southeast coast. It is six metres (20 feet)
in diameter and its edge is marked by a low kerb of stones.[6]

Such kerbed cairns are found in the Western Isles and on the mainland. They were built throughout the Bronze Age until about 1,000 BC, and where excavated, often contain cremated human remains in a pit or cist. There are no convincing standing stones or stone circles, although there is a circular arrangement of stones on the south coast. Pottery that may date to the Bronze Age was found in the excavation of a mound in Mingulay Bay, as discussed below.

After the uncertainties of the earlier prehistoric occupation of Mingulay, we are on firmer and more certain ground in the Iron Age, the period from about 500 BC to about AD 500 in the islands. Four roundhouses have been identified in Skipisdale, the southern valley, where there are abundant remains of built structures and field systems (plate 22). The buildings are concentrated in two complexes, one on the north side of the stream draining the valley (where there were two adjacent roundhouses),[7] and one on the south.[8] The roundhouses are up to 12 metres (39 feet) in diameter with stone walls up to two metres thick, and standing more than a metre in height in places. They would have had conical thatched roofs. Stones from the roundhouses have been reused over time to build irregular clusters of smaller structures, in some cases joined together. Some of these may have been sheiling huts from relatively recent times (see below). A team from Sheffield University conducted a small excavation in the southern complex, and identified three building phases. The earliest was the roundhouse, which may have been of the 'wheelhouse' type, in which the interior is divided up into sections by lengths of radial walling, like the spokes of a wheel. In the second phase, sub-rectangular buildings were built over and outside the east wall of the wheelhouse. Finally, a small sub-rectangular building was built adjacent to the west wall of the roundhouse. The roundhouse, constructed of massive blocks, appeared to have been built on an earlier mound. Iron Age pottery has been found in soil ejected from rabbit burrows at both sites. The southern complex is enclosed within a large semi-circular enclosure, probably for livestock, the stream draining Skipisdale completing the enclosure.

The fourth roundhouse in Skipisdale is high up on the north side of the valley. Stones from it have likewise been reused for various structures, the most recent being a pen for a ewe and a lamb in the 1920s or 30s.[9] There is a complex system of field walls in Skipisdale, and some of them were probably contemporary with these houses. Some of the stone dykes are buried in peat and the vegetation they enclose is heathland so it is a very long time since they were used for cultivation or pasture (see below).

There could be many more Iron Age houses on Mingulay. The RCAHMS identified twelve sites as 'settlement mounds', these being multi-period sites occupied over long periods. They are grass-grown mounds of stone and soil, up to 20 metres (65 feet) across and 1.8 metres high. Most of them are situated in the Mingulay Bay area and Skipisdale, and the eastern slopes of Hecla between the two.[10] One of them, in the sandy area east of the Chapel House on the edge of the village, was excavated in 1996 as part of the Sheffield University work. The site has been known about for many years, as the western edge has been exposed by erosion. The visible eroded section, with pottery, burnt stone, charcoal, animal bones and shells eroding out of it was a typical midden deposit, representing domestic occupation debris and food waste. Some students from London University excavated part of it in 1971, and recovered typical Hebridean Iron Age pottery.[11]

The Sheffield archaeologists excavated the eroding western section down to the underlying sand. The midden material was in two distinct layers, and within these there were layers of wind-blown sand. There were sections of walling at various levels and it is likely that the site had been a roundhouse. The pottery sherds had mostly come from bucket-shaped cooking vessels. Some pieces had been decorated with incised lines and cordons (raised bands of clay). The decorated pottery, from the upper levels of the site, is datable to approximately

200 BC to AD 100. Some of the sherds from the lower layer could be Early Bronze Age in date (c.2500–1500 BC). The midden deposits lay directly on a sandy surface on which there were grooves created by ploughing. This showed that this sandy area had been cultivated in prehistoric times, and that it became the site of a rubbish dump soon after it was last ploughed. A fragment of saddle quern – a stone with a depression worn in it by the action of grinding grain with a smaller stone – found in the eroding face of the midden in 1980 shows that the creators of the midden were growing grain.

The animal bones found represented the remains of animals that had been eaten, and some of the bones bore butchery marks. Sheep were the most common, and a high proportion had been killed as young lambs. Cattle were also eaten very young. It was common practice in the Highlands and Islands until recent times to slaughter stock in the autumn, because of the lack of grazing or fodder over the winter. Also present, in very small numbers, were bones of red deer (perhaps imported as a joint from elsewhere, such as South Uist), common and grey seals, and pigs. Fish bones were of species which could be caught close inshore, using lines from the shore or from small boats: tope, conger eel, pollack, cod, saithe, sea bream, ballan wrasse, ling. Bones of five species of bird were found: duck, Manx shearwater, cormorant, shag and great black-backed gull. The faunal assemblage at the Mingulay site was broadly similar to other excavated contemporary sites on Pabbay, Sandray and Barra, although no cetacean (whale) remains were found at Mingulay, unlike the other sites. However, the proportion of very young sheep and cattle was much higher than at other sites and it was considered that a farming economy based on slaughtering animals so young was unsustainable. The specialist analysing the assemblage considered it 'very unusual' and 'perplexing'. However, the excavated area was very small and the bones recovered may not be a representative sample from which to draw conclusions. The proportion of fish bones suggested that fish were not a major part of the diet, but the same caveat about the sample applies; small fish bones were not recovered because sieving was not used. Shells of shellfish were not mentioned in the report, but were abundant; a sample taken in 1980 included mussels, scallops and limpets.

The site lies in an area which appears to have been occupied over a long period in prehistoric and perhaps later times. Pieces of worked flint, burnt stone, animal bone, shells, and sherds of crude pottery abound; stone structures, including field walls, are being exposed by shifting sand. Flint pebbles occur naturally in the islands, brought from the mainland by ice sheets. Most of the finds of worked flint are undatable but one piece is characteristic of the late Neolithic and early Bronze Age. The use of flint continues into the Iron Age in the islands.

Another Iron Age site is the mound on which the post-medieval settlement described below is built. This site matches the description of a place recorded by Alexander Carmichael from information from a local informant in 1867: 'Totachain Ghreotais, the remains of some large circular building. Circumference 16 yards. On the side of a hill facing the sea – southeast. The foundations visible only on lower side. Over this and behind, the remains seven shielings. On low side the foundations visible about 2 feet.' Totachain (correct spelling Tobhtaichean) means ruin of a building, or wall ledge.[12] Although the site is bigger than noted even if the 16 yards refers to diameter rather than circumference, parts of an arc of walling are visible on the north and east sides. It is very likely to have been a roundhouse, and Iron Age pottery has been found there.

Further ancient finds were described in 1911 by a Mr Wedderspoon, a sanitary inspector. He described a shell midden adjoining, or perhaps forming part of, the knoll occupied by the graveyard; it contained shells, split bones, teeth, 'hammerstones split by fire', and two 'basin stones', presumably saddle querns or trough querns, which are similar. No sign of this midden remains. He also recorded the discovery of a small stone bowl and what appear to have been querns, during the digging of the foundations of the modern chapel, which, he said, was 'on the site of an older building, of which nothing remained but a shapeless heap of stones'. Saddle and trough querns are normally thought to be prehistoric, but the presence of a trough quern in a village house, and of another outside a house on Berneray, may indicate otherwise. Goodrich-Freer also mentions the finding of 'stones and ashes' on the site of the chapel, and pottery was found in soil survey pits in 1975. This site was clearly occupied sometime in the past, perhaps in prehistoric times, perhaps in medieval times prior to the legendary 'plague', which will be discussed in the next chapter. In 1898 Father Allan McDonald examined 'ashpits of old village that existed before the plague killed off all the inhabitants – found a broken spoon of bone and lots of rough clay pots'.[13] He was not referring to the modern chapel site, so he may have meant Wedderspoon's midden.

A site usually ascribed to the Iron Age is Dun Mingulay, the cliff-bound peninsula at the southwest end of the island.[14] Dun means fortification, (in Gaelic it can also mean 'fortified place'), and duns are the most common and most visible type of ancient monument in the Hebrides. They are massively built, often with double walls with a gallery between, in easily defendable positions. They are usually roughly circular, and in some cases, known as brochs, the walls were carried up to a considerable height. In the larger islands, Atlantic round-houses, as duns and brochs are collectively called, are spaced out in their own 'territories', but the smaller islands generally only have one (Vatersay has two, but it may have been two separate islands at that time).[15] Mingulay is exceptional among the main islands south of Barra in that it does not seem to have had an Atlantic roundhouse. The name 'Dun Mingulay' refers to the peninsula and not to a structure. There is merely a short stretch of walling on top of a natural rock face across the narrow neck of the peninsula; in places it is a couple of metres (6 feet) thick and now less than one metre in height. If it is Iron Age the site would be termed a promontory fort. Dun Mingulay could have served as a refuge, for people or livestock, in an emergency. While Mingulay lacks a defensive Iron Age site, it has at least six roundhouses, whereas none have so far been identified on Berneray and Pabbay.

The cliff-bound islet of Gearuim Mòr off the southwest coast has the remains of a building on it, variously identified as a dun or a chapel.[16]

The middle centuries of the first millennium AD are as much a 'dark age' in the islands as in the rest of Britain. The period is referred to as 'early Christian' or 'early medieval', and in eastern Scotland, 'Pictish', the Picts being the inhabitants of Scotland north of the Lowlands. In the Outer Hebrides Pictish finds are rare, and Mingulay's neighbour Pabbay boasts one of only two incised slabs, or symbol stones, found in the islands; the majority of these stones have been found in eastern Scotland. This stone can be dated to the eighth century, and bronze pins dating to the seventh century have also been found on Pabbay. Pabbay's Iron Age dun was occupied at this time. Possible finds of this period on Mingulay are mentioned by Wedderspoon: 'Several ancient coins and bronze pins were found in the graveyard some years ago, and sent to Castlebay to be disposed of.' Their location on the site of what may already have been a chapel and graveyard suggests this period. In succeeding centuries the Pictish culture and language were submerged by the Gaelic-speaking Scotti, or Scots, Celtic people from northern Ireland who had begun to settle the western seaboard in the early centuries AD. They founded the kingdom of Dalriada, which united with the Pictish kingdom in the ninth century.

Celtic Christianity of the type introduced from Ireland by St Columba in 563 was based on the monastic ideal. The early monasteries consisted of chapels and cells within a 'cashel' or boundary. Very few such sites are known, but it is possible that Cille Bharra ('Barr's Church') in Barra was such a monastery.

(The name Barra is thought to derive from St Finbarr or Barr, traditionally believed to be the sixth-century Finbarr of Cork, but more likely to be the early seventh-century St Finbarr of Caithness, a Gaelic Scot.) Some early monasteries had hermitages or retreats on nearby islands, and Pabbay may have served such a purpose. The name Pabbay (Gaelic Pabaigh) is derived from the Norse for 'Hermits' Isle', indicating the inhabitants at the time of the Norse raiding and later settlement of the Hebrides which began in the late eighth century. An Irish monk, Dicuil, said of the Hebrides in about 825: 'Some of these islands are small; nearly all alike are separated by narrow channels; and in them for nearly a hundred years hermits have dwelt, sailing from our Scotia. Now, because of these robbers the Northmen, they are empty of anchorites.' Pabbay's Pictish symbol stone bears a simple cross, added at a later date, and three other slabs bear crosses which could date from this or a later period; a cross-incised slab has also been found on Berneray. If Pabbay was used as a retreat it is possible that other islands were too; they all had chapels in later times, and it is possible that these were early in origin or replaced early ones in the more settled times after the early Norse period.[17]

Mingulay's chapel was mentioned by Monro, High Dean of the Isles, in 1549, and the memory of its site was retained. The officers of the Ordnance Survey were informed in 1878 of the traditional site of a chapel, dedicated to St Columba, with graveyard attached.[18] This was the knoll, occupied by the graveyard, next to the stream in the village, and the corner of a building is now visible on the knoll.[19] The dedication to St Columba does not imply an early date, nor does it indicate any particular connection with the saint, who is not recorded as having visited the Outer Hebrides. Graveyards on all four of the other main islands south of Barra are similarly the traditional sites of chapels, though only on Mingulay and at Cille Bhrianain, on a tidal island off Vatersay, are there clear visible remains. (On Vatersay itself, St Mary's graveyard has recently been identified as the site of a chapel.)[20]

There is another site with religious associations, Crois an t-Suidheachain, meaning 'cross of the seat (sitting place)'. It occupied a level area in the hillside above the road approaching the landing place at Aneir. The site was described and sketched by Muir in 1866, described by Carmichael in 1867, and sketched by the RCAHMS in 1915, but details and measurements vary.[21] It has not been recorded since 1915, and nothing is now visible. Muir described it as 'the Cross . . . a curious though greatly reduced antiquity'. From the two earlier accounts, it seems that it consisted of three or four rectangular structures within a circular enclosure of loose stones 13–14 metres (42–45 feet) in diameter. Carmichael gave the local name for the structures within: Leapaich Challum Cille, St Columba's bed. He noted that the structures were built of stones set on their sides or on edge, and some were large; the interiors were 'hollow, like a trough or box'. There was a central structure, 3 metres (9 feet 9 inches) long internally, a smaller one about 2.2 metres (7 feet) long, to the north, both aligned east–west. Associated with the latter structure, Carmichael described an 'altar, a raised rude square of masonry about 3 feet high and 3 feet square' where priests celebrated worship after the Reformation when they couldn't operate openly. However, elsewhere in his notes Carmichael describes Crois Chaluim Chille (Columba's Cross) as having these dimensions and 'at one side a large massive stone and this was the altar'. This altar was perhaps the 'cross' referred to by Muir and other writers. A 'mass stone' is remembered as having been built into one of the gable ends of a house built in modern style north of the school in the early years of the twentieth century; it is not far from the Cross, which may have provided a suitable quarry, and may account for the tradition. There was at least one other structure, southeast of the central one. The largest structure could be the 'traces of a building which is traditionally believed to have been a place of worship erected by a disciple of St Columba' described by the Ordnance Survey. Jolly refers to 'a cairn above the south

landing place, called St Columba's Cross, being looked upon
as sacred'. Father Allan McDonald, on his visit in 1898,
searched 'for remnant of old cross at Crois an t-Suidheachain
but failed to find a trace. Measured the remains of what appeared to be monastic cells at this spot. Michael Macneil later
on informed me that there was a leabaidh cràbhaidh 'a bed of
devotion' (probably a cell) at this spot.' [22]

So while the religious associations of the site are beyond
doubt, we can only hazard guesses as to its origin. If the central
structure was a chapel, two others could have been monastic
cells. The site would then resemble a miniature cashel of Early
Christian times, or, without the cells, some early chapels in
Argyll that are similarly small and within enclosures. An al-
ternative possibility is that some of the structures – at least
one of which seems to have consisted of large blocks of stone
– may have originated as the chambers of a megalithic tomb
of Neolithic type; or as the cists for single burials associated
with cairns of Bronze Age type.

Another possible reference to the Cross is found in Martin
Martin's account of 1695. He says: 'there is in this island an
Altar dedicated to St Christopher, at which the Natives perform their Devotion. There is a Stone set up here, about seven
foot high, and when the Inhabitants come near it they take
a religious Turn round it.' Was this 'altar' the Cross? Or a
standing stone? No other site in Mingulay or Berneray seems
to match this.

With the advent of the Norse, or Viking, period in the
Hebrides we are once again on firmer ground. The period
began at the end of the eighth century with violence and
plunder, and monastic establishments were favourite targets.
Being on the sea route from Norway to Ireland and the Isle of
Man, the Hebrides were used as bases for raids further south.
According to one of the Norse sagas, which cannot be regarded
as historically accurate, the first Viking to come to Barra was
Onund Wooden-leg. He came in 871 with five ships, drove out
a local ruler, Kiarval, and stayed for some years, plundering

in Scotland and Ireland. According to the saga, 'they went on warfare in the summers, but were in the Barra Isles in the winters.' Some time later Onund arranged a marriage between a relative and a Barra woman from a family which had been established in the Hebrides for two or three generations. Graves of these early settlers have been found in Barra, dating from the ninth century, before the Norse were converted to Christianity. A gravestone found at Cille Bharra bears a cross on one side and a runic inscription to the deceased on the other, a clear indication that Christianity survived in Barra and had been adopted by the incomers by the eleventh century.[23]

As time went on the raiders from Norway became settlers, for it was land they lacked at home and which they wanted in the similar environment of the Scottish islands. The settlement was on such a scale – especially in Lewis, and Orkney and Shetland – that their language became the predominant one, certainly for topographical names. Although Gaelic reasserted itself after the Norse lost political control of the Hebrides in the thirteenth century, the place names survive (subsequently Gaelicised, the Gaelic forms then being Anglicised) and remain the principal legacy of the period. Other evidence is in the form of folklore in which the Norse feature, and the system of land ownership in the islands before the nineteenth century which was based on the Norse pattern.

A large number of the place names in the Barra Isles are of Norse origin (or are compound Norse-Gaelic), as are the names of the islands themselves.[24] The name Mingulay is thought to derive from the Old Norse *mikil*, meaning big, and *ay*, meaning island. In Gaelic it is Miughalaigh or Miùghlaigh, pronounced something like 'mew-ul-eye', which accounts for the form Mewla given in a seventeenth-century source.[25] Monro's version of 1549 – Megaly – is the earliest known; Martin Martin, 1695, gives Micklay. The current spelling and pronunciation in English has drifted further from the Gaelic than in other cases, possibly because of the various forms used by early writers and map makers.

The majority of Mingulay's known place names are coastal.[26] They are descriptive or refer to an association, such as fishing. The commonest Norse element is the suffix -*geo* from Old Norse *gja,* chasm or cleft in a cliff. This is found in names such as Sloc Heisegeo, *sloc* being Gaelic for inlet or chasm, perhaps a later addition, the *heise* element being obscure. The suffix -*mul* is Old Norse for headland or island, and is found in the precipitous sea stacks off the west coast; in Liànamuil the first element is Old Norse for flax (significance unclear), in Arnamuil it is Old Norse for sea eagle or Arni (personal name). The suffix -*nish* derives from Old Norse *nes*, 'point', as in Bannish, 'white point', on the southwest coast. Inland, the hill Hecla is Old Norse for 'hooded shroud'; there is another cone-shaped Hecla in South Uist. In Biulacraig, the great cliff, the final element *craig* is derived from *creag*, the Gaelic for 'cliff'; the origin of the other element(s) is obscure, but the word order is Norse. In Skipisdale, Gaelic Sgiobasdail, the southern valley, the final element is derived from Old Norse *dalr,* valley, the first element being derived from Old Norse for ship, a reference perhaps to the landing place at its outlet.[27]

One place name of Norse origin is very significant, for it indicates a Norse settlement. Father Allan McDonald recorded it as Suinsibost and there are other variations which locate it in Skipisdale. The suffix -*bost* is common in some former Norse areas, and is derived from Old Norse *bolstaðr,* meaning farm. The first element of Suinsibost could be the Norse personal name Sveinn. A Gaelicised variation is Sumhsabaist in which case the first element could be derived from *sunnr* or *sunstr*, meaning southerly or most southerly, which would be a highly appropriate name given its location near the south coast.[28] If that is the case it could have been so called to distinguish it from a settlement at Mingulay Bay. The place name is important, as no other derivatives of *bolstaðr* are known in the Barra Isles. The only other Norse settlement name in the southern Barra Isles is Sheader, on the west coast of

Sandray. The strip fields on the north side of Skipisdale could date from the Norse period (see below). The Gaelic names probably date from a later period, and many also indicate their economic association. For example, at the northern end of Mingulay is Ard nan Capuill, 'headland of the horses'; off the north coast is Sgeir nan Uibhein, 'skerry of the eggs' (of seabirds); and in Bàgh Shleitadh is Sloc na Muice, 'inlet of the pig', meaning sea-pig or whale.

A story about a Viking attack on Mingulay was told by Nan MacKinnon of Vatersay in 1961:

I heard this story recently from Michael, son of Donald. Evidently long ago one of the shepherds was up on the hill looking after his sheep and what did he see but the Viking ships heading towards Mingulay. And he returned to tell the rest of the people, that is everyone in the village, that they were arriving.

They all knew very well that slaughter was their intent. He made everyone in the village aware that they intended to take over the place. So they all gathered, everyone there, old and young, small and large, and they all took with them everything that could be taken, sticks and wood, anything that they thought would injure and kill the Vikings.

They gathered – but anyway before they climbed up – it was at Leac Leite that they came ashore, that is the Vikings, at a place called Leac Leite [where a steep gully meets the sea in Bàgh Shleiteadh on the west coast]. Evidently there is a steep slope to Leac Leite. The Vikings had climbed to the top of the slope before they met and then battle commenced.

Six of the Vikings were killed. And when they killed them they buried them where they were and they placed stones over the graves. But anyway the old men used to say to the young boys who went to the hill for peat, for fear that they removed the

stones from the graves, they told them repeatedly,
every time that they went to the peat, they all carried
a stone which they threw on the cairn. And the cairn
is still there to this day. And the remainder of the
Vikings went, oh yes they did.[29]

The Hebrides and the Isle of Man formed the Kingdom of
the Isles from the ninth century. The Norse grip weakened
in the twelfth century with the emergence of a chieftain in
Argyll, Somerled, who expanded his territories to the islands,
including Barra. The Hebrides remained under nominal
Norse control until 1266, when they reverted to the Scottish
crown, and were ruled by Somerled's descendants, the Lords
of the Isles.

The Scottish clans originated in the period between the
twelfth and fourteenth centuries. The Gaelic word *clann*
means 'children', and in medieval Highland society the term
referred to a grouping who claimed kinship with, and owed
allegiance to, the hereditary chief. The clan owned a particular territory within which all property was held by the
chief on behalf of the clan; the clan members or tenants paid
rent for land in kind and in military service. Sometimes the
chief leased portions of land known as 'tacks' to his close
kinsmen – 'tacksmen' – to whom tenants paid their rents;
Mingulay is not known to have been a tack, but Vatersay and
Sandray were in later centuries.

By 1427 the MacNeils had emerged as the 'chiefs' of Barra,
for in that year they were granted the Barra Isles by the Lords
of the Isles. They had probably been the chiefs for some time,
however, though their history is obscure. They themselves
claimed descent from Niall Naoigiallach, 'Neil of the Nine
Hostages', King of Ireland in the fourth century AD, and they
believed that the 21st chief, Neil, came to Barra in the eleventh century.

As for ecclesiastical history, the Roman diocesan system of
church organisation was introduced in the twelfth century.

The chapel at Cille Bharra became the parish church and the parish was within the Diocese of the Isles, the bishops being based successively in the Isle of Man, Skye, and Iona. Many of the chapels in the Hebrides, including the present one at Cille Bharra, were built at around this time, which could be when the chapels in the islands south of Barra were built.

The village at Mingulay Bay was the only centre of population in the nineteenth century, but there are other settlement sites and individual buildings from earlier times, broadly termed post-medieval. There is a tradition that Skipisdale was inhabited at one time. There are clusters of small ruined buildings in Skipisdale, as described above. Some of these are sub-rectangular and could have been dwellings. There are also individual buildings in Skipisdale and in the formerly cultivated land along the coast to the east. Some of the field systems in Skipisdale and to the east could be contemporary with these settlement sites, perhaps using or continuing to use earlier field boundaries; they are clearly earlier than the lazy-beds.[30]

Also among the clusters in Skipisdale there are small round or oval buildings which could be shieling huts. The folklore collector Alexander Carmichael was told, in 1867, that the Mingulay people 'used to leave their houses [in the village of Mingulay Bay] early in summer and went to Susabeist and then to Ghreotais'.[31] Susabeist was in Skipisdale; Ghreotais was east of there. This seems to be a description of a custom which was common throughout the Highlands and Islands, whereby people would take their livestock to grazing areas away from the growing crops near the permanent settlements and live in shieling huts, where they would make butter and cheese. Some of the huts have small 'annexes' possibly used for storing such dairy products. In Carmichael's day Skipisdale was well cultivated, as there are lazy-beds all the way from there round the coast to Mingulay Bay; they probably date from the second half of the nineteenth century when the population was at its height. The tradition he recorded probably

dates from a time when Skipisdale was not intensively cultivated, since the shieling system arose in order to keep cattle
away from growing crops.

Ghreotais, or Totachain Ghreotais, is the site of another
group of small buildings, on the lower eastern slopes of Hecla
near Hecla Point.[32] The complex consists of a coherent group
of six well-preserved buildings, probably dwellings rather than
shielings. They are square or rectangular, up to 3.4 metres
(11 feet) long, with rounded external corners and neatly
squared internal corners. A Sheffield University excavation
of one building revealed a stone bench around the internal
walls. No dating evidence was found apart from some Iron
Age pottery sherds which originated in the mound on which
the complex is built. Carmichael, or rather his informant,
described the buildings as shielings. Perhaps the informant
had no personal knowledge of shielings but was aware of the
practice in the past, and assumed the ruins were of shielings;
or perhaps the place was abandoned as a settlement but continued to be used in the summer. The settlement is situated
within a field system in the formerly cultivated area. As with
Skipisdale, the tradition may date from a time when that area
was not intensively cultivated.

A third settlement site was in the sandy area to the northeast of the village. To the east of the 'old' school there is a
small rectangular building, smaller than the village buildings
and not marked on the nineteenth-century maps; another is
incorporated into the north side of the enclosure surrounding
the school.[33] In the area there are field walls and small enclosures. As we will see in chapter 4, there was a tradition that
the village at the time of the legendary plague was in this area.
There are also isolated buildings along the south coast and
one on the northeast coast near Rubha Domhain.[34]

In addition to these settlements there are the remains of
small round or oval huts which have been interpreted as
shieling huts. They are found on hill slopes away from cultivated areas, singly or in groups, mostly in the southern half of

the island. There is a group of seven, either side of a stream, on the higher northeastern slopes of Hecla.[35]

The long history of land use is documented in the complex field systems in the valley opening onto the bay, around the eastern slopes of Hecla and in Skipisdale. The RCAHMS surveyors identified four phases of development of the field system.[36] The earliest phase comprised small irregular plots defined by upright boulders, found in Skipisdale, on the southeastern slopes of Hecla, and to the west of the 'new' school. This phase may date to the Iron Age, as we know that the island was well populated then.

These fields were superseded by narrow strip-fields defined by low earthen banks, the best preserved being on the north side of the valley of Skipisdale, where they are aligned down-slope. These fields are of great interest as they are the only known examples in the Western Isles. Such fields are known in Shetland where they are thought to be post-medieval; the Mingulay ones predate the fields associated with the post-medieval settlements in the third phase and may be Norse, although there is no actual evidence of date.

The third phase comprised irregular field systems delimited by earthen head-dykes faced externally with stone – the head-dyke being the boundary between the enclosed land and the moorland – which surround the post-medieval settlements such as the two in Skipisdale, and those near Hecla Point and Mingulay Bay.

In the final phase, the head-dyke systems were joined to-gether by successive dykes incorporating new pieces of land, and combining all the improved land into one system. This is the system that was in place by 1878 when it was mapped by the Ordnance Survey, and remained largely unchanged (see map 3). It may have been established in the middle of the nineteenth century following the resettlement of the island after the clearance of 1835. The best land was on the south side of the valley west of the village, and this was divided into croft strips which would have been ploughed. Elsewhere, on the poorer soils on the east and south slopes of Hecla, crops were grown on lazy-beds (cultivation ridges, see chapter 5). Also in this phase, a new dyke was built across the 'waist' of the island from Bàgh na h-Aoneig and down the valley towards the village, dividing it into a predominantly grazing area to the south and a predominantly peat extraction area to the north.

So there is ample evidence of human occupation of Mingulay going back perhaps five thousand years. Occupation was not necessarily continuous, but, given the attractions of Mingulay, it is very likely to have been so.

3

The People and their Culture

The people exhibit the usual double type of race characteristic of the Islands and Highlands – the dark-skinned, dark-haired, dark-eyed, firm, and bilious Celt; and the light-haired, fair-skinned, blue-eyed Teut, descended from the invading Norsemen – but the races are now much mingled. The men are, in general, short and well-knit, with the broad shoulders and stout arms of all fishermen. They are generally pleasant in countenance, with healthy, bronzed complexions, but shy in eye and manner, the effect of their seclusion. They are frank and outspoken when addressed, but mostly wait to be spoken to; and mild and respectful in tone. They have an intelligent expression, greater than might have been expected in the circumstances. The women, so far as I saw them, were remarkable for neither good nor bad looks, but the girls were amiable looking, and some were bright and comely ... The people are singularly retiring, and distrustful if not suspicious of strangers, even more than the St Kildans.

Such were William Jolly's impressions, based on brief visits as a school inspector. Ada Goodrich-Freer and a female companion stayed for at least one night in 1898, and, being

women and being dependant on the islanders' hospitality (and
being accompanied by someone the islanders knew, Father
Allan McDonald, though Goodrich-Freer did not reveal that
in her account), had rather different experiences:

> They welcomed us with the utmost cordiality, and
> their kindness and cheerful readiness to take any
> trouble for our pleasure or convenience, we can
> never forget. So far are they from exploiting the
> stranger, as is the custom in St Kilda, that we had
> the greatest difficulty in persuading them to take
> payment even for laborious services, and to prevent
> them from robbing themselves to give us such neces-
> saries as added greatly to our comfort.

T.S. Muir, who visited Mingulay very briefly in 1866, was less
flattering:

> The people, like their houses, look, in great part,
> exceedingly poor; and that their minds are in no
> way better conditioned may be readily guessed, since
> the only instruction they have, religious or secular,
> is what is laboriously driven into them at a school
> that was instituted . . . by some benevolent ladies
> connected with the Free Church.

The Mingulay people – *na Miughalaich,* as they were known
– were of traditional Barra Isles stock in terms of their culture, religion (Roman Catholic), and language (Gaelic). The
surnames were those common in the islands, first recorded
in 1805 when the registers of the church at Craigstone,
Barra, begin: MacNeil, MacPhee, Campbell, MacLean and
MacDonald. MacNeil was the most common and a John
MacNeil was recorded as early as 1745, as a witness in the
enquiry into the Jacobite uprising in the Highlands of that
year.[1] Two more names, MacKinnon and Gillies, appear in

the 1830s, and another, Sinclair, in the 1860s. A number of others had only a brief presence. The written records only give names in English, and because the number of surnames and Christian names was limited amongst the islanders, it is not always possible to identify individuals. There were, for example, at least six Donald MacNeils in 1896.[2] In everyday life, surnames are relatively insignificant and little used in Gaelic. People (of both sexes) are identified by their own, their father's and their grandfather's Christian names or nick-names, giving a patronymic such as Iagan Dhòmhnaill Nèill, 'John of Donald of Neil', as John MacKinnon, the joiner, was known. This gives people an acute sense of genealogy, history, and community. The name of the first-born child would be chosen by the father, the second by the mother, and so on.

Some of these families were known for certain characteris-tics. The various families of MacPhees, who claimed ultimate descent from the legendary Kenneth whom we shall meet in the next chapter, were descended from Donald (Dòmhnall Iain), known as Dòmhnall Mòr ('Big Donald'; many of his descendants were also big!). He married Anne MacNeil in the 1820s and they had three sons who all had large families. The MacPhees were regarded as scholarly, and two of Donald's grandsons, Neil (Niall Chaluim, whose father appears in plate 12) and Donald (Dòmhnall Dhòmhnaill or Dòmhnall Bàn, fair-haired Donald), were exceptional. Neil MacPhee (1874–1927) acted as scribe for the Vatersay raiders from 1908 onwards. He was equally at home writing in English, a foreign language, as he was in Gaelic, the writing of which was taught as a school subject only towards the end of his school career. He was known as 'The Scholar' in Vatersay where he lived from 1908. He kept a copy (or perhaps a draft) of every letter he wrote, in letterbooks, and these show that he was not afraid to challenge any politician who did not support the raiders. He also composed songs, and one of these is given in Appendix 2.

Neil's cousin, Donald MacPhee (Dòmhnall Bàn, born 1870, plate 13), was interested in the traditions of the island, which he wrote down in Gaelic and English. He led prayer meetings and services in the absence of the priest, but was reprimanded by the priest for going too far for a lay person. Another cousin, Mary MacPhee (Màiri Iain Dhòmhnaill, born 1866) was a great storehouse of Mingulay traditions, folklore and songs. She passed these on to her daughter, Nan MacKinnon of Vatersay (Nan Eachainn Fhionnlaigh, 1902–82), who became famous for them and was recorded extensively by the School of Scottish Studies. Nan was born in Kentangaval, Barra, and moved to Vatersay in 1908; she never visited the island she knew so much about.

The MacKinnons came to Mingulay in the 1830s, when two, both Donald, married Mingulay women. The Donalds were first cousins from Tangusdale in Barra, where the family was known as *na Greusaichean*, 'the shoemakers'. The men were craftsmen in wood too, and Dòmhnall Nèill Nèill (1811–88) and his son John, born 1858 (plate 24), continued this tradition in Mingulay. John's name crops up again and again in the tape recordings as the builder of a modern house and a water mill, a maker of spinning wheels, furniture, church fittings, a plough and a boat, and even as a tailor. He must have been one of the better off of the islanders. Donald and his descendants held the post of 'constable', or landlord's representative in the community, a post that in Mingulay seems to have been informal.

Sinclair was not a local name, and originates from Duncan Sinclair (Dunnchadh Dhòmhnaill, 1805–74), a Protestant from Appin in Argyll, although his forebears were from Caithness. He was employed as a gardener by Dr MacGillivray at Eoligarry House, Barra, and later as a shepherd in Vatersay by MacNeil of Barra, examples of a Protestant outsider being employed in preference to a local Catholic. He married Mary MacNeil of Mingulay in 1833 and they had seven children. Each parent seems to have wanted the children to follow their religion, with the result that some of them were baptised by both Protestant and Catholic clergy; the children all grew up as Catholics, however. At some time between 1841 and 1845 the family moved to Berneray, where Duncan remained as a crofter. He must have had an education himself, for he was concerned about his children being educated, and seems to have taught them himself.[3] He was also interested in the antiquities of the islands; in 1866 he pointed out the Mingulay 'Cross' to Muir, who said that Duncan 'regarded the object as something very astounding'. Three of his sons were used as authorities – almost the only native ones – on the place names of the southern islands by the Ordnance Survey in 1878. Duncan's son John moved to Mingulay with his Barra wife in about 1868, attracted, perhaps, by the school which his children could attend, as well as by the croft he took on. Another son, Andrew, also moved to Mingulay on his marriage to Catherine Campbell (Catrìona Nèill Eachainn) of Mingulay; another, Donald, lived in Pabbay for a time, and another, Peter, remained in Berneray. The story is told that one of Duncan's brothers wanted to leave money to his Berneray nephews, but when he discovered they were all Catholic, he decided instead to leave it to the town of Oban, where Sinclair Drive is named after him.

These few examples show that intermarriage among the people of the various islands was common. In the fifty-six marriages of Mingulay people which took place in Barra parish between 1855 and 1907, twenty-six of the partners were from Barra (many from Tangusdale in particular), twenty-one from Mingulay, four from Berneray, four from Pabbay and only one from outside the parish – John Finlayson, the schoolteacher. There must have been many more marriages to outsiders, held in the spouse's parish, but it was rare for such couples to settle in Mingulay, not surprisingly! In one case, the wife, Margaret Milne, was from Peterhead, where she probably met her Mingulay husband, Neil MacDonald, when he was there during the herring-fishing season. Before the people of Sandray and Vatersay were evicted in 1835 and 1850 respectively, there were marriages between them and the Mingulay people too. Marriages between Catholics and Protestants were permitted, though not approved of, and the ceremony had to be a Catholic one for the Catholic to remain in the Church. Of the marriages between Mingulay people, many were inevitably between cousins, second cousins being the closest permitted if the bishop granted a dispensation. It may be noted that not one person was recorded in the censuses between 1861 and 1901 as 'blind, deaf and dumb, imbecile, idiot, lunatic'. A number of illegitimate births were recorded. In one case, around 1850, the name of the father, from Mingulay, was given, which was most unusual. He and the mother, from Barra, had two children. Such cases occasionally occurred when one party was Protestant, and social pressure made it difficult for the couple to marry. In this case, however, both were MacNeils, and so this explanation is unlikely. Marriage between people from different islands partly accounts for the movement of people between the islands, which was common right up until the desertion, other factors being eviction or moving for reasons of work or education.

Nearly all of these marriages took place in Barra, and this was normal before 1855 as well. They were performed at the Church of St Brendan at Craigstone until 1888, when the Church of Our Lady, Star of the Sea, Castlebay, opened and became the favoured place. Of the six exceptions, four took place in Mingulay (in the 1870s and 80s), the others in Pabbay and Berneray. Two marriages were held on the same day in November 1871, one in Mingulay and one in Pabbay, and this must have been arranged with the priest. It was risky for the priest to commit himself to going to the southern islands for a particular time, because of the unpredictable conditions of the sea and weather. Father Allan McDonald

> once went to Mingulay to hold service, meaning to return in the evening and to marry a young couple in Barra the next day. Over seven weeks passed before he could get back. He spent the time in religious

exercises among the people, and in collecting old lore; and the marriage party spent it in dancing, singing and composing songs on the anxious bride and groom.[4]

Families were often large, with up to ten or even more children, though not all children survived. The census returns between 1841 and 1901 show that three generations sometimes shared a house; one house had eleven inhabitants in 1861. By contrast, some households consisted of only one or two people, usually unmarried or widowed. Some families had young adults, mostly female, living with them, described as domestic servants. These may have been relatives, but it is curious, as there is no tradition of servants among the ordinary people in the islands; the Barra returns are similar in this respect. Unmarried daughters are also often described as servants, while teenage boys above school age are usually described as fishermen. Men's occupations are almost invariably given as crofter or fisherman, but there are a few exceptions such as boat carpenter, shoemaker, and sailor.

In reality the men were all crofter-fishermen, and were fowlers, builders, joiners and many other things too. Women's occupations are described simply in terms of their husbands' or fathers' occupations, even though some worked in their own right as gutters in the herring industry in later years. Women did as much of the croft work as the men, if not more, and not only when the men were away fishing. They also had their own work to do – food preparation, making cloth and clothing, and child rearing.

In terms of numbers, the earliest population figure is fifty-two in 1764,[5] and in 1794 eight families were recorded (see Appendix 1). [6] By 1841 the population had doubled to 113 in eighteen families, the highest of the smaller Barra Isles. The peak was reached in the 1880s: 150 people in thirty-four families were recorded in the 1881 census, but many men were away fishing at the time, as in previous years, so that the censuses are likely to be underestimates. There are four higher figures: 180 people in 1873, 164 in 1883, 160 in 1888 and also in 1896.[7] The population declined to 135 in thirty families in 1901, and the evacuation began in 1907.

Society was patriarchal: men held the titles to crofts, although there were cases of widows or single women being the tenants. Only men signed the 1896 petition for landing facilities and the deed of agreement for the derrick provided.[8] The men made the day-to-day decisions, and from the middle of the nineteenth century at least there was a nominal 'leader' in the constable (landlord's representative). In the last decade or so Michael Campbell, nicknamed 'Teac' (Mìcheal Nèill Eachainn, born 1867) emerges as a prominent person, and was the leader of the Mingulay contingent of the Vatersay raiders in 1907. He had been a teacher in Berneray and could speak English.[9] Because of Mingulay's remoteness, the factor (estate manager) from 1840 onwards rarely visited and was not the ogre he was to the people of Barra. The most important single figure in the people's lives, however, was the priest of Barra, whose role was not only pastoral. He was involved in the provision of the landing derrick in 1901, and in the final desertion.

The community was close-knit and self-contained, and island life was communal and co-operative, as it had to be. Families would help each other with tasks such as digging the arable land in spring, peatcutting, building, and families or individuals in need would be taken care of. Fishing and waulking (fulling cloth) were communal activities done by men and women respectively. The whole community helped in the landing of the boats. In the absence of regular visits from the parish priest, the people held their own services and prayer meetings. In the long winter evenings people gathered in someone's house for the *ceilidh* – storytelling.

Being close-knit did not mean that the community had 'the least possible intercourse with the outer world', as Jolly maintained. In the later nineteenth century, fishermen sold fish in Glasgow and in Ireland, and both men and women worked in the herring industry on the east coasts of Scotland and England. Many men worked in Glasgow in the winter, and earlier in the century had worked at the harvest in the Lowlands. And even Jolly admitted that 'the food supply is supplemented from Glasgow'.

The whole community would take part in special occasions such as weddings and funerals and in annual festivities. The wedding was preceded, some weeks earlier, by the *rèiteach* or betrothal ceremony. The custom in the Barra Isles was for the prospective groom to go to the house of his bride-to-be to seek the approval of her father. He was accompanied by a friend or relative who might become the best man at the wedding, who would extol the virtues of his friend to the father. The father's approval was a mere formality, for preparations for the celebrations, which followed immediately, were well under way.[10]

The wedding ceremony and celebrations would last at least two days, for the couple had to go to Barra for the wedding itself, and the celebrations followed their return to Mingulay. Mary Campbell described the wedding celebrations of John Sinclair (Iagan Iain Dhunnchaidh) and Anne Campbell (Anna Dhòmhnaill Chaluim) in April 1902.[11] The party began in the afternoon of one day and continued into the next day. It was held in the bride's house, and everyone who could, attended it (at a time when the population was about 135!). Two or three tables were set end to end, and the couple were welcomed to the first table, with their closest relatives next to them. Children sat at their own table or on the floor, young ones with their mothers. The best man and another man gave out the drams of whisky, and two girls waited on the tables with food: soup, meat, kail, followed by tea. The brother of the groom made a speech praising him. They then adjourned to the house next door for those who had come from a distance to change their clothes, and in the other end of the house the dance started. They danced to the bagpipes, played by two or three pipers in turn; there was no fiddler. There would be another meal later, with tea, wine and drams.

Most weddings occurred in autumn and winter, presumably because people were busy with fishing and croft work in spring and summer. This would have made it harder to arrange a date and to invite people from other islands, because of the weather being even more unpredictable than usual at those times of year.

Catherine MacNeil described funerals in Mingulay.[12] There would be a wake the first night after the death, when people would gather in the house of the deceased, and stay up all night saying prayers and telling stories, and food was served. In Barra, the body, wrapped in a shroud, was placed in the coffin which was brought to the house in the morning, and a requiem mass was held in the church. In Mingulay, the people had to take the funeral service themselves; one of the elders would perform this function, probably in the deceased's house. The coffin, which was blackened instead of being covered with a cloth, was then taken for burial in the graveyard, and the men who carried it were given tobacco.

There were various annual festivities and associated customs. At New Year children went round the houses reciting poems, and were given barley bannocks in return.[13] At Hallowe'en children stole cabbages. The story is told of three girls who were raiding a vegetable garden one Hallowe'en night when they saw a youth they thought they knew; he ran off, and they followed. However, they thought there was something evil about the youth, for he could walk up the sides of rock with ease. The girls crossed themselves and returned home. They found the youth they thought they had seen at home, where he had been all the time. They later told the priest, who said they had done the right thing.[14] This must have happened in the 1820s or 30s. There were numerous religious holidays throughout the year, some associated with the cycle of the seasons and crops. On St Michael's Day, at the end of harvest (29 September), the people made a special dish, a chicken and barley soup.[15] No agricultural work was done on St Patrick's Day, 17 March.[16] All saints' days seem to have been school holidays.

The Gaelic culture of the Mingulay people was of the Barra tradition, a tradition expressed in stories, songs, beliefs and superstitions and customs. Some examples of these have been recorded, first from about 1860 when folklorists, finding that knowledge of cultural traditions was fast dying out on the Scottish mainland, scoured the islands. They found that the inhabitants of Barra and Mingulay had retained more of their culture than almost any others. This was due partly to remoteness, and partly to their being Catholic, as explained by Samuel Johnson who regretted that he had not got to any Catholic islands, where the old ways survived, on his tour of the Inner Hebrides in 1773: 'Popery [Catholicism] is favourable to ceremony; and among ignorant nations, ceremony is the only preservative of tradition. Since Protestantism was extended to the savage parts of Scotland, it has perhaps been one of the chief labours of the Ministers to abolish stated observances, because they continued the remembrance of the former religion.'[17] But while some rejoiced in this survival, others condemned it as evidence of cultural 'backwardness', and their Catholicism also as 'backward'. For instance, the report on education in the Hebrides of 1865 said of Barra: 'The natives are far behind, as might be supposed, in knowledge and culture.'[18]

The storytelling tradition of Gaelic society is remarkably rich and varied. The clan chiefs had bards and *seanchaidhean* or *shennachies* (oral historians) who maintained clan traditions, and there was also popular lore. These stories are of various types: heroic, historical, supernatural; many of the heroic stories, such as those of Ossian, a legendary Irish warrior-poet, are variants of stories known throughout the Highlands and Islands and in continental Europe. Storytelling was the main occupation during the long winter evenings, when people would gather at someone's house for a *cèilidh*.

The cèilidh was an informal and impromptu gathering, quite different from the formal occasion the term is applied to today. Its participants were mainly men, and men were the reciters; the listeners would mend the fishing nets of the householder, while the women of the house got on with carding and spinning wool. Stories often took hours, even days, to recite; Catherine MacNeil remembered her grandfather Malcolm MacLean (Cadaidh) telling a story lasting three days.[19] Hector MacLean of Islay, who took down stories for the collector John Francis Campbell, wrote of storytelling in the islands in 1860:

> In the islands of Barra, the recitation of tales during the long winter nights is still very common. The people gather in crowds to the houses of those whom they consider good reciters to listen to their stories. They appear to be fondest of those tales which describe exceedingly rapid changes of place in very short portions of time, and have evidently no respect for the unities. During the recitation of these tales, the emotions of the reciters are occasionally very strongly excited, and so also are those of the listeners, almost shedding tears at one time, and giving way to loud laughter at another. A good many of them firmly believe in all the extravagance of these stories.[20]

MacLean wrote to Campbell from Barra on 30 September 1860:

> I was over at Minglay last week and saw Roderick MacNeill who is so celebrated among the people here as a story teller. I have written several of his tales which appear to me to be remarkable for vivid and painted dialogue. He is an animated and spirited old man and though crippled to a certain extent by rheumatism his vivacity is not the least damped

and the vigorous activity of his mind is not the least
impaired; 74 and not a trace of dotage. He hobbles
about bareheaded and barefooted and is said not to
have worn shoes for the last fifty years. He tells his
tales with extraordinary effect being a capital natural elocutionist using pause, emphasis, gesture and
inflection of the voice to express passion sentiment
and character fully as well as though he had been
trained by some of the best actors of the day . . . He
has many stories borrowed from other sources than
Highland but he gives them all a Highland form.[21]

Campbell himself met and painted MacNeil (Ruairidh
Dhòmhnaill, died 1875) (plate 20), while storm-bound in
Mingulay with Alexander Carmichael in 1871.[22] Campbell
referred to him as 'Ruairidh Reum', or 'Rory Rum the Story
Man', 'on account of a hogshead of rum he found on the shore,
from the contents of which he nearly died'.[23] Carmichael later
wrote:

MacNeill was then ninety-two years of age. He
had never been ill, never had shoes on, and never
had tasted tea. His chest was as round as a barrel,
and measured forty-eight inches in circumference.
He had been an extraordinary 'rocker' after birds,
moving about on precipices of eight hundred feet
sheer down to the sea, where a goat or cat might
hesitate to go. So powerful was the man that wherever his fingers could get insertion in the crevices of
the rock he could move his body along the face of
the precipice without any other support.[24]

Carmichael also recorded the following anecdote:

Ruary an Ruma. Strange. The school servant gave
him a cup of tea. He declared that once and but once

only did he ever taste tea before. Is there another
man of 88 in Britain who can say the same? I asked
him how did he like the tea. His reply, translated
from the Gaelic was – By God this is good. But I'd
prefer sugar in hot water than this! [25]

According to Carmichael, MacNeil and two South Uist
storytellers 'expressed regret that they had not a better place
in which to receive their visitors, and all thanked them for
coming to see them and for taking an interest in their decried
and derided old lore. And all were courteous as the courtier.' [26]
Campbell described MacNeil as 'the best climber [i.e. fowler]
in Minglay till he got past work'. [27] By the time of their visit,
MacNeil was living with his daughter Anne MacNeil, the
midwife, whom we will meet in chapter 9. As will be seen in
the next chapter, he was not native to Mingulay, but had come
from Greian, Barra, and before that, from Sandray, where
he was living at the time of his marriage to Flora MacNash
(Floraidh Iain) in 1815. The accounts of MacNeil are very
valuable, as they are the only ones of a native islander.

Hector MacLean, in another letter to Carmichael, wrote:

There is another man on the island Donald McLean
red haired with very peculiar features. The face is
nearly as broad as it is long, the nose is low and
thick, the mouth is large, the chin and forehead very
broad. He is very fancy in manner and his tales I
understand are very fancy but I was disappointed
for the day I thought of having him he was off to
another island to cut hay. The people of this island
are a peculiar and isolated community, remarkably
kind and polite. They are very sprightly and fluent
in conversation. The boys and girls are wonderfully
old fashioned very modest and very polite. They
address seniors with ease and assurance free from im-
pudence on the one hand and from mauvaise honte

on the other. I envy them in this respect. . .these
children passed me leading along at ease their tiny
ponies with a couple of bunches of sheaves attached
to each they all addressed me in a manner extremely
winning and agreeable.[28]

Superstition and belief in the supernatural was as much
part of life as the islanders' Christian faith. Stories of the
supernatural, such as those of the *each-uisge* ('water horse'),
were common in the islands. A water horse was believed to
have lived in a bottomless well in a hollow near the summit of
MacPhee's Hill. It had been foretold that a beautiful maiden
would be strangled in a contest between man and beast at this
spot. A certain Finlay, son of Iain, son of the Black Fairy was
searching for sheep on MacPhee's Hill when he heard fairy
music, and a beautiful fairy appeared. He fell in love with her,
although he had his own sweetheart, and he would meet her
in the hollow on the hill. One day the water horse came out of
the well and overpowered Finlay, shouting, 'Death upon thy
head, O Finlay, son of man!' His former sweetheart, hearing
his cries, rushed to the place, to find the water horse about
to drag him into the well. She cried, 'Oh God, dear Finlay,
sorry I am for your plight this night! On hearing the name
of the deity, the fairy vanished, the water horse strangled the
maiden, and dragged Finlay into the depths.[29]

There were stories of 'second sight', or the foreseeing
of future events, though Mary Campbell knew of no one
with these powers in her day.[30] Goodrich-Freer travelled to
Mingulay to seek evidence of this, though she doesn't say
what she found there. In one of the stories, a girl was lifting
a creel of peats on her back when she saw a strange man
standing before her. As they talked, she saw a boat some miles
away capsize, and all its occupants were thrown into the sea.
The girl cried out, but the stranger assured her that what she
had seen bore no relation to the present; the grandparents of
those thrown overboard were not yet born. The girl returned

home and told her story, and the people named the area where the boat capsized Cuan a' Bhòcain, 'Sea of the Ghost'.[31] It was in this area that a boat from Pabbay was lost with all hands in 1897, but the story, of course, originated long before that.

Fairies and ghosts were very real to the islanders. The fairies could be good; for instance, Michael MacPhee and some others gathered the harvest of a man in difficulty, who, when he discovered this, thought the fairies must have done it.[32] But more often the fairies were to be avoided, and measures were taken to avoid them; mothers used the threat of the fairies to keep their children in order.[33] The fairies lived in knolls, and their music was often heard.

The singing of song was part of everyday life. There were love songs, songs in praise of people, songs of historical events, and songs of the supernatural. There were work songs to accompany all sorts of rhythmical and repetitive activities – spinning, weaving, waulking (fulling cloth), preparing food, milking, ploughing, rowing. Waulking songs, described in chapter 8, are thought to have originated in the sixteenth and seventeenth centuries, and have features that are unique in Western Europe. Once widespread in western Scotland, they survived in South Uist and the islands of Barra into the twentieth century. The subjects of the songs touched on every aspect of the old way of life, and served to keep memories of it alive.[34] The source of some of the songs in the nineteenth century was the collection of Father Angus MacDonald, priest of Barra from 1805 to 1825. When he left to become Rector of the Scots College at Rome he gave his collection to the young John Campbell (mac Nèill) of Mingulay. Angus MacDonald's successor wrote to him in 1830 saying that Campbell was 'all the winter nights amusing the Mingalay people with your library of songs'.[35] He could be the same person as the 'Eoin, an old man on Mingulay' used as a source of Angus MacDonald's poems by Father Allan McDonald of South Uist and Eriskay.[36] As well as singing the traditional songs, people would compose songs about particular events. The song about the adventure of the Mingulay man in Appendix 3 was composed by Allan MacLean, priest at Craigstone, Barra, between 1837 and 1840.[37] Singing was not accompanied by musical instruments; the bagpipes, the only instrument mentioned, accompanied dancing.

Mingulay's most famous song – outside Barra and Vatersay that is – is 'The Mingulay Boat Song'. But neither the words nor the melody originate anywhere near Mingulay; it is a romantic invention of the twentieth century. It was devised in 1938 by Glasgow-born Sir Hugh Roberton, who was very fond of the melody of Creag Ghuanach, a song from Lochaber, which celebrates a crag near Loch Treig. He needed a sea shanty, and so he adapted the music, chose the romantic name Mingulay, and composed the words. It was to be sung in F, slowly and rhythmically.[38]

Hill you ho, boys; let her go boys;
Bring her head round, now all together.
Hill you ho boys; let her go boys;
Sailing home, home to Mingulay.

It is ironic that this song should be the only well-known song associated with the island, and, for many, the only reason they have heard the name Mingulay at all.

4

Chiefs, Landlords, Tenants

Access to land for growing food and pasturing animals was a basic necessity in the Highlands and Islands, and land tenure and the people's relationship with those who owned the land is a fundamental element in the history of the area.

As we have seen, Barra and its islands were held by the MacNeils from at least as early as 1427. One of the best known of Mingulay's legends concerns the origin of the people and their holdings, and the role of the chief. Every version of the story, written or oral, differs in details but the basic elements remain the same. This is Nan MacKinnon's version, just as she herself wrote it:

> This happened in the fourteenth century. MacNeil of Barra, who was in Eoligarry House at the time, was wondering why the Mingulay people weren't coming over to visit Barra as usual. So he sent a boat over to Mingulay to investigate, but when the boat arrived at Mingulay, there was no sign of life on the island, so the older men who were on the boat ordered a young lad of 17 to go ashore and find out what was wrong. The young lad was no other than the eldest son of Kenneth MacPhee, who was only a baby in arms when his father fled from the island of Eigg, at the time when St Francis's cave was set on fire by the

MacLeods of Skye. The boy did as he was told. He entered all the houses in the village, but they were all dead. He was in such a state after finding them dead that he called out at the pitch of his voice, before he got near the boat, 'Oh God, they're all dead.'

'In that case,' one of the older men called out to him, 'if it's a plague that killed them all you've got a stomach full of it already, so you'd better stay where you are.'

The boy cried and begged them to come back, but they wouldn't and he was left on the island alone for six weeks on end. His father, Kenneth MacPhee, was wondering what happened to his son, and walked all the way to Eoligarry to ask the Chief what happened. But after getting there, the Chief wouldn't answer. So MacPhee got very angry and told the Chief if he wasn't willing to tell him the truth about his son, he would suffer for it, and threatened to pull his house down. So the Chief had to be honest about it all, and told Kenneth MacPhee that his son was left on the island of Mingulay in case he would carry with him any of the plague or whatever disease that killed the Mingulay people. And the Chief told him to pick his own men and go to Mingulay and that the island would be theirs free of rent as long as any of his generation lived.

And Mingulay was rent free till such time as the Gordons bought Barra. So there were no survivors of the Plague, as it was called. The boy that was left there alone is said to have lived on the sheep that he killed with his pocket knife, and shellfish. And the hill that he used to climb to see if there was any sign of a boat coming is called 'MacPhee's Hill' to this day.[1]

While a number of details are at variance with known facts – the MacNeils didn't move to Eoligarry until the eighteenth century, and Mingulay was not rent-free before 1840! – and it is easy to dismiss the legend as no more than that, it is quite possible that elements are true. The entire population could have been wiped out by an epidemic, for epidemics were common right up until the last years; the population of St Kilda was greatly reduced in 1724 by a smallpox epidemic. According to another version related by Nan MacKinnon, the village was burnt down and rebuilt on a new site, astride the stream, where it is now; again, this is plausible, for houses visited by 'plague' have been abandoned within living memory in Barra.

The folklorist Alexander Carmichael recorded the tradition that the village at the time of the plague was in the sandy area to the northeast of the present village. He named the place Cnoc-Conain san Creagan rua meaning 'rabbit hill by the red rocks/little red rock'.[2] After the people left for Vatersay they would return to Mingulay for visits and would pay their respects at the graveyard in the village and then at the site of the former village. In 1898 an islander said the old village could have been on the site of the new chapel, for 'stones and ashes' were found while digging the foundations.[3] Carmichael records the story that after the old houses were burnt, the people 'built new huts down on the strand' but 'had to remove on account of the encroachment of the sea . . . Ruary saw a man to whose house the sea was approaching. He left his old mother in his hut and had not got six yards from the house when a sea came and left not one stone.' A wise old man advised the new colony to build their houses on each side of a running stream and that no such calamity would ever happen again.

Another record of the story dates from about the same time as Carmichael's visit, when a visitor noted:

> Tradition relates that the island was colonised 314 years ago, but the whole colony was swept off by some epidemic. The next colony, acting on the

advice of a medical man, paid more attention to the
necessary sanitary conditions, and built their houses
on the side of a small stream which flows through
the township. [4]

The link with the Eigg massacre – in which the MacLeods
of Skye suffocated the MacDonalds of Eigg by lighting a fire
at the mouth of the cave they were hiding in, in a revenge
attack – provides an indication of date; its supposed date
was about 1577. This would make the plague near enough
Martin's time, about 1695, for him to have mentioned it, but
he didn't, and there are no other contemporary references
to it. Some versions of the story give Colonsay as the place
MacPhee came from.

The MacNeils were not the only overlords of the islands
south of Barra. In the earliest account of Mingulay, about
1549, Sir Donald Monro, High Dean of the Isles, describes it
as 'Inhabit and veill manurit [cultivated], guid for fishing and
corne, perteining to the Bishope of the lyles'.

There are various references to the connection of the
southern islands with the Bishops, giving rise to the term
'Bishop's Isles'. The 'five isles of Barray' are listed in a rental
of the bishopric of 1561;[5] Martin Martin, writing about
1695, says they were 'held of the Bishop', but elsewhere he
says that Barra 'and the adjacent lesser islands belong in
property to MacNeil . . . He holds his lands in vassalage of
Sir Donald MacDonald of Slate' (Sleat, Skye). This refers
to MacDonald holding the 'superiority' of MacNeil's lands,
which confuses the picture still further. J.L. Campbell has
found that, earlier in the seventeenth century, 'the lease of the
teinds of the Bishop's Isles were held by Sir Dugald Campbell
of Auchinbreck. In 1617 the Bishop of the Isles complained
to the Privy Council that the tack duty had not been paid
by Sir Dugald since 1611. In 1623 Ruairi Mor MacLeod of
Dunvegan gave a lease of these teinds to Neil Og MacNeil [of
Barra]; they had been assigned to Ruairi Mor by Sir Duncan

(? Dugald) Campbell of Auchinbreck.'[6] This complicated and confused picture suggests that the islands were not of great importance to anybody, and exactly what their attraction was is not clear.

According to an account of 1620, the MacNeil, the 'Master or Superior' of the southern islands, received as duty 'half of ther cornes, butter, cheese and all other comodities which does Incres or grow to them in the yeare. And hath ane officer or serjeant in everie Illand to uptake the samen.'[7] Martin Martin says much the same, adding, 'the Steward of the Lesser and Southern Islands is reckoned a great Man here, in regard to the Perquisites due to him . . . the Measure of barley paid him by each Family yearly is an Omer, as they call it, containing about two Pecks.' (A peck is a variable unit of volume.)

Martin has a lot to say about the islanders' relationship with MacNeil, which, while it is not always entirely credible, is worth quoting here. 'The Natives never go a fishing while Mackneil or his Steward is in the Island,' he maintains, 'lest seeing their plenty of Fish, he might take occasion to raise their Rents.' To suggest that MacNeil would have been so deluded is absurd, especially if, as Carmichael says, he stayed for a month in Mingulay, on either side of Lammas Day (August 1st).[8]

MacNeil is portrayed by Martin as a paternalistic clan chief in the best tradition, fulfilling his obligations to his tenants and ensuring their support:

> When a Tenant's Wife in this or the adjacent Islands dies, he then addresses himself to Mackneil of Barray representing his Loss, and at the same time desires that he would be pleas'd to recommend a Wife to him, without which he cannot manage his Affairs, nor beget Followers to Mackneil, which would prove a publick Loss to him. Upon this Representation, Mackneil finds out a suitable Match for him; and the Woman's Name being told him, immediately

he goes to her, carrying with him a Bottle of strong
Waters for their Entertainment at marriage, which is
then consummated.

If a tenant died, the widow likewise applied to MacNeil for
a new husband, and if a cow was lost, MacNeil replaced it.
MacNeil also took in elderly tenants and maintained them
until their death. Of the islanders, Martin Martin says:

> The inhabitants are very Hospitable, and have a
> Custom, that when any Strangers from the Northern
> Islands [of Barra] resort thither, the Natives, imme-
> diately after their Landing, oblige them to eat . . .
> this Meal they call Bieyta'v, i.e. Ocean meat, for they
> presume that the sharp Air of the Ocean, which in-
> deed surrounds them, must needs give them a good
> Appetite. And whatever Number of Strangers come
> there, or of whatsoever Quality or Sex, they are
> regularly lodg'd according to ancient Custom, that
> is, one only in a Family; by which Custom a Man
> cannot lodg with his own Wife, while in this Island.
> Mr. John Campbel, the present Minister of Harries,
> told me, that his Father then being Parson of Harries,
> and Minister of Barray . . . carry'd his Wife along
> with him, and resided in this Island for some time,
> and they dispos'd of him, his Wife and Servants in
> manner above mention'd: and suppose Mackneil of
> Barray and his Lady should go thither, he would be
> obliged to comply with this ancient Custom.

Another source for these early times is Alexander
Carmichael, writing in 1883. 'Of old,' he says, 'the crofters
of Miuley paid their rents in birds to MacNeil of Barra. These
birds were principally the young of the shearwater, and called
by the people, Fachaich, "fatlings". The land was divided into
crofts called Clitig, Feoirlig, Leth-Pheighinn, and Pheighinn.'

The Pheighinn or Penny Croft paid two barrels of 'fachaich' rent, the Leth-Pheighinn or Halfpenny Croft paid one barrel, and so on. Carmichael said that the people were not allowed to collect the birds until MacNeil's arrival in mid-July. His assertion that 'probably not less than twenty barrels of these birds went to MacNeil yearly' is hard to believe, as there can never have been enough holdings to pay such an amount. The system of land tenure described by Carmichael, based on 'pennylands', was Norse in origin and was common in the Hebrides. As we will see in the next chapter, the way the land was worked in these pre-crofting times was known as 'runrig'; the arable land was held in common by the tenants, and shared out at intervals according to their rental.

How long the payment of rent in kind went on in the Barra Isles is hard to say. By 1764 the Mingulay rent was £12,[9] which, if there were eight holdings as there may have been thirty years later, meant an average of £1 10s per holding per year. The islanders could have paid this from the sale of feathers, cattle and fish.

In addition to rent, MacNeil could expect military service from his tenants, and it seems that Mingulay men served their chief in this way in the Jacobite uprising of 1745, which he supported. Goodrich-Freer told a story heard from an islander relating to this time:

> There was about this time a soldier, who had been in the '45, who belonged to Mingulay. He was great uncle's son to Ian yonder, the son of Hamish, and he had some money, and the soldiers were coming after him. His brother advised him to put away the money in case of what might happen, but he said 'they've not done with me yet'. However, he was surrounded by soldiers, and Captain Scott (whose name is execrated in these islands) ordered him to be shot, and he was robbed and murdered at the back of the house where the stackyard is.

Captain Scott, with some more of his hind, went off in a ship to Tiree. He was only just in time, for his superior officer, on coming to Mingulay, was shocked to hear of his brutality, and said that if he had been there, it was Scott himself would have been shot.

There is another story, recorded by Alexander Carmichael from Roderick MacNeil in 1866, about a Mingulay man who had fought in the '45 (possibly the same man as in the story above). Captain Scott came to Mingulay, and 'without trial, judge or jury hanged the man. The man whose name was Iain mac Fhearachair ic Mhurachidh ic Neill was remarkably big and strong . . . the man had been living in a cave long previous to this. His own brother had to show [the soldiers] where he was.' The hill above the southern edge of the village is known as Cnoc na Croicheadh, 'Hill of the Gallows', i.e. where a hanging, perhaps this one, took place. Some time after this incident, a vessel anchored in the bay. The people feared it was Scott returning, so they fled to the hills. One old woman was unable to keep up with the rest. She threw herself on her knees on the hillside. The story relates that for ten days there were 600 soldiers between Mingulay and Barra 'destroying and tearing anything. Not a cow nor a sheep not even a hen did they leave. All was destroyed as if the wing of ravage had swept over these peaceful isles.' While in Mingulay the soldiers 'amused them[selves] by flaying the cattle of the people alive and allowing them then to run mad about the island'.[10]

A story concerning James Grant, priest in Barra at the time of the '45, is quoted by Goodrich-Freer. Grant had sought refuge from the government soldiers in Mingulay, from where he tried to escape to the mainland:

It was at nightfall that he set sail, and when he got to Vatersay he went ashore to enquire news, and heard that the red soldiers (the Hanoverians) were in

Barra, so he returned to Mingulay, and went alone
to the cave of Hoisp [near the end of the cliff-bound
peninsula of Dun Mingulay]. The red soldiers came
to Mingulay, and the first two men they met were
put under oath at the point of the sword. The first
man said he had seen the priest leaving the island
the day before, and the second said he had seen him
come back and go over the hill. The soldiers struck
the first man on the face with their muskets, and his
nose was crooked till the day of his death. The other
man they took with them, and they got the priest,
and he was bound, and brought down to the village,
and thrown into a barn near the house where John
MacKinnon, son of Donald, son of Neil, now lives.
Two young lads came in, one after another, where
he was, and he asked the first to bring him some
thatch to put under him, for the ground was very
wet; and the lad went out, but was unable to return.
And he asked the second to bring him an egg, but
he too could not return. Thereafter the priest was
taken away, and the next thing they heard was that
he had been made a bishop [of the Lowland District,
at Aberdeen].

According to tradition, the boy who led the soldiers to their
victim was haunted with guilt and heard voices, the priest's
voice, the people said, until the day he died. He is remembered
as Dòmhnall Mòr nam Bòcan, 'Big Donald of the Ghosts'.
He went to New York to escape the voices, but the voices
followed him, and followed him back again.

Another version of the story tells how a soldier who had
been in the '45 was hiding in the cave with Father Grant, and
they both gave themselves up when they heard that Captain
Scott threatened to burn the houses. The soldier was hung.[11]
So it seems likely that various elements of various stories were
recorded variously!

There were dramatic changes in the Highlands and Islands in the eighteenth and nineteenth centuries. The old clan system crumbled during the eighteenth century, the death blow being the repressive measures following the defeat of the Jacobite uprising of 1745. The clan chiefs, deprived of their traditional status and role, and, increasingly, leading expensive lifestyles in London and Edinburgh, needed regular cash income. In the islands and parts of the mainland they achieved this by establishing commercial ventures such as kelping – extracting an alkaline ash from seaweed to use in the soap and glass industries – fishing and sheep farming. In order to accommodate the huge number of kelpers needed by the industry, chiefs divided up the former commonly held arable land into individual parcels of land called crofts, their tenants being called crofters. Because the tenants had a cash income – indeed the conditions of their tenancy forced them to work for the proprietor – the crofts were deliberately kept small, insufficient to support them alone. Eventually, the clan chiefs were forced to sell up altogether, and by the end of the eighteenth century few were left in possession of their ancestral lands.

In Barra the MacNeils survived until well into the nineteenth century, although their traditional role was reduced to that of mere landlord. The last chief, Colonel (later General) Roderick MacNeil, who ruled from 1822 until 1836, felt no sense of compassion or responsibility to his tenants. Until about 1828 he was an absentee landlord, being an officer in the British army.[12] MacNeil had inherited massive debts and obligations from his father, which he attempted to pay off by adopting a much more commercial – and tyrannical – policy towards his estate and tenants. His tyranny has been largely forgotten because that of his successor, Gordon of Cluny, was better documented[13] but in some respects MacNeil was even worse. Kelping had been introduced in the 1760s,[14] and the crofting system between about 1815 and 1820.[15] When the market for kelp collapsed in the 1820s the crofters could no longer pay their rents, but MacNeil raised the rent anyway. He evicted crofters from fertile land, such as on the west coast of Barra, to make way for more profitable sheep, and settled the tenants on barren land such as on the east coast. Such 'clearances' as they became known, were a feature of Highland and Island history for over a century. Some people sought better lives by emigrating, largely to Nova Scotia, Canada, a process which had begun in the later eighteenth century. MacNeil established Castlebay as a fishing village, for the processing of cod and ling, and threatened to evict fishermen from their holdings if they sold their fish in Glasgow or to passing vessels, rather than in Castlebay so that he would get his cut.[16] He ordered his factor (estate manager) to sieze crofters' cattle, even if they did not owe him any rent, and, on more than one occasion to kill the crofters' sheep.[17]

And what of Mingulay all this time? Although isolated, and having no kelp, it was not unaffected: the population, rent and number of crofts all increased in the early decades of the century. In 1794 Mingulay had eight families (possibly eight holdings)[18] which could have meant a population approximating to the fifty-two recorded in 1764. In 1811 there were nine holdings, and in 1836, 11.[19] People evicted from elsewhere in the Barra Isles settled in Mingulay. For instance, Roderick MacNeil, 'Rory Rum the story man' and his wife Flora (MacNash, from Greian in Barra) arrived in about 1825 from Greian, from where it seems that they were violently evicted. MacNeil was recorded in 1871 as saying that:

> My fresh new house was burned over my head, and I burned my hands in rescuing my dear little children. Oh the suffering of the poor folk! The terrible time that was! The land was taken from us, though we were not a penny in debt, and all the lands of the townland were given to the lowland farmer beside us ... my people were scattered, some of them in Australia, some of them in Canada.[20]

Another victim of eviction, from Caolas, Vatersay, was reported in 1831. Father Neil MacDonald of Barra wrote to
his predecessor, Angus MacDonald: 'Poor Neil Bane (i.e. Bàn,
'fair') is evicted to Mingulay with 18 or 20 head of cattle, he
is not pleased.' The next sentence reads: 'It is reported that the
poor creatures will at Whitsunday be sent elsewhere, except
Neil Campbell, who will have no more allowed him than one
cow.' [21] It is reasonably clear that this refers to Mingulay, and
there was a Neil Campbell there at the time, whom Angus
MacDonald had known; but the threat may not have been
carried out immediately.

Some Mingulay people decided to seek better lives in
Canada; between 1807 and 1828 at least twenty are known
to have emigrated.[22] When the first schoolteacher arrived in
Mingulay in 1859 he was asked to read letters people received,
and some were from Canada.[23]

The Mingulay people got a taste of MacNeil's brutality
in 1835. In a desperate attempt to stave off bankruptcy, he
invested heavily, using borrowed money, in building a factory for reprocessing kelp, producing 'enhanced kelp', with a
higher alkali content, for use in making soap.[24] This would,
in theory, sell for a higher price than the product of the first
stage in the process, thus making the venture worthwhile. It
would be sold in Liverpool, where the MacNeils had business
interests. The factory was called a 'soda manufactory' at the
time, and it is remembered in Barra oral tradition as making
glass. The factory was built by the shore at Northbay, Barra,
near the site of the later priest's house. It began production
in about 1833. MacNeil instructed all his crofting tenants in
Barra to supply the factory with kelp – he even forbade them
from using seaweed as fertiliser on their crofts – and set many
of them to work at the factory. He must have paid them in
some way, perhaps with food, for it was reported in 1836 that
'he raised the rents [of the crofts] because he gave the tenants
work at the soda works and thus in a manner had their labour
for nothing'.

MacNeil hatched a monstrous plan: he evicted the people from the southern islands, and sent some of them, the people of Berneray anyway, to Northbay to work in his factory. The minutes of meetings and the annual reports of the Commissioners of Northern Lights document the events, as the evictions affected the operation of their lighthouse on Berneray. The 1834 report states that 'the laird of Barra having removed the few families who once resided upon it [Berneray] and stocked the island with sheep . . . The tenants have been warned to remove from the neighbouring island of Mingalay.'[25] By March 1835 this threat had been carried out:

> the nine families chiefly fishermen who inhabited it at the time of the establishment of the light having been removed to the island of Barra . . . the neighbouring Isle of Mingalay has lately been depopulated in like manner . . . the removal of the inhabitants from Mingalay has been felt as a great inconvenience at Barrahead. Two active young men who attended as boat men here have also been forced to go to Barra and are now stationed at Castle Bay.[26]

The annual report for 1835 states that 'in the arrangements with the laird of Barra this and the neighbouring islands were converted into sheepwalks so that for a time there was not an inhabitant within 13 miles of the lighthouse by water. In the course of last year, however, a family or two have come to reside on one of the neighbouring islands,' [27] perhaps Mingulay. Thirteen miles (21km) includes Vatersay, and while the crofting tenants may well have been evicted from there, it is unlikely that the tenants and workers of the two Vatersay farms were (Vatersay Farm was run by General McNeil himself at the time).

Far from being MacNeil's salvation, building the factory was a financial disaster and precipitated his ruin. It had not had time to begin making a profit when one of MacNeil's creditors, Colonel John Gordon of Cluny, Aberdeenshire, demanded the repayment of a loan. MacNeil could not pay up and he was declared bankrupt in September 1836; the estate was put in the hands of trustees and the factory stopped operating. According to the lighthouse report for 1837, 'Since the estate has been put under trust, several of the families have returned to their old habitations.' Some of them may have returned by 24 June 1837, when the *Edinburgh Courant* reported that 'The destitute condition of the inhabitants of the Barra Isles has sent them forth in greater numbers and at an earlier period this season than in former years to hunt for food among the cliffs of Barrahead. One of these adventurous and brave fellows having lost his hold, fell into the sea from a height of 600 feet.' It is not clear from this whether the writer meant the inhabitants of Berneray only or of other islands. Some islanders must have stayed on in Barra because the 1838 annual report states that 'the inhabitants of Lighthouse Island have returned after sojourning three or four years on the main island of Barra at the laird's kelp-works.'[28] Since the works had stopped operating in 1836, they must have been detained in Barra for some other reason for the last year or two.

The islanders were probably accommodated in the 'barrack room' which is mentioned in an inventory of the factory in November 1836; indeed, it is hard to explain this room otherwise, because workers living in Barra would not have been provided with accommodation.[29] It is recorded, in a separate source, that 500 people worked at the factory in 1836, although this must have included crofters supplying kelp, as the site was not big enough for such numbers.

Although the crofters of all five southern islands were evicted, for some of the year 1835 at least, the people of Berneray bore the brunt of MacNeil's tyranny. Since it is unlikely that he gave them a choice in the matter, this looks like a case of forced labour, the only such case known in

Scotland. There were plenty of instances of brutality and inhumanity carried out by landlords (or their agents) on their tenants during the period of the clearances – of which those in Sutherland were notorious – but none as extreme as this. The full extent of MacNeil's excesses has only come to light as a result of research in recent years. In Sandray's case, the evictions were permanent: the island became a grazing island for the farm of Vatersay, and some of the former inhabitants ended up on Mingulay.[30]

It is remarkable that there is no oral tradition either of this traumatic period for the islanders, or of people from the southern islands working at the factory. Alexander Carmichael noted down dozens of historical stories, traditions, anecdotes, and place names with historical associations, including Roderick MacNeil's account of his eviction from Greian, but he did not record any mention of these events only thirty years before his time. The only source is the lighthouse records. Carmichael evidently revered General MacNeil's memory as the last of his line (MacNeil died in 1863), for he wrote in 1883 that 'he was adored by his people who, with the fidelity of their race, ruined themselves in trying to save him from ruin. They gave him their all.' So perhaps he did not record everything he heard; it is unlikely that he was right about the islanders' feelings about MacNeil, for Barra people, giving evidence to commissions of enquiry later in the century, were clearly resentful of the treatment their families received. Carmichael did, however, record a tradition dating from the time: on a boat trip round the island he was told that at Falamhuilt, somewhere on the southeast coast, 'the people tied and hid their wedders [sheep] from MacNeil on a ledge but they were all washed away and drowned. The last Colonel [i.e. MacNeil] took away the cattle of the people when he was becoming bankrupt although not in his debt.'[31]

Mingulay may have been resettled by more people than had left it. The population census of 1841 recorded 113 people in twenty-one families. We know who some of the newcomers were, from oral tradition and from the dates and places of birth of children whose baptisms were recorded in the registers of St Brendan's Church, Craigstone, Barra. Neil Gillies (Niall Eòghainn) from Glen, Barra, and his wife Flora (MacNeil), came from Glen. Donald MacKinnon (Dòmhnall Nèill Nèill) and his wife Flora (MacNeil), who was from Mingulay, came from Allasdale in Barra. His cousin Donald MacKinnon from Tangusdale, Barra, and his wife Marion (MacDonald) from Mingulay, moved to Berneray from Tangusdale before settling in Mingulay. John MacNeil and his wife Mary (MacNeil) came from Sandray. John MacLean and his wife Anne (MacNeil) came from Berneray. Whether or how much the movement of people around the islands at this time was dictated by the estate is unclear; the trustees of the estate had more urgent things to be concerned with, such as to sell it. The ancestral estate of the MacNeils of Barra was put up for sale in 1837, and sold in 1840.[32]

The increase in population was not matched by the increase in the number of holdings, now crofts; there were nine in 1810, and eleven in 1836, only three more than in 1794 (if there really were eight then), and it is not known whether new land was made available. The rent increased dramatically, from £12 in 1764 to £42 in 1810 and £82 in 1836, an average of nearly £7 10s per croft.

The Barra estate, together with South Uist and Benbecula, was bought in 1840 by the above-mentioned John Gordon who, like all the new owners of former clan lands, had a purely commercial interest in his lands and tenants. He was, however, one of the worst, and when, in the years between 1846 and 1851, the failure of the potato crop due to blight caused famine in the Highlands and Islands, he became notorious for his meanness in providing relief in the form of grain (to sell, not to give away), and 'food for work' schemes. These schemes resulted in public works such as the building of roads.[33] Gordon continued, on a larger scale, his predecessors' policy of evicting destitute tenants to create sheep farms.

Many of these emigrated voluntarily, but others were literally forced onto emigration vessels, creating scenes similar, as one observer reported, to slave catching on the West African coast. Most of these emigrants went to Quebec and Montreal.[34]

How the Mingulay community fared during the famine years can only be imagined; in Barra, the winter of 1846–7 saw the people reduced to near-starvation, eating their seed corn, and there were outbreaks of cholera.[35] The Mingulay people may have been better off; perhaps, having a variety of food resources, such as seabirds, they were less dependent on the potato. A possible candidate for a 'food for work' scheme is the road which connects the village with the landing place, built by 1861–3.[36] A track which runs along the western slopes of MacPhee's Hill may also have been built at this time, to ease access for ponies fetching peat. As will be seen in chapter 15, Gordon apparently supplied food for his tenants in Berneray during the famine years, so perhaps did the same for other islanders. Neil MacNeil in Pabbay, however, was well enough off to actually contribute to a fund for the 'relief of destitution in the Highlands and Islands'.

An incident occurred in 1847 that may, or may not, be an indication of the dire straits the people were in. Seven men from Mingulay and two from Pabbay were imprisoned in Inverness for offences for which they were tried at the Criminal Jury Court in Inverness, as the *Inverness Courier* reported on 31 August: The men were

> charged with the theft of ropes, sails, spars, seamen's chests, clothing, and provisions on 29th April, from a Danish vessel, the *Helena* of Sonderburg . . . on her voyage from Belfast to St Domingo was caught by a storm, dismasted and water-logged and driven to the neighbourhood of Barrahead, where her crew went ashore exhausted with fatigue, leaving the vessel at anchor. In this state the prisoners plundered her . . . they pled not guilty. . . The jury unanimously

found them guilty, and they were sentenced to four
months' imprisonment.

The Mingulay people were again threatened with eviction,
in 1851. In November 1850 Duncan Sinclair, a resident
of Berneray who was employed as Occasional Assistant
Lightkeeper at the lighthouse of Barra Head, wrote to his
bosses: 'Mr MacLellan, tacksman Vatersay, is going to take
a lease of three islands, that all the tenants are to be removed
off them at Whitsunday, and he told me himself that Colonel
Gordon offered him the three islands . . .'[37] Sinclair went on
to talk about Berneray specifically, so it is clear that the other
two were Mingulay and Pabbay, as Sandray was already peo-
ple-free and part of Vatersay Farm; the crofting tenants of
Vatersay had been evicted in 1850. However, it seems that
the MacLellan plan did not go ahead, because there are no
further references to it in the lighthouse records. If it had, all
five southern islands would have formed a single grazing unit.
   Mingulay's population continued to rise, to 114 (twenty-
three families) in 1851, and 145 (twenty-five families) in
1861. There may have been some immigration in the 1850s of
people evicted from elsewhere, such as Vatersay, as there had
been earlier; John MacLean and his family came from Pabbay.
   Despite Gordon's well-known and well-remembered out-
rages, some of his initiatives deserve credit: he reduced the
small tenants' rents considerably, and increased the number
of crofts (though not necessarily the total area of land for
crofting). The rent for Mingulay was reduced from £82
among eleven tenants to £48 16s 8d among nineteen tenants
by 1845, averaging just over £2 10s.[38] The former rents were
fixed, as seen above, when the crofters were working at the
kelp factory, but had not been reduced when it closed. So
the reductions seem to have been a belated recognition of a
gross injustice, for which Gordon himself was not responsible. The last Gordon proprietor, Lady Gordon Cathcart,
inherited the estate in 1878, about the time of her last visit in

her fifty-four-year 'rule' from her Berkshire home.[39] She was accused of indifference to the plight of cottars (landless squatters) in Barra, but in reality it was her factor (estate manager) who ran the estate.

At one time the Mingulay people had their own 'benefactress of the island', a Mrs Knight, mentioned by John Finlayson in 1888, but nothing more is known about her.[40]

Compared to the upheavals of the first half of the nineteenth century in the Barra Isles, the second half was relatively peaceful. But in other parts of the Hebrides evictions and other injustices continued, and it was as a result of continuing pressure by and on behalf of crofters and cottars that the government was forced to act. A Royal Commission – the Napier Commission as it became known – was established in 1883 to 'inquire into the condition of the crofters and cottars in the Highlands and Islands of Scotland'. The Commission took evidence at various locations, including Barra, from crofters and cottars themselves as well as estate officials and others; it also surveyed each croft. It was the first attempt to address grievances that had been ignored by the establishment – because its own members, the land-owning classes, had been largely responsible for them – since the collapse of the old order.

The estate factor, Ranald MacDonald, gave evidence as to conditions in Mingulay in 1883:

> The island of Mingalay, which was said to be a pretty good island, is found to be most unsuited to the people, if we judge by their circumstances and the amount of their arrears . . . They are upwards of ten years' rent in arrears, and in consequence of the difficulty of getting to the island, they have enjoyed for some considerable period a certain amount of Home Rule, and the result in Mingalay has certainly been most prejudicial. The man who was a sort of constable there met me when I was last in Barra, and

> told me of the state of the people, and I was really
> sorry that they should be left in such an island; but,
> in consequence of their attachment to the locality,
> and the difficulty of even recommending crofters to
> leave one place and go to another, they must just be
> left there. Latterly, however, they found the place so
> unsuitable for them that I had several applications
> from Mingalay people to come over to prosecute the
> fishing here [Barra]. I told them that those who were
> good fishermen would certainly get a share of what
> was proposed to be a sort of club farm for Castlebay
> ... [if they would] ... disencumber themselves of
> what really interferes with the continuous prosecu-
> tion of the fishing.[41]

by which MacDonald meant having more land than would
suffice to grow potatoes and graze a cow. In other words,
to give up crofting and fish full-time, which the people did
not want to do, and anyway, fishing was impossible in winter
because of the sea conditions. In these respects the islands
could not be compared to the Scottish east coast, the model
with which MacDonald was comparing Barra unfavourably.

A small number of Mingulay people did, in fact, move to
Glen, Barra, in or before 1883, but as cottars; and a few others
took part in a scheme of the type referred to by MacDonald,
in Garrygall. When asked why the people had left Mingulay, a
Barra crofter said: 'The island is so stormy that they could not
live there; and there are too many there already.'[42]

William Jolly said at this time that 'When overtures were
lately mooted in regard to their possible removal to superior
holdings and better soil, they would not listen for a moment
to such treasonable suggestions.' This could be his version
of MacDonald's story, adjusted somewhat to fit his romantic
portrayal of the islanders as firmly rooted to their ancestral
home; but perhaps he did know about some plan which is
otherwise unrecorded.

At this time (1883) there were twenty crofts, paying between £1 10s and £5 rent annually; the total rent was £57
7s.[43] The population was at its peak – over 160 – as was the
number of cottar families; there were fourteen more families
than crofts in 1881. These cottars were usually relatives of
crofters who had missed out when a croft passed to another
family member. They paid no rent and, being landless, often
depended more on fishing; in Mingulay, however, it is likely
that there was little distinction in practice, and that they
shared the work and produce of relatives' crofts.

The result of the Napier Commission was official recognition, for the first time, of the grievances and needs of the
crofting population, and led to the passing of the Crofters
Holdings Act of 1886. This gave crofters security of tenure
of land and dwellings, and was a landmark in crofting history. A Crofters Commission was set up to assess rents and
compensate tenants for improvements carried out on crofts;
the lack of such reward had always been a disincentive to
making improvements. The Mingulay tenants applied in
1887 to have their rents assessed, which involved detailing
such work.[44] When the commissioners visited the island four
years later, 'they found', wrote John Finlayson, 'that the
people, though on oath, concealed a large part of their live
stock. This criminal action might have biased the decisions,
so that the reduction [in rent] on this island was only 10%
whereas in all the Hebrides it reached 37%.[45] (The average
reduction in Barra was 35%.) Most of the rent arrears, totalling £1,064 in 1891, were cancelled; almost nothing had
been paid in the previous ten years, and one tenant owed
about forty years' worth. The arrears were the highest in any
community the commissioners came across in the crofting
counties.[46] Arrears soon built up again. In 1897 Finlayson
wrote: 'The few who used to pay regularly don't pay now
because they find that those others who don't pay are not
punished or evicted. Want of discipline is a great fault in this
instance.'[47]

In 1906 a government investigator singled out Mingulay for condemnation for non-payment of rents and rates in the Uists and Barra, finding that neither had been paid for some years. He blamed this on the islanders' unwillingness, rather than inability, to pay, but he also said that 'no attempt has been made to make a collection . . . the previous factor, by personal visits and threats of legal diligence, succeeded in recovering a fair proportion of the rents in arrear.' He went on, 'Mingulay has never paid a penny in rates, yet it gets the benefits from the rates of school buildings, education, poor relief and vaccination. It seems to me that an example, even at considerable cost, of a recalcitrant ratepayer in Mingulay might probably be beneficial.'[48]

It is doubtful whether the Crofters Holdings Act or the rent reductions made much difference to the Mingulay people, having had security because of their isolation, and having paid rent only irregularly. But they must have made a psychological difference, and this may have led Finlayson to declare in 1889 that 'the crofters are getting very assertive now. They don't scruple to argue a point with the factor. 30 years ago a wink or wince from that bugbear was enough to kill or settle a crofter.'[49] The Act did nothing for the cottar population of the Highlands and Islands, as it did not allow for the creation of new crofts. This omission was addressed by the establishment in 1897 of the Congested Districts Board, which was to fund, in addition, projects such as improvements to roads and harbours. It was this agency which funded the Mingulay derrick and bought Vatersay for crofting use, as we will see.

5

A Living from the Land

> Mingula is a rough hilly island, but everywhere there
> is good pasture, and the little cultivated patches be-
> side the village appear to thrive better than could be
> supposed in a place of the kind.

So wrote Muir in 1866, capturing the two elements of the
land-based economy. The traditional Hebridean economy
was a largely subsistence one, based on a combination of
agriculture, stockraising, and exploiting the natural resources
of the sea and seashore. This was the case in Mingulay from
early times until the nineteenth century, when the population
became too high for the island to support, and the people
had to supplement their income from other sources. Most
of the information we have on crofting – which is how the
land-based economy was organised from the early nineteenth
century – relates to the last few decades of the community's
life.

Although only a small fraction of the land area of Mingulay
was suitable for cultivation, it was fertile. The best land was
at the head of the bay and on the lower slopes of the main
valley, as can be seen by the lush green pasture there today.
The soils in these areas are based either on boulder clay or on
sand blown from the beach, and would have been fertilised
with seaweed and manure. There are traces of cultivation

on the poor peaty soils around the southeast coast as far as Skipisdale, where there is more good land.

Until the early years of the nineteenth century, agriculture would have been practised under a system found all over Europe and known in the Highlands and Islands as 'runrig', whereby the arable land was held in common by the tenants, who shared it out at yearly or longer intervals. The advantages of this system were that each tenant would, over a period of time, get a share of the best land, and that working and maintaining the land was a communal responsibility. But there were many disadvantages. The land, though fertilised, was overused and crop rotation was unknown. There was little incentive for tenants to improve land that they knew they would soon lose. There were fewer field walls, so straying animals were a problem.

As described in the previous chapter, crofting was introduced to Barra by 1816, though perhaps not to Mingulay until some years later, and the arable land was enclosed with stone dykes into plots, or crofts, rented by individual crofters. Elements of the old runrig system seem to have survived in Mingulay, however, as will be seen. The complex field system which was surveyed for the first Ordnance Survey map in 1878 and which survives to this day probably dates to this period of enclosure, or perhaps to the early 1840s when more crofts were created. Traces of earlier field systems and boundaries can be seen in places (see chapter 2), for example, a stone dyke running in a southwesterly direction from the village, through the later strips and along the northern slopes of Càrnan. Each croft consisted of some arable land and some pasture for animals, distinct from the common grazing which was the whole of the rest of the island. Arable and pasture land were located in different places according to suitability of the soil, and proportions of each varied according to croft.

Detailed records of the crofts in 1891[1] show that the tenancy of the crofts had become very complicated by then, and was not a simple matter of one tenant renting one croft.

Many crofts were divided into fractions – quarters, halves, even thirds – each one rented by a different tenant who might have several fractions as well as, in some cases, one or more whole crofts. This was the case in Barra too; the division of crofts originated when a crofter divided up his croft for a son or daughter, but there came a point when no more sub-division occurred, and there was presumably none after the Crofters Act of 1886. In Mingulay, the rents paid by each tenant remained the same from the middle of the nineteenth century (with reductions in 1891), and the number of tenants remained at nineteen or twenty.[2] Eleven crofts were recorded in 1836, nineteen in 1845,[3] sixteen and a half in 1856,[4] twenty in 1883,[5] and twenty-three in 1891. The increase after 1883 may have been a result of the Crofters Act, but the Ordnance Survey maps show that there was no significant change in the stone dyke boundaries (though some boundaries may have been of walls of turf, as was the case in Berneray; if so these were not marked on the maps) or in the total crofting area after 1878. There was great variation in total areas of crofts: from a little over one acre (0.4 hectares) to over sixteen acres (6.5 hectares), this croft being shared by three tenants. There was equally wide variation in the amount of land rented by each tenant. Donald MacKinnon, the constable, had the largest amount of land, about fourteen acres.

The total area of the crofting land was 137 acres (55.5 hectares), almost 10 per cent of the area of the island, of which forty-two acres were arable and sixty-five pasture. The remaining thirty acres were described as 'common machair', for arable use, in which eight tenants had shares; machair is light sandy soil such as that in the main valley, but where this common machair was is not clear. This appears to be a survival of the old runrig system, and there were similar survivals in Barra at this time. Once laid out, the croft boundaries – the stone dykes anyway – would have remained largely unchanged. On the death of a crofter, the croft nor-mally passed to a relative. The croft land was divided from the common grazing by the head dyke, made of stone and turf, and stout enough to keep animals out. From the details of improvements to crofts submitted with applications for rent reductions in 1887,[6] it seems that crofters were responsible for maintaining their own sections of head dyke. Other improvements included land drainage by means of subsoil drains, and clearance of stones.

The best arable land, on the south side of the main valley, was divided by low dykes into narrow strips, perhaps originally one per croft (see map 3 and plate 19). The soil here is sandy, and although the eastern part inland from the beach was naturally so, towards the peaty hills some sand may have been brought in, and the land cleared of stones, all at great cost of labour and time. This area only accounts for about one third of the total described as arable; the rest was scattered about the area shown on the maps as being enclosed, such as the area north of the village and beach, and around the southeast coast as far as Skipisdale. Most of the latter is peaty ground, but some of it was cultivated in strips called lazy-beds *(fiannagan)*, an unfortunate term, for the labour involved in making them was immense.

The strips were made by digging parallel ditches down a slope every couple of metres (6 feet), laying the peaty material on the intervening strips, then adding manure, perhaps shell sand, and seaweed, though Mingulay never had much of that. The result, common throughout the islands where damp ground was cultivated, was best suited to potatoes; indeed, lazy-beds became widespread only after potatoes were adopted on a large scale in the Hebrides from the middle of the eighteenth century. The potato's tolerance of poor soil and its high yields made it the most important food crop at a time of rising population in the late eighteenth and early nineteenth centuries. It could be said that the potato was partly responsible for this rise, and the poorer people became so dependent on it that, when the crop was struck by blight in the 1840s, famine ensued (the blight, a fungus spread by the wind, rotted the tubers in the ground).[7] The Mingulay lazy-beds almost certainly date from the nineteenth century when the population was at its highest.

The arable land was fertilised in spring with seaweed, carried from the shore in sacks and fish baskets,[8] manure from the byres, and peat ash from the fireplaces and hearths; in later years fish guts brought from Castlebay were used as an unsatisfactory substitute for seaweed, which was not plentiful.[9] Martin Martin said, in 1695, that 'the Natives . . . fasten a Cow to a Stake, and spread a quantity of Sand on the Ground, upon which the Cow's Dung falls, and this they mingle together, and lay it on the arable Land'. The land would have been ploughed with spades of two types found in crofting areas. The *cas-chrom*, bent spade or foot plough, had a long iron-tipped blade fitted at an angle to the shaft for extra leverage, and it was particularly suitable for stony ground and lazy-beds. The *cas-dhìreach* or straight spade was used for the lighter sandy soil, the operators working in teams. Michael MacPhee remembered seeing both types in Mingulay,[10] though by the time of the desertion they were being made obsolete by spades of modern mass-produced type. According to Father Allan McDonald, the *cas-chrom* was used by men on lazy-beds, the *cas-dhìreach* used by women on the lighter soils in South Uist and Barra.[11] The women would have been obliged to do work which may have been traditionally men's, when the men were away fishing in spring and summer. Only John MacKinnon (Iagan Dhòmhnaill Nèill) used a horse-drawn plough, which he made himself, as his croft was less stony than others. He also ploughed for Michael MacNeil (an Rìgh, 'the King')[12] (plate 24).

The first seed to be planted was sprinkled with holy water, and a blessing was recited: *Dia a chur buil is buaidh is toradh is cinneachdainn air* – 'May God send result, success and fruit and growth.'[13] Crops grown in the last years were barley, rye, small- or black-oats, potatoes, cabbages, carrots, and turnips (the last for winter fodder; hay was also cut for fodder).[14] Some of the vegetables were grown in enclosures in the village. Barley was traditionally the main crop grown, but was overtaken by the potato, as we have seen. Mingulay potatoes were said to have been the best in the Hebrides.[15] The other vegetables were probably also introduced relatively late, though Martin Martin mentions the parsnip in Mingulay, which he describes as 'lately discovered'. Crop rotation was practised in crofting times, and it is not clear whether particular crops were grown on particular soil types. Planting, generally done by women, was finished in May or June, and the crops needed only weeding, by the women, until harvest in August or September. The cereals were cut with sickles and, in later years, scythes (larger than sickles, operated with both hands). There was always a rush not to be the last with the harvest as that person was said to 'have the *cailleach*' (old woman), a belief common in the Hebrides. The cereals then had to be processed to separate the grain from the ears and husks, and ground.

In the eighteenth century it was common practice in the Hebrides to pull up the crop by the roots and set fire to the ears, a handful at a time, dashing them on the ground at the critical time to shake off the grain before it too burnt. This was known as *gradanadh*, 'graddaning', and was condemned by contemporary observers as being wasteful of the straw that could have been used as winter fodder or as thatch. In later years the Mingulay method was to dry the ears in a corn-drying kiln. Most of the crofters had a kiln, housed in a barn,[16] of a type common throughout the Highlands and Islands. The kiln consisted of a raised platform with a large stone-lined bowl sunk into it, to the bottom of which heat was brought from a fire, via a flue. The ears, detached from their stalks, were placed on a piece of sacking suspended from a plank straddling the bowl (in other areas more commonly placed on straw or sacking over sticks placed across the bowl), and dried for a couple of hours. The ears were then winnowed – thrown up into the wind so that the chaff (husks) was blown away and the grain fell to the ground or floor of the barn.[17] The barns were provided with an opening in the wall opposite the door, so creating a through draught suitable for this purpose.

Apart from some barley which was eaten in grain form, the grain was ground into meal. In early times, and perhaps even into recent times, grain was ground in saddle querns as described in chapter 2. In later times the rotary quern or hand-mill was used. This consisted of a pair of flat circular stones: a fixed lower stone, and an upper stone which was rotated on an axle set in the lower stone, by means of a handle on its edge. The grain was fed into the quern through a hole in the centre of the upper stone and the resultant meal was scattered around the edge. This was women's work, often done in pairs: one feeding in grain, the other grinding. These querns were made of local stone as late as the last decades, as John MacKinnon is believed to have made one. A third method of processing barley was to pound it in a stone 'mortar', with a wooden mallet, to remove the inner husk. One of these stones survives against the outside front wall of one of the newer houses. It is a rough cube, with a conical hollow 15 centimetres (6 inches) deep, of a type found more widely.[18] The pounded grain was called *cnotag*, and was used to make a chicken dish eaten on St Michael's Day (Michaelmas, 29 September).

Around the end of the nineteenth century, John MacKinnon built a mill on the stream a short distance above the village. He ground grain for the whole community, presumably for a fee, or a share of the meal, as poorer people continued to use the hand mills. Mary Campbell remembered sending four sacks of barley at a time to the mill. The building of a mill at this time is puzzling. Towards the end of the century most of the meal consumed in Barra was imported[19] and meal prices generally were falling. But landing imported meal on Mingulay was difficult, and, although this may have been eased with the construction of the derrick promised in 1899, this could explain the building of the mill. On the other hand, Mary Campbell said that meal was imported only when the locally produced meal ran out; also that a little white (wheat) flour was imported.[20] As in so many cases, the evidence is confusing. The mill may have been built in the 1890s, as Murray said there was no mill at the time of her visit in 1888, but it is odd that it is not marked on the 1901 map. Its life was short, for it had apparently been abandoned by 1905, when a photograph (plate 9) shows its roof to be in disrepair.

An unusual feature of the mill was its design. The surviving ruins show that it was built on the vertical, rather than on the much simpler horizontal principle, which had been common in the Hebrides for centuries. This is explained by its origin – it was a copy of a mill built on Berneray by a lighthouse keeper from Fife.[21] MacKinnon probably used some of the Berneray mill's parts, for this went out of use in the same period that MacKinnon built his. The wheel revolved vertically, powered by water brought in a channel from a point on the stream above the mill. The horizontal axle of the wheel powered, through gearing, the millstones in the mill itself. The stones were probably quarried from an outcrop about 200 metres west of the school buildings.[22] Sometime prior to 1975 the millstones were removed from the mill and now lie near a house in the northern part of the village. Another possible use of the mill was as a kind of lathe. There is a tradition that the mill was used for wood turning, which would make sense, as MacKinnon made spinning wheels and furniture; however, water-powered lathes are not known to have existed in western Scotland.

It was common throughout the Highlands and Islands for the use of both querns and mills to be forbidden by proprietors, forcing tenants to use the proprietors' own mills, for a fee. This was the case in Barra, where the sites where querns that had been seized were dumped in the sea or in lochs are remembered. It is hard to imagine that this rule could have applied to the outlying islands; querns were in common use in Mingulay and Berneray, and Berneray had a mill, as noted – the only one, apart from the proprietor's mill at Loch an Duin in Barra, shown on the maps of the Barra Isles of 1861–3 and 1878.

Agriculture was always precarious in the Highlands and Islands, because of soil conditions, long winters, and crops being vulnerable to bad weather and disease; and its products often ran out long before the next harvest. Stockraising was of equal, and in earlier times probably of greater, importance. As I.F. Grant has said:

> The nature of the physical conditions of the Highlands of Scotland make them . . . more suitable for the raising of livestock than for the cultivation of crops, or perhaps one should say . . . the Highlands are less unsuitable for the raising of animals than for the growing of grain.

The Mingulay people kept cattle, sheep, ponies, poultry, and, before the end of the nineteenth century, pigs. The amount of grazing stock each crofter was allowed was theoretically fixed according to the number of shares in the common grazing each had, which varied according to their rental; this entitlement was known as the 'souming', but it was exceeded in many cases.[23] There were two points of access to the common grazing from the village which would have been used by cattle and ponies in winter: a northern one between the village and the chapel, and a southern one branching from the road south of the village. The crofters also had their own plots of pasture, and some of this was on the northern, steeper, side of the main valley, where plate 9 shows cattle, and barbed wire reinforcing a stone dyke.

Cattle were the most important animals, providing food – milk, butter, cheese and other products – throughout the year (although depleted in winter when fodder was short). This was particularly important during the spring and early summer when there was the danger of the produce of the land running out. The account of 1620 notes that butter and cheese were paid as rent,[24] and in 1820 butter and tallow were being sold,[25] though to whom is not recorded. Tallow is animal fat;

it was sold for 6d per pound (2½p per 0.45kg), and quantities of seven and eleven pounds were recorded. It was formerly used in making, for instance, candles, soap, and lubricants; Berneray Pabbay and Sandray also produced it, and it is known to have been exported from Skye in the seventeenth century.[26] It was among the products together with fish and, in Mingulay's case, birds and feathers, which were taken to Glasgow and elsewhere and bartered for commodities such as cloth, salt, and paraffin. Cattle were also one of the few commodities that could be sold for cash, with which to pay rent and buy necessities. In 1794 the average price paid for a cow in Barra was £2 5s,[27] more than enough for the year's rent; but the difficulty of shipping so large a beast as a cow from Mingulay probably meant that only calves were sold off the island. Until the nineteenth century the cattle in Barra were black (i.e. 'unimproved'); they were later bred with mainland types to produce the Highland cattle such as those seen in the 1905 photographs.

Most of the crofters had at least one cow, some many more, plus calves; eighty cattle were recorded in 1856[28] and seventy in 1883,[29] but these figures exclude cottars' stock. Most of the calves were sold when a year old at the cattle fair at Eoligarry in Barra, and buyers also came to the island. The cattle spent the summers outside on the common grazing or on the croft, and were milked and tended by the women. Catherine MacNeil said that in winter, from October to April, the cattle were housed at night (in the houses until the late nineteenth century, later in byres); the women still milked them but, since they were busy with spinning and other domestic work, the men tended them. Cattle were not eaten in later years, but Catherine MacNeil said they were in her grandfather's time, the beef being salted for winter use and shared out among the community.[30] Autumn slaughtering of cattle was common in the Highlands and Islands before the introduction of turnips in the eighteenth century made it possible to feed cattle in the winter.

Sheep were kept for their wool and for winter food, and in earlier times would have been milked. They needed the least attention of all the animals: they had the run of the common grazing all the year round, only needing to be rounded up for shearing in early summer and for dipping in late summer. Dipping, introduced in the late nineteenth century, involved everyone, including the children, who sometimes missed school because of it.[31] Most crofters had sheep, latterly of the Hebridean Blackface variety; there were 144 in 1856,[32] 140 in 1883[33] (crofters' stock only). They provided all the islanders' wool needs, and some were killed and salted for winter use, five at a time, Mary Campbell remembered (but not shared out as the beef was).[34] They were not sold off the island.

Sheep were regarded as sufficiently valuable for the people to go to extraordinary trouble and risk to land them on the precipitous sea stacks of Liànamuil and Arnamuil to graze their summits. MacQueen mentioned this in 1794, and as late as 1887 Harvie-Brown recorded that there were about five sheep on Liànamuil, and twenty on Arnamuil, which the people had cleared of puffins to preserve the grazing.

Ponies of the Barra breed were kept to carry the peat down from the hills in creels, in the summer and autumn. This was their sole function: they didn't carry seaweed from the shore, or goods landed at Aneir, as Mary Campbell said that the road was too rough for them to use.[35] Most of the crofters had at least one pony, and these totalled thirty-two in 1856[36]. and thirty-five in 1883.[37] The ponies were hardy enough to be out all year round, but two crofters had stables in 1887,[38] so their ponies must have been stabled in winter. These would have needed feeding, and bearing in mind the scarcity of fodder (hay and turnips) in winter, and the limited amount of work they did, it is surprising that so many were kept. The St Kildans had ponies for a time, but didn't consider them worth the amount of grass they ate.[39] So it is probable that they were bred for sale, as was the case in Barra, where foals were sold at six months or a year old. Barra ponies were in demand, and mainland dealers would attend the horse fairs at Castlebay.[40]

Pigs were uncommon in the Barra Isles, but two visitors encountered young ones in houses in Mingulay: Walker in about 1869 and Murray in 1888. Poultry was kept in the houses and outside: John Finlayson kept hens 'on the hill' and complained of crows getting at the eggs.[41]

The land also provided peat, which had been used as fuel from prehistoric times in the Hebrides. Mingulay was fortunate in having plenty of peat, unlike its neighbours, and there was no restriction on its use. Most of the peat was dug from the western and northern hills. The peat on the northern promontory (an Aird) was said to be the best, although it was the furthest from the village. A track which runs along the steep west side of MacPhee's Hill, as already mentioned, is believed to have been made to enable access for ponies.

Getting peat was a family activity that went on throughout the summer. Cutting began in May.[42] The peat was cut from vertical sections into brick-shaped pieces. The turf was first cut off with a spade, and the peats may have been cut with a special spade which had a blade at right angles to the main one; this was known as a *treisgeir* in Barra, where it was in common use. The waterlogged peats were laid out on the ground for a few weeks for the water to drain off, then laid upright against each other to continue drying. When hard and dry, they were carried down to the village directly; alternatively, they were built into stacks (see plate 12), to be taken down to the village when needed. In boggy areas stone platforms or stances were built for the stacks, to keep the peats dry.[43] These platforms are the most numerous of the man-made structures on Mingulay; there are more than 300 of them, a contrast with the other islands which have very few. They form one of the largest collections of such platforms in those areas of Scotland where peat was dug. They are found on Càrnan and MacPhee's Hill and especially on the plateau-like high ground between the two. Here the peat has been stripped from huge areas, leaving large expanses of bare rock. The platforms are rectangular or oval, up to seven metres (23 feet) long, and construction methods vary. A series of rectangular platforms, defined by large stones set on edge, were interpreted by Sheffield University investigators as possible Bronze Age burial monuments. It is very likely that some of the platforms were built out of earlier structures. Some of the platforms have remains of walling on them, presumably built around peat stacks to stop peats blowing away in gales. Alexander Carmichael noted this in 1866, and drew a comparison with the custom in St Kilda. He also noted that the Mingulay peat was not good; and he saw several stacks near the edge of Biulacraig.[44] The majority of the platforms probably date from the second half of the nineteenth century when the population was at its highest and peat was being dug on an almost industrial scale. However, the tradition of building such platforms goes back earlier: there are twenty four platforms on Berneray, which date to before 1828, because we know that by then the people of Berneray were getting their peat from Mingulay.

The peats were carried down to the village by ponies, in creels, made from rods of black willow known to the islanders as *caol dubh;* it grew on the shores of Loch Sunart on the mainland, and was collected by the fishermen when fishing there. The rods used for the creels carried by ponies and people were thinner and more pliable than those used for lobster creels. The creels had one flat side for ease of carrying on the back, and were held, when carried by people, with one hand over the shoulder, and the bottoms were flat to ease loading on the ground.

The peats were built into big stacks in the stackyards of the houses, thatched with turf. A family might get through eight or nine stacks during the year, for the domestic fire was always kept burning.

Agriculture and stockraising, the elements of crofting, were therefore an important part of the island economy, but could not have supported life on their own; fishing, which we will look at next, and fowling together complete the picture. Crofting declined in relative importance in later years as fishing developed, and the sale of produce is not mentioned after 1820.

6

Fishing and the Sea

The male portion of the population follow the
calling of fishermen, and have the reputation of
being industrious, skilful, and persevering.

This was one of the statements in a petition the islanders sent
to the Secretary of State for Scotland, as will be seen.

In historic times, fishing was fundamental to the economy
of the Barra Isles. The abundance of fish in the surrounding
seas – amongst the richest of the Scottish west coast – made
fish an important food item, and, in later years, cash earner.
The earliest writers mention fishing, but a detailed picture is
available only for the last twenty years or so of the community's life.

Until the seventeenth or eighteenth centuries, fishing from
the Barra Isles was for home consumption, but by the end of
the nineteenth century it had become an important industry
based in Castlebay, Barra. Fishing from Mingulay was always
handicapped by stormy seas and the lack of a landing place
or anchorage for boats, but it was profitable, and the island's
last inhabitants were engaged in fishing.

By the end of the nineteenth century there were three types
of fishing from Mingulay: line fishing, herring fishing and lobster fishing. Fishing by line, for white fish – mainly ling, also
cod, skate, halibut and monkfish – in the seas around Barra

Head was the longest established. The lines were fitted with hooks so many fathoms apart, and baited with fish and shell-fish. They were taken to sea coiled in baskets, set on floats and buoys, and then left, to be hauled in later in the day or the next day. There were great lines, for catching ling in deep water, and small lines and hand lines for catching flatfish in shallower water. In 1900 four boats carried between them thirty great lines, each averaging 600 yards (546 metres) long; twenty-four small lines, 240 yards (218 metres) long, and twenty-four hand lines, 60 yards long. Each boat had four or five crew.[1]

The white fishing season lasted from March or April until August; the Barra men started in February but the conditions for launching and landing boats made this impossible from Mingulay. This was one of the complaints set out in a petition from the islanders to the Secretary of State for Scotland, ap-pealing for improved landing facilities, in 1896.[2] It was sent via their MP, James Baillie, who may have written it; there were a few errors of fact in it, suggesting that the writer was not local. It was signed by sixty-five of the island's men and boys, the teacher John Finlayson, and the Barra priest, James Chisholm; the first signatory was Michael Campbell (Teac), who may have organised it. The petition pointed out that 'many of the fishermen migrate for the season to the small island of Boreray [i.e. Berneray] where the access is much easier, and there they erect temporary huts and cure their fish.' There was a curer in Berneray who bought the catches, but Ealasaid Sinclair said some curing was done in Mingulay, probably for home consumption.

The method of curing in Barra was described by Walker in 1764:

> When they bring the Fish ashore, they split and wash them and cleanse off the Blood and Slime with Heather Brushes. They then lay them in small Heaps, upon the rocks with a Layer of Salt between each two Layers of Fish. They are allowed to ly in this

manner for two or three Days, when they are again washed in Sea Water, and laid out on the Rocks to dry: and in good Weather, they will be sufficiently cured in eight or ten Days.

In about 1867 curers from the Scottish east coast developed Castlebay as a fishing port,[3] mainly for herring, the only such port in the Outer Isles south of Stornoway, Lewis. Before this, and to a lesser extent afterwards, the fishermen of the Barra Isles took their catches to Glasgow, Tobermory (Mull), and Northern Ireland for sale or barter, returning with goods unavailable in the islands. The fishermen sometimes got stranded by bad weather along the route; on one occasion a crew spent nine days on the island of Coll helping a farmer with the harvest. The trade from Barra was described by Walker in 1764, and may have begun the previous century when trade between the Hebrides and the mainland first became significant.[4] The last MacNeil of Barra, General Roderick, attempted to get a cut of the profits of this trade from Barra, which may have been written into the terms of the tenancies of the crofts. His successor, Gordon of Cluny, complained in 1846:

My fishermen persuaded me to supply them with tackle, that they might prosecute their calling, and be thereby enabled to pay their rents, but ... they sent off their fish clandestinely to Glasgow, from where no money was brought back, but boat loads of raw-grained whisky, to be retailed in the islands. When I could get no rent, and saw my authority so completely disregarded, 1 made the best bargain I could with a fishing company from Lerwick, and instructed my factor to see that they got all the fish at the agreed price, the company giving the fishers oatmeal and tobacco for their own use, and a tally for what more they might have earned ... as credit for their rental.[5]

From 1867 onwards, the fishermen sold most of their catches to the curers at Castlebay. The curers were merchants, or employed by merchants, and the fishermen contracted to sell to a particular merchant who paid them in credit at his shop. This so-called 'truck' system was controlled by the merchants; it 'keeps them in a kind of slavery with the dealers with whom they have to do', said Mrs Murray in 1888. The fishermen continued to sell some of their catches on the mainland and in Ireland, where they presumably got better prices. Donald MacPhee (Dòmhnall Bàn) said that in the later years the fishing industry suffered from the depradations of trawlers from the East Coast regularly fishing illegally within the 3-mile limit, reducing catches and incomes. He said this was one of the reasons behind the decision to leave.[6]

Fishing from the shore on the island's east coast with bamboo rod and line was also popular, using seagull feathers rolled up as a fly, known as *maghar*. Flounder and saithe could be caught in the bay, which John Finlayson reckoned to be the best place for flounder in Scotland.[7] Saithe (cuddies) were also caught in shallow water using a method described by Michael MacPhee:

> They had a thing they called *tàbh*: that was made with a big hoop of osier and two ribs in the middle crossing over each other. And on top of these ribs was a net, fixed round the rim of it. A great long handle, roughly ten feet. And they would go to the craigs with the *tàbh*. The first thing they had to do was to go and gather *soll*. They would crush the *soll*. Well, soll is what they called limpets, whelks, winkles and little things like that pounded up together. When they had pounded that up they would call it ground-bait. They would let down the *tàbh* into the sea: they would scatter the ground-bait over it, and the cuddies would come to the bait. When they saw there was enough round the bait, they would

raise the *tàbh* and the poor little cuddies were in the
middle of it.[8]

This method was used in other islands. Saithe liver oil was
used as fuel for the lamps in the houses; the oil of the dogfish
was used for curing sick cattle.[9]

The rich herring stocks around Barra were hardly exploited
until Castlebay's development as a port in 1867, due to the
lack of adequate boats and nets; nets were needed because
of the small size of the fish, in contrast to white fish. At first
the fishing was monopolised by east coast fishermen who had
the larger boats and nets needed, and local men were hired as
crew. By 1880 the Barra men were able to buy boats of their
own, worth £400 fully equipped, with loans from merchants
and the landlord, Lady Gordon Cathcart.[10] In 1894 two of
these larger boats appear in the records for Mingulay (which
start in 1888), and their purchase, if they were the first, suggests growing prosperity. They were between 30 and 45 feet
(9–13.5 metres) long, half-decked and single-masted, and
had a crew of five or six. They would carry up to thirty-five
drift nets each, twice as many as the smaller boats previously
used. The crews slept in the boats at Castlebay at night, and
at weekends left them there and rowed home in smaller boats,
as they were too big to beach on Mingulay. Donald MacPhee
(Dòmhnall Iain Dhòmhnaill) had one of these boats, the
Snowbird, 40 feet long.[11]

The herring were sold to the curers at Castlebay. During
the herring season, from May to July, the village became a
bustling metropolis, with hundreds of boats, and dozens of
curers, based there. The industry provided work for thousands
of people, on shore as well as in the boats. Thus Mingulay
men were employed as carters and labourers, and in making
and mending the nets, as well as on the boats themselves.
The women worked in teams of three gutting the herring
and packing them in barrels with salt for export to Glasgow
and thence to the Continent and Russia. The work was hard

and the conditions unhealthy from the stinking offal, and the sleeping accommodation in wooden huts was primitive and insanitary.[12] There were eighteen gutters from Mingulay in 1904, the highest number recorded, but none after 1908. There was also a herring station in Vatersay from about 1867 to 1892.[13]

The herring migrate in July round the north coast of Scotland and into the North Sea. The east coast boats followed them, again with hired crews: twenty Mingulay men were so employed in 1892. Roderick MacNeil and one other man from Mingulay went right down the English coast, into the winter. The women also travelled to the east coast ports and as far into England as Lowestoft, gutting and packing. Mingulay boats pursued the herring as far as the sea lochs of the mainland and Skye, and the men spent the autumn fishing there.

Fishing for lobsters around the Barra Isles also developed late in the nineteenth century when it became possible to transport them live to southern cities by steamer and rail. It was carried on from Mingulay in relatively shallow water, from March to October, by the older men who didn't want to follow the herring. Boys were taken out in the boats to get their sea legs before embarking on more arduous work. The lobsters were caught in creels made from black willow *(caol dubh)*, which grew round the edges of the sea lochs of Skye and the mainland, and were brought back by the fishermen when fishing there. The creels were made with a solid wooden base, with the rods bent over from one side to the other. This frame was then covered with netting, and an opening was left for the lobster to climb in. 210 creels were recorded in 1895, sixty in the last season, 1912. The creels were set, baited, on the sea bottom and marked with buoys. They were checked daily and the lobsters were taken to Castlebay for sale once a week, and the men were paid in credit at the merchant's shop.

There were various superstitions associated with fishing. It was believed to be unlucky to go out on a Monday on the first day of the season. It was also believed to be unlucky to meet a woman on the way to the fishing. The skipper of a boat once saw a mermaid; he ordered the crew to turn back, but never told them why.

At one time the Mingulay people caught basking sharks, formerly called sun fish, *cearban* in Gaelic. These huge harmless creatures swim close to the surface in summer and would have been easy targets with harpoons. The naturalist Harvie-Brown wrote in 1888: 'Forty or fifty years ago many "cearban" came into Mingulay Bay and the natives killed large numbers for the sake of the oil found in their livers. The natives found this lucrative, so much so, that they procured harpoons on purpose by steamers from Glasgow.' Writing of Barra in 1840, Nicolson said that the shark hunters 'received a premium from the Board of Trustees for Fisheries; but this productive source of wealth has been discontinued, from their inability to procure the necessary tackling.' Premiums were offered as an incentive to fishermen catching all types of fish. Winners of a £1 premium for catching sun fish were recorded in 1819. Hector Campbell of the *Kelly*, Mingulay, sold 60 gallons (272 litres) of oil, while Roderick MacNeil of the *Mary*, Sandray, one of four Sandray men mentioned, sold 295 gallons (1341 litres).[14]

The boats used for line and lobster fishing were latterly of the type used on the Scottish east coast, as seen in plate 13. Boats between 18 and 30 feet (5.5–9 metres) in length were used for line fishing up to about 8 miles (13 kilometres) west of Barra Head, with a crew of five or six; the smaller ones, under 18 feet, were used closer inshore. The recorded number of boats varies; in the 1890s there were six or seven, thereafter four or five (including the two herring boats). In 1903 one of the smaller boats was called the *Provider*, owned by Donald MacPhee (Dòmhnall Bàn) (shown in plate 13), another was the *St Peter*, owned by A (?Angus) MacNeil.[15] John MacLean (Barnaidh) also had a boat. These boats were presumably purchased, but John MacKinnon is said to have made a small boat, and his father also made boats; the cradle used for boat building was still visible in the village in 1949.[16]

The east coast boats were a big improvement on the locally made Barra boats which they superseded. Walker, visiting Barra in 1764, was critical of the 'smallness and insufficiency of their Boats, by which they are kept idle during a great part of the fishing Season, as they dare not venture abroad in them but when the Weather is very moderate; and they are likewise extremely defective in Lines and fishing Tackle'.

MacCulloch described the boats in 1816 as

> very peculiar . . . the boatmen are their own builders, purchasing the timber from the northern traders. They are extremely sharp, both fore and aft. They have no floor, but rise with an almost flat straight side . . . from their lightness, they are almost as buoyant in a bad sea as a Norway skiff.

Shellfish were not eaten in recent times, according to Catherine MacNeil, but sand-eels were eaten, and used as bait for lythe. Michael MacPhee described how he caught sand-eels:

> It was by night you caught them, at night time at low water with a spring tide . . . we had a sickle called a *corran shìolag* . . . we would go to the beach and start making furrows with these sickles, sinking them about six inches into the sand, until we found a sand-eel. When you found one, you set your foot against the sickle and pulled it up very gradually to your foot and held it there. Then you put down your hand into the sand and caught it and put it in the bucket . . . some of them were about thirteen inches long . . . They were good to eat . . .[17]

Fishing was always a hazardous occupation in seas with

treacherous currents between the islands, and with unpredictable weather. In 1858 a boat and its crew of five from Tangusdale, Barra, was lost off Mingulay,[18] and in 1897 a boat from Pabbay with five crew – most of the island's men – was lost in a storm south of Barra Head. This disaster is said to have led to a loss of confidence among the Mingulay people, and to have been a reason for the decision to evacuate. It was suggested in about 1866 that a breakwater be thrown across the west end of the sound between Mingulay and Berneray to create a harbour of refuge for fishermen.[19] This might have seemed a good idea on the map, but is quite absurd to anyone familiar with the islands and the raging seas. (It is a fascinating idea, though: had it been possible, Mingulay's southern valley, Skipisdale, where there is a landing place, might have been resettled and could have developed into a curing station.) Mingulay's biggest drawback was the lack of a landing place and anchorage, as will be seen. These difficulties were behind the applications by some of the fishermen for crofts in Barra in 1883.

Despite these drawbacks, fishing was profitable, and Mingulay was used as a base even after the last inhabitants had left. Although the majority of the people had left in 1907–8, and most of the rest in 1910, the records show that twelve fishermen and boys were working from Mingulay in 1911 (as in the previous two years), and ten in 1912.[20] They must have lived there only during the fishing season, for only six of the eleven people living in Mingulay in April 1911 were men. 1912 was the last year that fishermen were based there.

The economic and social impact of the fishing industry, particularly the herring industry, on Mingulay must have been considerable. For the first time many islanders – between thirty and fifty in the twenty years up to 1907 – were earning cash. Hired crewmen were paid a proportion of the boat's earnings: in a good year they could make £20–£30; in a bad year – which could mean glut as well as scarcity – almost nothing. The women could earn £4–£8.[21] The cash was used

to buy foodstuffs, cloth, kitchenware, tobacco and other commodities that in earlier times would have been regarded as
luxuries. Many people were now absent from the island for
long periods; those men who spent the winters working in
Glasgow can hardly have been home at all. Inevitably, extra
cash and less time meant that crofting and fowling, which
coincided with the fishing season, declined. Travelling to
other parts of Britain would have opened the islanders' eyes
to how other people lived, and led to dissatisfaction with their
own lot. It was ironic that while fishing brought prosperity to
the community, it contributed to its decline and death.

With the increasing dependence on fishing, and on the outside world in general, the lack of a landing place or anchorage
became more serious. The fishermen were, said the 1896
petition, 'very much handicapped by having at the end of the
day's fishing to drag up their boats high and dry on the rock
[beach was meant] without any mechanical appliances, and in
launching them again the crews are compelled to wade breast
high, the wading being repeated on their return'. Mingulay
Bay is too broad an indentation to provide much shelter from
the swell and wind, especially if from the south or east. There
are two points in the bay where people and goods could
be landed on the rocks: one on the south, Aneir (probably
meaning 'landing place' in Gaelic; it was not one particular
spot but comprised an outer one, Aneir a Muigh, and an inner
one, Aneir a Stigh); and one on the north. The state of the
sea and wind determine which can be used, but a calm sea is
needed for both. Boats themselves had to be landed on, and
launched from, the sandy beach, which, being exposed and
steeply shelving, was often difficult, dangerous, or impossible,
as the 1839 disaster related in chapter 1 shows. This, and the
need to haul them up the beach, limited the size of boat that
could be kept at Mingulay, hence the herring boats were left
at Castlebay. To land a sailing boat, the men had to furl the
sail, collapse the mast, move the ballast (beach boulders) to
the stern or jettison it, and ride the boat up the beach with a

wave.[22] The whole community helped haul it up the beach, on planks. During Robert Adam's stay in 1905 a sudden storm blew up and the islanders – mainly women and old men, the younger men being away fishing – rushed to haul a boat out of reach of the sea. Adam realised that the people could not go on much longer like this.[23]

When the boats were in regular use they were left on the beach beyond the high-water mark, but during the winter the smaller ones were dragged up a grassy slope above the rocks in the middle of the bay and secured in shelters from the gales.[24] These shelters (known in Barra as *bara*, 'barrow'), are boat-shaped enclosures of stone slabs embedded upright in the turf, and ropes were passed between opposing stones over the upturned boats. The three surviving shelters could accommodate boats up to about 6 metres (18 feet) long. They were used in recent times although they could be much older; such structures are well known in the former Norse areas of Scotland such as Orkney and Shetland, where they are known as noosts or nausts, but that does not imply a Norse origin. Other nausts can be seen as seaward-facing scoops on slopes above the beach, for instance on the side of the gully opening onto the southernmost section of the beach.

In adverse conditions, which could last for weeks or even months at a time in winter, it was impossible to launch a boat or land an incoming one, leaving the islanders completely cut off. It was common for visitors to be marooned there, and, conversely, for islanders to be stranded in Barra waiting to come home. As related in chapter 3, Father Allan McDonald was once stranded on the island for seven weeks. The story is told of two men who went to Barra together, one to return after a short stay, the other to go to New York (!). The latter returned after three months to find his friend still waiting to get home to Mingulay. On another occasion conditions in the bay forced the islanders to resort to the desperate measure of carrying a boat over the island to Bàgh Shleiteadh on the west coast, where it is possible to launch a boat, to get a doctor from Barra. The sea, once a highway, had become a barrier.

The Mingulay people were fortunate in having a regular, bi-weekly postal service, in the last years anyway, as the Post Office had an arrangement with the lighthouse boat. In 1905 Peter Sinclair of Berneray, the 'Barra Giant' was the postman for the southern isles and in 1907 and 1908 James Stewart, who lived in Mingulay, was a postman.[25] The lighthouse boat, which sailed down once a week in summer, once a fortnight in winter, may have been made use of in other ways by the islanders, if the Northern Lighthouse Board allowed it. In the later nineteenth century the fishermen would have gone to Castlebay regularly in spring and summer with white fish and lobsters, and would have brought back supplies, but otherwise a boat would go over only every six to eight weeks.[26]

In 1897 Dr Ogilvie Grant, Medical Officer for Inverness-shire, said it was easier to get to America than to Mingulay. He went on to say of the inhabitants of Mingulay (and Eriskay):

> They are all hardy fishermen, well known for their skill. They have not been clamouring claimants for doles, and they badly require landing places to carry on their occupation. I am not likely to forget the difficulties I experienced when landing at Mingalay, or, when leaving it, I found that I could not get back to Castlebay, and had to take refuge from the storm in the Island of Bernera, and be for days the guest of the kindly lighthouse keepers; but my difficulties were trifling compared with the difficulties experienced by the people in landing their provisions. I was informed that it was no unusual occurrence for them to have to throw their bags of meal into the sea and drag them ashore by means of a rope. This, no doubt, is a state of matters that will soon come to an end owing to the institution of the Congested Districts Board.[27]

This prophecy was to be fulfilled little more than a decade later, though in a manner not, perhaps, anticipated by the doctor – the desertion of Mingulay and the Board's purchase of Vatersay. In the immediate term, however, an attempt was made to alleviate the problem. Although a government commission had been informed of the situation in 1890,[28] nothing had been done, hence the islanders' petition, six years later. It called for the government's assistance in making a 'boatslip with a boat-hauling convenience', for the building of which they offered free labour, and it concluded with the hope that 'your lordship will lend a favourable ear to the cry of a sorely-distressed community'. Again nothing happened, but the following year, 1897, the Congested Districts Board was created, with a remit which included the provision of piers, roads, etc., and an appeal by Barra Parish Council got things going.[29]

The Board's engineer established that building a boatslip as requested, or a pier, was not feasible, the bay being too exposed and its floor too sandy. He supported an islander's suggestion of a crane or derrick which would hoist boats right out of the water, of a type which the Board had installed elsewhere. But, somehow, this ambitious concept was downgraded to one of merely hoisting loads, cattle and passengers into and out of boats. This rendered the whole project much less useful, but – and this must explain the change – it would be considerably easier and cheaper.

Arguments over the upkeep of the derrick once completed delayed the project still further, and it was not until March 1901 that the go-ahead for its construction was given. It was eventually agreed that the islanders would be given the derrick as a gift, and that they, with Michael Campbell (Teac) in charge, would be responsible for its upkeep. The men were to provide free labour, although, as Father James Chisholm of Castlebay, who had agreed to act as mediator between the Board and the islanders, pointed out, they were 'not accustomed to such work'.

The derrick was erected on a platform, blasted out of the rock and completed with concrete, a short distance east of the landing place at Aneir (see plate 14). Concrete steps linked the platform to the road, which was extended from Aneir, and to a small corrugated iron store. The derrick, made of wood and iron, was supplied with boxes for goods, canvas slings for cattle (though how cattle were meant to get to the platform is not clear), and a basket for people. On one occasion, it is said, some boys gave an old man who was being plucked from a boat more swings than he had bargained for. An iron ladder was supplied, presumably to fix to the platform edge for people to climb up from arriving boats in order to operate the derrick, and to climb down into departing boats, but it was never fixed. The engineer reported that the sea had been too rough to do it, but he had arranged that John MacKinnon would fix it, under the supervision of John Finlayson. The ladder can be seen on the road on the right of the photograph, and today reposes further along the road.

The derrick was completed in September 1901. The engineer reported that 'the principal part of the inhabitants were present and expressed in loud terms their appreciation of the crane and surroundings as a great convenience to the island and its inhabitants'. But within a few months there were problems: Father Chisholm informed the Board that the concrete surface of the platform was disintegrating, exposing the shingle packing underneath. The Board claimed this was due to the local sand being unsuitable, but an islander blamed poor workmanship. The Board were irritated, and nothing was done, as the photograph seems to show.

Shoddy workmanship was not the only defect of the derrick. In 1903 a Board official reported an islander as saying that 'the crane is in the wrong place and is very little used and, generally, he was rather strong in his language about the way things had been done'. A glance at plate 14 shows what the islander meant about the derrick's positioning: it was too far from the sea for a boat to approach safely, except in very calm conditions. None of the tape recordings mentions the derrick. The photographer Robert Adam was not landed by it, although he was taken off from it;[30] the fact that the ladder was never fixed is further evidence of its lack of use. An official of the Board wrote in 1908 that 'great difficulty is experienced in shipping stock, and a like difficulty in landing supplies',[31] an admission, probably inadvertent, of the failure of his own agency's project.

So while the derrick may have had its uses, the biggest problem – what to do with boats – remain unresolved. With better planning and more resources, it may be that a more substantial and useful structure could have been installed, but it is doubtful whether the winching of boats would really have worked in such an exposed situation. A winch for hauling boats up the beach, as originally requested, might have been more useful; the Board installed these in various places for only £25.[32] Ideal solutions, such as excavating a harbour and building a breakwater or pier, would have been very costly for such a small community. Lady Gordon Cathcart would not have invested in a community that did not pay rent, and she, and the Congested Districts Board, may in any case have foreseen its eventual demise.

7

Catching the 'Feathered Tribes'

> Immense flocks of sea fowl frequent these rocks
> in spring, and, like the inhabitants of St Kilda, the
> people here add considerably to their means of living
> by their annual attacks upon the feathered tribes.

So wrote Mr Ross, a visitor to the school in 1868.[1]

Seabirds and their eggs must have made Mingulay attractive to settlement from early times. Unlike fish, birds and their eggs could be taken without any special equipment, although latterly instruments were used. The birds were taken not only for food, but were used to pay rent, and their feathers were sold for cash. Fowling declined in the late nineteenth century, but continued until the desertion on a big enough scale for birds to remain an important item in the diet.

Martin Martin, writing about 1695, said that the people 'take great Numbers of Sea-Fowls from the Rocks, and salt them with the Ashes of burnt Sea-ware in Cows Hides, which preserves them from Putrefaction'. He went on to describe fowling on the stack of Liànamuil:

> The Rock Linmull . . . is almost inaccessible, except in one Place, and that is by climbing, which is very difficult. This rock abounds with Sea-Fowls that build and hatch here in Summer, such as the

Guillemot, Coulter-neb [Manx shearwater], Puffin, etc. The chief Climber is commonly call'd Gingich, and this Name imports a big Man having Strength and Courage proportionable. When they approach the Rock with the Boat, Mr Gingich jumps out first upon a Stone on the Rock-side, and then, by the assistance of a Rope of Horse-hair, he draws his Fellows out of the Boat upon this high Rock, and draws the rest up after him with the Rope, till they all arrive at the Top, where they purchase a considerable Quantity of Fowls and Eggs. Upon their return to the Boat, this Gingich runs a great hazard by jumping first into the Boat again, where the violent Sea continually rages; having but a few Fowls more than his Fellows, besides a greater esteem to compensate his Courage.

A century later, in 1794, MacQueen wrote of Mingulay and Berneray:

The inhabitants catch some of them [the birds] in the rocks, which they think very good eating, and from which they get very fine feathers, these feathers they sell for 6d the lb in the country [Barra] as they never had them in such quantities as to send them to a public market.

In 1820, the feathers were fetching 9d per pound (4p per 452g). Several men were recorded as selling large quantities at a time (to whom is not recorded), though none so large as the 109 pounds (49 kilos) sold in Greenock by a man from Pabbay, who had probably got them from Mingulay.[2]

The sale of feathers, for beds, was mentioned again in 1840.[3] There is a tradition that at about this time Mingulay boats sailed to the Isle of Arran in the Clyde with feathers and salted birds, and returned with salt, flour, paraffin and drugget cloth (a mixture of linen or cotton, and wool). Arran did produce salt and cloth at this time, so the tradition may be true.

Birds, mainly young shearwaters *(fachaich),* were also used to pay rent to MacNeil at one time, as we saw in chapter 4; and according to John Finlayson, 'Fulmars were so good that MacNeil the chief had to be supplied with some.'[4] In more recent times gulls' feathers were rolled into flies for use in fishing from the shore with rods. Parts of the birds may have been put to other uses; in other fowling islands, for instance, bones were made into pipe stems, stomachs into tobacco pouches, beaks into thatching pegs, and the skins of necks were made into footwear.[5]

Only in later years do we have details of species caught and catching methods, from the tape recordings, and from the naturalists Harvie-Brown (who quoted information from John Finlayson), Elwes, and Walker. The main species caught were guillemots, razorbills, puffins and cormorants. Some of the Gaelic words for the birds were specific to Mingulay, or variants of terms in wider use, such as the general word for birds, *peataichean;* they are given here in their singular form.[6]

Guillemots *(langaidh)* and razorbills *(duibheineach)* are cliff dwellers. They take up residence on ledges in May and lay a single egg on the bare rock. Finlayson wrote:

> The female guillemot often allows itself to be caught by the hand, but that only at the time when the young one is nearly being hatched. The guillemots and razorbills are so blinded by their affection for their young that, during the week before and the week after the little ones are hatched, they allow themselves to be captured in hundreds. The way of capturing them practised in Mingulay is by a lasso [noose] of horsehair stuck to the top of fishing rods.[7] There is no use trying to lasso guillemots on a shelf visited before. In this case the bird is educated and

will not allow itself to be taken. I let down a climber
years ago to a shelf never visited, and he captured all
the birds with his hand without loop or lasso.[8]

The noose was known as the *dul gaoisne* ('hair loop'), and
the method, known as *ribeadh* ('snaring'), was used in many
fowling islands (see plate 3). Puffins *(peata-ruadh* or *bùigtre)*[9]
sitting on ledges could also be taken in this way; they could
also be dragged out of the burrows on the cliff tops or ledges
in which they nest, by hand.[10] Young kittiwakes (*seagaire*,
old ones *crahoileag),* also cliff dwellers, were regarded as a
'favourite dish', according to Elwes in 1868.[11]

Another method of catching birds was used when a strong
wind blew against the cliff face and was forced upwards,
particularly up gullies in the cliff. Birds trying to settle on
ledges were whirled about, in such a way that a man, sitting
or lying on the cliff top with a wooden pole about five metres
(15 feet) in length, could strike the birds from below. A blow
on the body would not harm the birds, but a hit on the head
would stun them; they were thrown back to the cliff top where
another man wrung their necks. This method was known as
stearradh,[12] and was also used by fowlers from Lewis on the
Shiant Islands in the Minch,[13] and on Ailsa Craig in the Clyde.[14]

Eggs could be taken in the knowledge that the birds would
lay again. Finlayson continued: 'All the species lay several
times again if their eggs are lost. I have seen the same shelf
robbed three times of its eggs. The time allowed between
each lifting may be fifteen or sixteen days.'[15] This would have
had the advantage of prolonging the breeding, and catching,
season, which ended with the departure of the majority of
the birds in July. Sgeir nan Uibhein (correctly Uibhean, now
normally spelt Uighean), Skerry of the Eggs, a low islet off the
northeast coast of Mingulay, was presumably a source of eggs.

Although Martin and Finlayson mentioned the use of
ropes, in general the fowlers 'do not seem to have used ropes
as they do in St Kilda, but to have clambered among the rocks

like goats', as Alexander Carmichael wrote in 1883. His description of how one of the fowlers, Roderick MacNeill, did this has been quoted in chapter 3. It is not perhaps surprising that 'this desperate robbery', as the Rev. Alexander Nicolson described it in 1840, 'has cost some of the natives their lives'. Accidents were rare, however; only one death in the final fifty years is known to have occurred while fowling, that of Finlay MacNeil, aged eight, in 1878. He was collecting eggs on the low cliffs at the northeast corner of the bay, and fell into the sea. The accident was witnessed by members of his family, including his sister, who never got over the shock. Another reason for descending the cliffs was to retrieve sheep that had wandered along grassy ledges, and would end up in the sea if not rescued.

Catching cormorants (*sgarbh,* young ones *odhragan*) required different tactics. These birds occupy the lower levels of the cliffs and coastal rocks, and are more accessible by boat. Michael MacPhee described how the men would go out at night with oars covered with cloth to quieten them. Once the sentinel cormorant had been dispatched with a twist of the neck, the rest could be killed while asleep.[16]

We have two figures of numbers of birds that could be taken: 600 in six to eight hours using the pole method in Berneray in 1868;[17] and 2,000 guillemots in a day's raid on Liànamuil by men from Pabbay in 1887.[18] There are no detailed figures such as exist for St Kilda, where over 100,000 birds were taken annually, and tens of thousands of eggs weekly during the season.[19]

Some of the birds were cooked and eaten fresh; Walker described how they were 'plucked, boiled, and the flesh gnawed off by the men, but is not much relished by us, as it is tough, red and fishy-tasted: the eggs when fresh are delicious, those of the razorbill and guillemot having a rich orange yolk, and the white of a semi-transparent opal colour'. Most of the birds were preserved for use in the autumn and winter. Young cormorants were singed and salted, and dried 'as hard as a tangle', said Mary Campbell.[20] Other birds were plucked and hung to dry, presumably in the houses and barns. In earlier times they may have been dried in small stone huts, the remains of which can be seen in places near the cliffs, perhaps comparable to the 'cleits' of St Kilda. Roderick MacNeil reckoned dried puffin to be 'as good as smoked ham'.[21] Another opinion was that young puffins were especially tasty, also old ones if boiled for an hour.[22] Puffins were not always so good; in 1899 John Finlayson wrote: 'This season the young puffins were in such a lean condition as to be unfit for the kitchen. One year all birds were inedible – too dry, even dogs wouldn't eat them. This is due to scarcity of spawn on the fishing grounds.'[23] The eggs were preserved in barrels, in salt. Dr John MacRury related a story, in 1894, of

> a former minister of Barra who was one day visited by a native of the island of Mingalay. The minister asked the man what kind of birds they had in the islands, when he got the following reply – in the native language of course: 'You could eat three puffins, two razorbills, but the guillemot would satisfy you to your heart's content.'

Fowling declined in the last decades. MacRury continued: 'Numbers of the puffin, razorbill and guillemot used at one time to be salted and stored up for winter use by the natives of the southern islands but at present this practice is not so common.' Carmichael said in 1883 that 'the people do not now kill many birds, being too much occupied otherwise'; by this he must have meant fishing, which coincided with the fowling season. Harvie-Brown noted in 1887 that an old man, Rory Campbell, still occasionally went down the cliffs, but was the only one who did.[24] Ten years later John Finlayson wrote: 'Up to ten or twelve years ago, people here made a trade of getting birds and eggs from the rocks. There are no professional climbers now. Long since I dropped it.'[25]

The islanders are unlikely to have known that after 1869 most of their fowling operations were made illegal by the passing of the Preservation of Seabirds Act, which outlawed the killing of all seabirds except young unfledged ones, between April and August. The Act was aimed at bird hunters in search of feathers for ladies' hats, but Mingulay's remoteness preserved it from the raids suffered by other bird stations. No voice was raised on behalf of the islanders to exempt them, as happened in the case of the St Kildans.[26] Fowling did continue, however, as the islanders recorded on tape talk about it in detail. Alexander MacKinnon is remembered as being a fowler in the last years. Robert Adam and his companions performed a useful service on their visit in June 1905 by catching birds (see plate 3) at a time when most of the men were away fishing.[27]

8

The Village: Walls and Work

The village was the centre of island life. It lies at the head of the beach of Mingulay Bay, astride the main stream running into the bay. The grey stone walls remain, like the bleached skeleton of a long-dead animal, and, with the help of early maps and photographs, the tape recordings, and visitors' accounts, it is possible to flesh out the bare bones and to say a good deal about it and the domestic work of its inhabitants.

The village occupies an ideal settlement site: the ground is firm and dry, being gently sloping boulder clay, the southern part at least is relatively sheltered from the southwesterly winds, and it is close to water and a landing place for boats. The site had probably been used for hundreds, if not thousands, of years, though not necessarily continuously. Compared to most Outer Hebridean settlements, in which houses were, and are, scattered on crofts or wherever the land permitted a house to be built, the village is large and exceptionally compact on account of the limited space available. Enclosed on most of its landward sides by rising ground, and clinging to the edge of the beach, it is easily imagined as the 'picturesque huddle of rude dusky huts' seen by Muir in 1866. Like the village on Hirta, St Kilda, it is tremendously evocative of a way of life gone for ever; but unlike the latter, planned and built under outside influence, it is a truly Hebridean township.

The importance of the remains of the village was recognised by its being scheduled under the Ancient Monuments Act by Historic Scotland in 1997. It was described as being 'of national importance as one of the finest examples of an "unimproved" isolated settlement complex surviving in the Western Isles'.[1]

The village in its present, final form consists of about fifty buildings, associated walled enclosures, the graveyard and the chapel; along the road to the landing place southwards there are about ten more buildings and the school (see map 3). The present layout of buildings presumably originates from the population expansion in the middle and later nineteenth century, and was established by the time of the first Ordnance Survey of 1878, after which there were only minor changes. It evolved haphazardly, with little regularity or consistency in the position of buildings, though the majority are aligned down-slope. The isolated buildings south of the main village may have been built at a relatively late date, when the best sites had been taken. Those west of the school appear on a map of 1861–3,[2] but the house next to the road doesn't; John Sinclair (Iain Dhunnchaidh) is known to have occupied this house (plate 8) in the last years, and he probably built it himself when he moved to Mingulay from Berneray in about 1868.

The enclosures around the houses served as stackyards for the peat stacks, and as vegetable gardens, and some of them were built of peculiarly massive upright blocks. The early photographs show a network of paths, now disappeared; the road to the landing place, however, is still very much in evidence. The road is surprisingly wide and well built for its comparatively short length, and for the small population it served; and the terrain it crosses is not particularly rough. It seems unlikely that the islanders would have built it on their own initiative, and it is possible that, as suggested in chapter 4, it was built during the famines of the 1840s when many public works were undertaken in the islands.

With the exception of two gabled houses of 'modern' type, the domestic buildings – houses, byres for cattle, and barns – are variants of the traditional Barra Isles type. Contemporary observers compared the Barra type unfavourably with houses in the islands to the north, with such phrases as 'a disgrace to a civilised country', 'the worst in the Hebrides', and 'of a most miserable description'.[3] But the houses were very practical and well adapted to the conditions. The thick drystone walls were built up to the same level all round, the doors being about 1.6 metres (5½ feet), or less, high, and topped with lintels. The walls had an outer and inner face of stone, with a core of smaller stones and earth. The outer face leant inwards and the corners were rounded to withstand the weight of the roof. The rounded (hip-ended) thatched roof was supported by driftwood rafters which rested on the inner face of the wall, leaving a terrace running round the wall top and ensuring that there was no overhanging roofing for the wind to play havoc with. It also meant that the rain drained into the wall, leading to permanent dampness. The rafters and smaller timbers were covered first with a layer of overlapping turfs, then a heavy thatch of straw, or marram grass from Pabbay (as in plate 5); the thatch was then secured with ropes of marram (superseded by hemp in later years), which were weighted with stones. The thatch was renewed every year,[4] and the old thatch and turf, its underside covered with soot, was spread on the agricultural land as fertiliser. A small building in plate 5 is roofed only with turfs, or peats, like tiles.

This form of construction was determined by available materials and the climate. The hip-ended roof was the only option in an area where wood was scarce and inadequate for a gabled, high-pitched and more lightly thatched roof, which would anyway have been unsuitable for the conditions. The crudeness of the construction meant that buildings could be modified, rebuilt, or added to easily. To add a barn, byre or house to an existing one, only three walls had to be built, the fourth being there already. Most buildings are in fact in groups, varying from two – such as house and byre – to ten, such groupings often being family units. Many cases of elderly parents living in houses built onto their adult sons' or daughters' houses are known. The form of construction also means that it is very hard to date buildings (with the exception of the improved houses described below), except to say that one might be older or younger than its neighbour. It is unlikely that any of them are of great age. Comparison of the earliest maps and photographs with the later ones and with the present remains shows that many buildings were modified or rebuilt, or new ones built on new sites in the last twenty years; there were some changes even after 1901. The last inhabitants of most of the houses are known (see Appendix 5).[5] Occupancy of buildings seems to have changed surprisingly often, and families were not necessarily fixed to particular buildings or their sites.

Until the later nineteenth century the houses would have had no windows or built-in fireplaces and chimneys; this type of house in the Outer Hebrides is often called 'black house', though this term was not local, and there is no one definition of it.[6] Windows appeared, if the censuses are reliable, between 1861 and 1871, when most of the twenty-five houses had two windows – to be precise, two rooms with windows – where there had been none ten years earlier (or perhaps the definition of the term had changed). Windows were described by Jolly in 1881 as 'small openings, often without glass', which must have been in the wall-top or at the base of the thatch. Later, some houses were provided with more substantial glazed windows, like those seen in the 1905 photographs (one can be seen in the 1887 photograph, plate 1); thirteen out of twenty-seven thatched houses in 1901 can be seen to have been improved in this way. Fireplaces – with stone or wooden lintels – and chimneys were also a late development. As late as 1883, according to Jolly, the fire was 'in the middle of the clay floor, and there is the usual hole in the roof for the smoke, which as frequently escapes by the door or oozes through the

thatch, and gives the dwelling, as MacCulloch truthfully puts
it, the look of "a melon bed in heat"'.

Some chimney stacks can be seen in the 1887 photograph,
and by the time of the desertion twenty-two houses had fireplaces and chimneys in one end wall, sometimes in both end
walls. There were other improvements in later years, such as
the use of dressed stone, and mortar. These were probably
inspired by the building of the new schoolroom in 1881, and
later the schoolhouse, the stone for all of which was quarried
using drills and wedges from outcrops west of the school
buildings; dynamite was used in the case of the chapel. The
front of one of the houses west of the school was rebuilt using
massive quarried blocks.

Two accounts of the interior of these 'unimproved' houses
are known. Theodore Walker and his brother stayed overnight
in what he called the 'chief hut' in 1869. He noted the 'peat
fire on the earth floor, filling the hut with blue eye-smarting
reek, through the gloom of which one sees the grandfather
and grandmother crooning over the fire, two calves, a fat
young grunter and sundry fowls, two cats and a dog'. They
ate 'haddock, with sea-oat cake and sour milk', and slept on
beds of straw and heather.

Mrs Murray provided a more detailed account, in the autumn of 1888.

> An old woman at her time-blackened spinning
> wheel, sitting on a lump of the naked rock beside
> the peat fire, which is burning brightly without
> smoke, in the middle of the clay floor; two children
> healthy and brown beside her, playing with a kitten;
> a hen mother and some chickens busy foraging for
> themselves over the clay floor; a small pig scratching
> his back under the bench of driftwood supported by
> turf on which we were sitting. A little table, but no
> dresser; one small chair, one three-legged pot, and a
> kettle, not to omit the never-failing friend of every

old wife in the kingdom, the brown teapot standing
by the fire. What more? A quern or hand-mill on the
table, in daily use still in an island where there is no
population to support a miller, and where the meal
is still prepared by two women grinding it painfully
in this primitive way. Three stout kists [wooden
chests], the property of the girls of the family who
had just returned from the fishing at Peterhead. This
is about all. Most of the houses have separate byres,
which are cleaned out twice a year, but this dwelling
was one in which the cows were tied up along with
the family in the same end of the cottage in four
stalls between the fire and the door. During our visit
the cows were in the fields, but there was plenty of
evidence to show where they lodged at night.

In time, we can assume that most, if not all, cattle were
driven out of the houses into their own winter quarters, and
there is no mention of cattle in houses in the last years. This
was one of the requirements of various public health acts that
were being enforced, with some success, in Barra in the 1890s.[7]
Byres were usually tacked onto houses, often, as Mrs Murray
observed with distaste, 'above the level of the dwelling, so
that the whole drainage had to soak through it into the house
below'. Perhaps fifteen to twenty of the smallest buildings in
the village can be identified as byres. The byres or cow ends of
the houses were used as toilets, and the beach was also used.
Intermediate-sized buildings would have been barns, which
most of the twenty crofters had; a few can be identified by
the hole in the wall opposite the door which was opened to
create a through-draught when grain was being winnowed.
There were also a few stables and workshops.[8] Other buildings which were not obviously houses, having none of the
'improvements', were dwellings even in the last years, and
even more of these must have been lived in earlier; thirty-four
houses were recorded in the 1881 census.

Two houses were built in 'modern' style towards the end of the community's life. One, in the village below the chapel, was built by John MacKinnon, the joiner, sometime after the 1887 photograph was taken and probably before 1898.[9] It was well built of dressed stone and mortar, and was gabled, having had a felt roof. The other, near the school, was even more modern in that only the gable ends were built of stone, the side walls having been of wood and corrugated iron. Tradition has it that this was built for Donald MacPhee (Dòmhnall Bàn) on his marriage, but as this was in January 1907, when the evacuation of the island had just begun, it is likely that the house had been built some time before. This style of house was becoming common in Barra, built with grants from the Congested Districts Board. A 'mass stone' was built into one of the gable ends, perhaps got from the site of the Cross nearby. The free-standing gables were so well built that they stood, unsupported, until a severe gale flattened them in 1989.

These improvements in housing reflect the general trend in the islands at this time, though Mingulay seems to have been in advance of Barra in this respect; there, the central hearth was still common in 1901, and cattle were still in some houses as late as 1907.[10] Many of these improved houses were built after the photograph of 1887 was taken, and the old school-room was rebuilt into a house after the new school was built in 1881. There are various possible reasons for this trend, as we have seen. The building of the school and chapel in modern style would have been a stimulus. Legislation such as the 1886 Crofters Holdings Act gave crofters security of tenure of their houses, which they now had an incentive to improve; and there were various public health acts from 1867. There was also increasing contact with the mainland, and the fishing industry created some prosperity.

The improved, cattle-free houses measured between 8 and 12 metres (26–40 feet) long and about 4 metres (13 feet) wide internally, and were divided into three rooms by wooden partitions. Inside the door, which was roughly in the middle of a long wall, was a small entrance lobby leading to the kitchen/ living room on one side and the bedroom on the other, with a small bedroom between, reached from one of the other rooms. In the kitchen there was a bench under the window, a dresser, full of dishes, a table and a few upright chairs. Cooking and baking were done over the fire.[11] The photograph of the interior of the house of John MacLean (Barnaidh) (plate 7) shows that the wall, which must have been rendered, was covered in newspaper which MacLean probably got from the east coast of the mainland when fishing there. This house was one of those built after 1887. In the bedrooms the family slept in box beds, perhaps fitted with roofs to keep out rain, and curtains to keep out draughts, and there were several people to a bed. Lighting was provided by means of the *crùisgean*, a simple lamp using fish oil. These were made of iron or tin, and used rush wicks. In later years paraffin lamps were used;[12] paraffin was got from Arran as early as 1850.

Furniture, spinning wheels and other items of wood were made locally from driftwood. All the men were practical, but the best-known carpenters were the MacKinnons, Donald and his son John. John had a 'sawpit' made of boulders on the shore below the school for sawing up driftwood, and he had a workshop in the village. He also made his own clothes, which was unusual for a man.[13]

The house was the centre of various activities – mostly carried out by women – such as food preparation and cooking, and making cloth and clothing. Food varied according to season; the staples were fish and seabirds (fresh or dried in both cases), seabirds' eggs, milk and milk products, potatoes, and grain in various forms. Mutton, chicken, eggs, seaweed, cabbage and other vegetables were also eaten. Ealasaid Sinclair said the people were never hungry in her day. Sheep were slaughtered in the autumn and the meat was salted for winter use. All edible parts were eaten – the stomach was used for puddings made with oatmeal, onions and suet. At one time cattle were also slaughtered in the autumn, when the meat, salted, would be shared out among the community. Chicken was eaten on St Michael's Day and Shrove Tuesday, when it was made into a soup with husked barley.[14]

Most food was boiled in pots hung over the peat fire; bannocks and scones were baked on girdles – flat iron pans – hung over the fire, or on a flat stone on the edge of the fire, as illustrated in plate 7. Bannocks were made from both barley and oatmeal; older people preferred the oat bannocks. A savoury and nutritious variety had cod liver mixed in. Soda scones made with imported white flour were also made; Ealasaid Sinclair said these were better made on a stone by the fire than on a girdle. Making the day's bannocks was the first job in the morning, after stoking up the fire; the previous night the glowing embers had been covered with ash – 'smooring' as it was called – to keep them alight. Robert Adam described his experience of Mingulay bannocks – the very ones, perhaps, in his photograph (plate 7):

> Our bread consisted of a huge girdle-scone an inch thick. So thick that, after being baked on the girdle, this round, flat object was allowed to finish the baking process by a long lean against the sooty kettle in front of the peat-fire. These mighty comestibles, when new, were easily chewed. A day or two old, they resembled crepe rubber, fearfully tough. How we were able to eat them then was by soup made of seafowl. When softened in this highly concentrated meat-juice, they presented no dental difficulties.[15]

Nan MacKinnon told a charming story about small oat bannocks called *bonnaich boise*, 'hand bannocks', which her mother, who was from Mingulay, used to make. When she had finished shaping the bannock, she used to put a small mark in the middle of it with her thumb. She explained why:

Before there were chimneys in the houses, they had a smoke-hole in the middle of the house, and this day, this woman had made a bannock; this was in the time of the fairies. And she'd made a bannock and set it up against the fire. And the fairies came to the door and she kept the door barred against them. And they looked down through the smoke-hole, and saw the bannock. And the fairies called down the smoke-hole: 'Little bannock with no dimple, rise up and open the door for us.'

The little bannock started moving and rolled away from the fire and struck the door, and the door opened and the fairies swarmed into the house. And ever since, every bannock they made they had to put a dimple in it with their thumb, and as long as there was a dimple made in it with their thumb the fairies could do nothing to it.[16]

Milk, besides being drunk, was made into butter and crowdie. To make butter, milk was put in a butter churn, a cylindrical vessel a metre (3 feet) or more in length, and agitated by means of a plunger pushed in and out until the butter separated out. As with other repetitive and rhythmical activities, this was done to the accompaniment of songs. Crowdie was a kind of cottage cheese made from buttermilk, the curds being produced by warming the buttermilk gently. Mrs Murray found that the milk and cream she was given in the Barra Isles sometimes 'tasted so of peat that we could hardly make it palatable'.

Food was eaten off chinaware in the late nineteenth century, and dishes were displayed on the dresser as well. The fishermen got it from the east coast when they were there fishing. Before that, wooden bowls were used, as noted by Miss Bird, a visitor to Berneray in 1863.

Various naturally occurring foods were eaten. Shellfish – cockles, mussels and limpets – were eaten in early times, and very probably more recently in times of hardship, though not in Catherine MacNeil's time. Sand-eels were eaten, as we have seen. Seals and whales may have been eaten if found stranded, though there is no mention of this in recent times, and the name of an inlet on the west coast may suggest that whales, or a whale, was caught or found there. Seals may have been caught, as they were in Barra, according to Hall in 1807. Silverweed, which grows in sandy soil around the bay, and seaweeds such as dulse, may also have been eaten in times of hardship. Edible mushrooms grow in profusion, and to an enormous size, on the more fertile ground, but these were, said Harvie-Brown, 'contemptuously left alone by the natives, and called *balgan buachair,* i.e. "spots made by dung"'. Only John Finlayson, the teacher, seems to have appreciated them: 'They are excellent for clearing down any flatulency or stomach burden. They are real cathartics and though I always go to extremes in their use, there is nothing like surfeit or nausea as a consequence.' Cattle liked them too, and Finlayson 'once had a race with a cow for a brilliant mushroom ahead of us'.[17]

Alcohol – whisky and wine – was drunk on special occasions such as weddings, and no doubt at other times too. It was Mrs Murray's opinion that the people had 'plenty to spend on tea, whisky and tobacco'. There was a whisky still in Pabbay at one time, and a jar believed to have been used for carrying its produce to Mingulay survives. Pipe-smoking was common among the men, and running out of tobacco during bad weather when it was impossible to get to Barra is said to have contributed to the men wanting to leave Mingulay.[18] At such times they would sniff the newspaper the tobacco had been wrapped in as second best.

An important part of a woman's work at home, especially in winter, was spinning, weaving, and making clothing. 'They manufacture all their own clothing from the wool of their sheep,' wrote Jolly in 1883. The fleece, sheared in summer, had to be washed in the stream, dried, and carded (to straighten the fibres) before it was ready for spinning. Before the mid nineteenth century, when spinning wheels were introduced to the Hebrides, wool was spun using the spindle. This was a shaft of wood, weighted at the bottom, which was spun, drawing the fibres into yarn. The spindle could be suspended from a distaff, a longer shaft of wood held in the crook of the arm, enabling the woman to spin while walking. By the end of the century, most households had a spinning wheel, made locally by the MacKinnons, who also sold them in Castlebay.[19] Donald made a set of eight from a single piece of oak driftwood, without using nails or screws, in about 1859 (see plate 21). Several of the MacKinnons' wheels survive.

Once spun, the yarn could be dyed in large pots using natural dyes derived from plants, lichens and seaweeds; and then woven into cloth. Not all the households had looms; Michael MacPhee said that only two, one all-female, had them, but they served the whole community.[20] Finally, the finished cloth had to be waulked (fulled or shrunk). The cloth was first soaked in human urine, to fix the dye, then laid on a broad bench or table with a row of about six women each side. The women on each side moved alternately, simultaneously crushing and kneading the cloth against the table. The action was conducted in a disciplined rhythm to the accompaniment of songs specially devised for this purpose. It started slowly but gathered speed until it reached a feverish frenzy. The 'leader' measured the progress of the shrinkage at intervals, using the middle finger as a measure.[21] Ealasaid Sinclair said there might be a waulking in each house in turn, say one every week of the winter. Mary Campbell said a waulking would start at four in the afternoon and might continue till three next morning, the women working in shifts. In one house, known as the *taigh-ceilidh* ('ceilidh house'), girls learned the waulking songs from the old woman who lived there. The waulking women were the best singers in Mingulay.[22] One of these was Nan MacKinnon's great aunt, Effie MacKay (Oighrig Iain Mhìcheil, maiden surname MacNeil, born c.1837).[23]

Alexander Carmichael, the folklorist, witnessed a waulking in Mingulay in 1866, at which he

> asked a beautiful girl to sing a certain song over again. She blushed and looked confused and abashed, and the women looked in an embarrassed way at one another. The leader said that were they to sing the same song twice at the same waulking the cloth would become thin and streaky and white as *rùsg na caora*, the sheep's fleece, and there was no knowing what mischief might not befall the wearer of the cloth or the singer of the song. The hands of these girls were small, the fingers tapered, the arms muscular, the girls themselves of medium height, strongly made, well formed, and well mannered.[24]

Cloth of varying thicknesses was produced. Lightweight, undyed cloth (*clò bàn*, 'white cloth') was used for men's underclothes. Lightweight cloth was also used for plaids, shawls and blankets. The heavier tweed (*clò gorm*, 'blue cloth') was used for men's trousers and waistcoats. In later years women wore skirts and blouses of imported drugget, a mixture of linen, or cotton, and wool.[25] Jolly wrote:

> The people seemed generally well clothed, wearing a thick, strong, heavy woollen stuff. The boys were clad chiefly in trousers and woollen shirts alone, sometimes with vests and cravats, but seldom with coats or jackets. Most of them had no bonnets, and their hair was matted into a coarse, thick felt, which formed a perfect, if more suspicious, substitute. The girls were better dressed than their brothers. They wore various materials, bright colours being much appreciated, as in all primitive communities, and many of them were clean and tidy.

Women's dress is well illustrated by plate 11. The woman and the girl are wearing skirts, blouses, and the small head-shawl *(beannag)*, which could be worn as a scarf around the neck or over the head. In some parts of the islands women wore the latter round the neck before marriage, and over the head thereafter. Women would have worn the great plaid *(plaide mhòr)* as an outer garment, covering the head as well; and, when in mourning, most of the face too.[26]

Fishermen wore blue knitted jerseys, as seen in plate 24. The patterns varied from island to island, which meant that, should the wearer drown, his home could be identified. In wet conditions they wore long smocks of oiled canvas.

All the men in the 1905 photographs are wearing boots, as is Catherine MacLean, and the younger children are barefoot. A visitor in 1905 remarked that 'the men were all booted, but the women were tramping over rock and sand in their bare feet'.[27] James MacNeil was described as a shoemaker in the 1851 census, though not again. He wouldn't have had any custom from at least one islander, his father-in-law, Rory Rum the storyteller, who was said in 1860 not to have worn shoes for fifty years.

The islanders were therefore largely self-sufficient not only in food, as seen in previous chapters, but in clothing, building materials, and furniture. Various items would always have been imported, such as anything made of iron, and in later years more and more items and commodities were imported as contact with the mainland increased and there was more cash to spend.

9

Sickness and Death

One of the features of the Barra population was its
physical excellence and powers of physical endur-
ance. It is astonishing to me how one can reconcile
this with their struggles, their low standard of nutri-
tion and their indifferent sanitation.

So wrote Dr Donald Buchanan, a native of Barra and a doctor,
in 1942. Dr Ogilvie Grant, medical officer for Inverness-shire,
was in no doubt about the principal cause of ill health among
the islanders. After a visit to Mingulay in 1892, he wrote:

There I saw that sad scene, alas, so common, a young
man dying of consumption, and when I left his bed-
side and breathed as pure an air as exists in the wide
world, I felt that here perhaps another human being
was being sacrificed to insanitation.[1]

Insanitary living conditions were a principal cause of the
vulnerability of the islanders to infectious diseases such as
typhoid, measles and influenza. Numerous outbreaks and
deaths are recorded in the later years. Dr Grant again:

The difficulties peculiar to the treatment of infectious diseases in the island districts are very great.

> The poverty of the districts has to be considered,
> their congested state, the ignorance and prejudice of
> the people, and their neglect of the most rudimen-
> tary attention to sanitation.[2]

Mingulay certainly was 'congested', as far as the village
was concerned. The houses were closely packed together,
and there were up to eleven people to a house. Until the
later years, cattle shared the houses in winter. Sanitation was
non-existent; the only privies were at the Board school, where
the risk of infection spreading among the children was high.
Household refuse was dumped outside the houses; in 1893
the county Sanitary Department issued all households in Uist
and Barra district with a written notice instructing them to
remove 'offensive middens, ashpits and dungheaps' at least
twenty yards from houses and wells, and to provide separate
accommodation for cattle.[3] It is unlikely that such instructions were taken much notice of in Mingulay, and as far as
the cattle were concerned, people had begun to build byres
already. A 'dung heap' was mentioned by Harvie-Brown as
being the last resting place of a snowy owl which had been
shot early in 1887, for the remains of which the portly naturalist made an unsavoury and unsuccessful search on his visit
the following summer. Contamination of water supplies, so
common in Barra, was not a problem in Mingulay, where
'most of the inhabitants, Dr Grant was told, take their water
for domestic purposes from Linique, well up the brae.'[4]
Linique (derived from Lianag, a green spot) was a pool above
the Chapel House, on the small stream running past it into the
bay. There appears to be a well between the house and stream
in plate 5.

A well-documented case of typhoid occurred in 1894 in
the family of Donald MacPhee (Dòmhnall Dhòmhnaill Iain)
and his wife Catherine (Catriona Ruairidh Eachainn). John
Finlayson, the teacher, reported as follows:

In July last typhoid generated somehow or another at Castlebay. A girl from this island unfortunately went across and put up for the night in the house where the fever was. She did this without knowing it was typhoid the children were sick with. The girl came back to this island, taking the disease with her. The people here got alarmed, and those houses nearest the infected family were deserted. The house was well kept isolated. In due time all the other members of the family, six in number, were infected. The father kept up as long as he could, but he should have been in his bed a week before. He could be seen walking out like a drunken man. I saw him fall down in the sand. He took to bed and died two days after. Alas, there was not a person in the island who would put him into the coffin.[5]

Dr MacRury, who arrived from Barra shortly after MacPhee died, continued the story:

On learning that none of the inhabitants, in spite of my persuasions, would enter the house to give assistance in putting the dead man in his coffin, I offered to do this myself, but found that the coffin could not be ready till next day, and as I could not wait so long the Reverend Mr MacKenzie then volunteered to do this, as he said he had to return to the island next day to discharge some professional duties.[6]

The case illustrates the dread of infection prevalent in the islands, which we have met already in the story of the 'plague'. This attitude was not understood in the south; an English newspaper, the *Daily Chronicle,* seized on the story, criticising the 'unkindly islanders' for their 'failure to act with common decency or courage'. It also shows the islanders' attitude to such occurrences to be on a spiritual rather than practical level, for when Donald MacPhee was dying, the islanders went to Barra to fetch the priest, not the doctor. They met Dr MacRury by chance, and he went with them; before returning to Barra, he instructed one of the daughters on how to look after the other patients and later sent medicines and disinfectants. When Catherine MacPhee died two days later, again nobody would go near the body to put it in a coffin. Help was sought from Barra, and the sanitary inspector, Donald MacLean (nicknamed 'an Sgarbh', meaning 'the Cormorant'), came to do it. Dr MacRury commented on the case: 'That such a state of matters should exist in any part of Great Britain today is scarcely credible.'

In January 1898 measles was brought by someone returning from Glasgow. Three adults, children of Malcolm MacPhee (Donald's brother), died, 'which disposes the people', wrote John Finlayson, 'to look upon the whole thing as a mysterious visitation and plague.' This time new legislation allowed Dr Grant to send a nurse, Nurse King, to the island; she believed that 'the deaths are simply due to not being properly nursed, want of cleanliness, and overcrowding'.[7]

There were numerous outbreaks of influenza, some fatal, and in 1899 John Johnston recorded in the school log book that an 'epidemic of mumps aggravated by an epidemic of harvest work reduces attendance'. He had trouble informing the doctor, so as to get the requisite certificate to close the school. Dr Grant stressed the importance of ventilation in the schoolroom, in order to reduce the risk of infection spreading among the children.

Smallpox may have visited the island at one time, but this was gradually eradicated throughout the country following the introduction of compulsory inoculation in 1864. Children were vaccinated between the ages of six months and three years,[8] and the Barra doctor would visit the southern islands periodically for this purpose. By 1906 the high cost of this was met out of the parish rates, which, a government report noted disapprovingly, the Mingulay people themselves never paid.[9]

Another cause of ill health in the islands was dampness, which was largely responsible for lung diseases such as tuberculosis, pneumonia, pleurisy, and whooping cough, which were often fatal. Dr Grant blamed, firstly, the coldness and dampness of bedrooms, and the contrast of these conditions to the heat of the living rooms from which the people retired to bed; and secondly, trudging over sodden hills to fetch peat, herd or milk cows, etc.[10] Fishermen spent long periods in wet clothes, and as a result, suffered from rheumatism as well.[11]

Most deaths in Mingulay occurred without a medical person being present, in which case nothing more specific than, for example, 'senile decay', or simply 'unknown' was given as the cause of death in the death register. There were occasional accidents, such as drowning or falling from cliffs, and we can assume that there were deaths of mothers in childbirth, though none are recorded. Infant deaths were common: of fifty-one babies born between 1890 and 1908, eight died when anything between a few minutes and over a year old. Compulsory civil registration of deaths, certified by a doctor, began in 1855, but it was seventeen years before the first death in Mingulay was certified. There had been a doctor, in private practice of course, resident in Barra since about the middle of the century, but it was not until 1890 that the foundations of a publicly-funded medical service were laid, in the form of a medical officer for Inverness-shire. He was concerned about the large number of uncertified deaths, which were due to the unwillingness or inability to pay a doctor for his services as much as, in Mingulay's case, to remoteness, and the islanders' attitude.[12]

A total of 125 deaths were recorded in Mingulay between 1855 and 1909. Some elderly people from Mingulay may have died in Barra, for tradition has it that people would go to live with relatives in Barra in their old age to be sure of getting the last rites from the priest on their death. The last death occurred in March 1909 (Mary MacPhee, Màiri Iain Mhìcheil, widow of John), but the last person to be buried there actually died in Sandray, as we will see.

The dead were buried in the little graveyard by the stream in the middle of the village (plate 10). This is a low oval hillock enclosed by a wall, with an entrance on the west. The graveyard had been used for centuries, being the site of the medieval St Columba's Chapel and graveyard. There are today about fifteen identifiable gravestones, merely unshaped slabs set vertically into the ground, and forty to fifty other stones which may be gravestones; and no doubt there are more under the sand which has overwhelmed the eastern edge of the graveyard since the desertion.[13] There are two free-standing concrete crosses, one a memorial to John MacPhee (Iain Dhòmhnaill Iain) who died of influenza in 1900, inscribed with 'in loving memory'. A third concrete memorial is substantial and very elaborate, unlike any in Barra; it can be seen in plate 10. It has an unfinished twin lying in an enclosure at the southern end of the village, where it must have been made, but it was never erected. They are obviously a pair, and must be relatively late, as the one in the graveyard does not appear in the 1905 photographs; but it is not known whom they commemorate. Three wooden crosses in plate 10 seem to be the same as the three white ones in plate 1 of 1887.

If there are, say, between fifty and seventy marked graves, there must be a great many more unmarked. There were at least 123 burials in the last fifty-five years, and perhaps hundreds before that; because of the graveyard's small size, later burials must have cut earlier ones. Many of the stones are in groups, presumably family groups, and the closeness of some on an east–west alignment suggest infant graves.

T.S. Muir was informed, by Miss Oswald of Barra Head Lighthouse, that (in 1866) the graveyard was 'in a most ruinous condition; there has been a wall of loose stones around it, but the cows and horses are allowed to graze in it, and it is covered with weeds. There are no tombstones in it more than some rude ones at the heads of graves.' By 1905, photographs show that the wall had been topped with a barbed wire fence, but a visitor in the same year noted: 'It would be very picturesque if only cared for. It is one mass of tangle and weed . . .'[14]

To return to the living: the islanders, of course, had their own forms of treatment using naturally-occurring substances; boils and sores, for example, were treated with a poultice of dock. Martin Martin mentioned 'a sort of Stone, with which the Natives frequently rub their Breasts by way of prevention, and say it is a good Preservative for Health'. This could refer to the 'font stones' described by Alexander Carmichael in the three islands in the 1860s. In Mingulay's case, the stone was kept in a water-filled hollow in a rock below the road where it passes Crois an t-Suidheachain. The hollow was known as St Columba's Well, and Carmichael called it a font. He was told that 'The stone in the font was always kept in the font. It was used to cure pains and gripes'[15] (see chapter 16). Some forms of treatment were based on superstition, and Jolly wrote of the treatment of the so-called 'king's evil', or scrofula (tuberculosis of the lymphatic nodes). He met a boy from South Uist travelling to Mingulay.

> It seems that in Minglay there lived a native, who was the last of seven sons in direct male descent without any intervening daughter. According to popular notions, this endows him with a power of curing the malady, like the once potent 'royal touch' which gave name to the disease. The supernatural physician enjoyed great local fame for the many cures believed to have been effected by him. He had already seen the boy twice, and this was the last visit that was necessary for completing the cure. It appears that he operated on the patient with no human eye to see, but merely recited a 'rhyme' or charm over the sore. He charged no fee, though a piece of silver must be presented as essential to good luck.

The belief in the powers of a seventh son (of a seventh son) was common in the Outer Hebrides well into the twentieth century. The silver was usually a sixpence hung around the patient's neck.

Women in childbirth were attended by 'midwives', who, although scorned by the medical authorities, were well regarded locally. There is even a tradition of a Mingulay woman, who had gone to live in Barra, returning to her native island for the birth of her baby in the 1860s. According to Nan MacKinnon, it was believed that the 'gift' of midwifery was passed down from mother to daughter, and that an ancestor of the last midwife, Anne MacNeil (Anna Ruairidh Dhòmhnaill, daughter of Roderick MacNeil, the storyteller, and Flora MacNash), received the gift from a supernatural man she met one night in Barra.

> No wife or mother died there in childbirth while she
> was there . . . she would stay up with them for three
> whole nights running on her own. Nobody dared
> to give drink or food or anything to the woman
> in child-bed, as they called childbirth, but herself.
> And when the three days were up and when she
> was certain that she was on the way to recovery she
> wouldn't come so often at all then, but she would
> call to see her each day after that.[16]

Anne MacNeil continued to attend births into old age when she could no longer walk. She moved to Sandray in about 1909 to be with her son John MacNeil and daughter Flora Gillies, and died there in April 1910. There being no burial ground in use on the island then, her body was taken to Mingulay for burial, the last one there.[17]

Another midwife was Isabella MacLean, who registered births she had presumably attended.

In general, then, Mrs Murray was right when she said that in spite of the various 'defiances of the laws of sanitation . . . the people in Mingulay are a healthy, long-lived people'.

10

The Ladies' School

In the education of the children, Minglay has long
been singularly fortunate.

So wrote William Jolly in 1883, referring to the fact that
Mingulay was the only one of Barra's satellites to have a
school. Not only were the islanders fortunate; the historical
record has benefited from the records of both the schools
which served the community in its last fifty years.

Until 1872, when education in Scotland became a state responsibility, basic education in the Highlands and Islands had
been provided sporadically by various religious and philan-
thropic bodies. For a few years at the end of the seventeenth
century Barra boasted one of only two Catholic schools in
Scotland at the time, its main function being to train young
men for the priesthood. A contemporary observer scornfully
remarked that Catholic parents in the west of Scotland would
sooner send their children to Jamaica than to Barra. At the
end of the eighteenth century, the Society in Scotland for the
Propagation of Christian Knowledge, founded to counter
Catholicism and the Gaelic language, set up a school. Then,
in the early nineteenth century, the Gaelic Schools Society,
which taught the reading of the scriptures in Gaelic, provided
itinerant teachers in Barra, and, in 1822, in Sandray.[1] By
1865 Barra had four schools: the parish school, a Church of

Scotland Ladies' Association school and two run by a new organisation, the Ladies' Highland Association. In the report on education in the Hebrides of that year, it was stated that 'The educational state of Barra appears to be behind that of any other of the Western Islands, not excepting St Kilda.'[2]

In 1859 Mingulay became the only other island in the Barra group to benefit from a long-term school, when the Ladies' Highland Association, also known as the Free Church Ladies' Association (Edinburgh branch) established a school there. This Association had been founded in 1850, seven years after the establishment of the Free Church of Scotland by disaffected ministers of the Church of Scotland. The reasons for the break were complex, but the power of landlords in appointing ministers, and the consequent failure of most ministers to condemn evictions by their patrons, were important factors.

The Association had three principal objectives: Firstly, to attempt to improve the conditions of the population of the Highlands and Islands after the terrible famines of the 1840s by providing schools (and, in poor districts, clothing to enable children to attend); secondly, to use the schools as a training ground for the young men being trained for the ministry in the new Church; and thirdly, 'to bear upon the popery [Catholicism] which still exists in some Highland districts'. Schools were established throughout the region, in Catholic as well as Protestant areas; Mingulay was the only solidly Catholic island to get a school, and the most remote. They were known locally as Sgoil nan Leadaidhean 'The Ladies' School'. The organisation was funded by private donations; fees were not charged, but local people were expected to contribute to the provision of buildings, and food for the teachers.[3] We are fortunate in knowing a good deal about the Mingulay school, which features in some of the annual reports of the Association.[4]

Mingulay seems to have got its school largely by accident. In 1857 one of the Barra Head lightkeepers appealed to the Association for a teacher. He 'promised that half the

PLATE 1. 'A picturesque huddle of rude dusky huts': the earliest known photograph of Mingulay Village, taken in 1887.

PLATE 2. The same view, 1987. There were several building developments, such as the gabled house, after the earlier view.

PLATE 3. The photographer's companion fowling with a noose on the end of a rod. On the right is the stack of Arnamuil, and beyond, Gunamuil and Dun Mingulay (1905)

PLATE 4. Mingulay's great cliff, Biulacraig, 229 metres high.

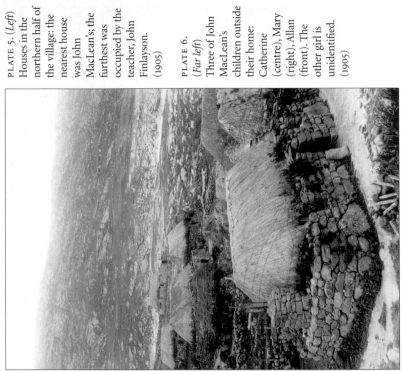

PLATE 5. (*Left*) Houses in the northern half of the village: the nearest house was John MacLean's; the furthest was occupied by the teacher, John Finlayson. (1905)

PLATE 6. (*Far left*) Three of John MacLean's children outside their home: Catherine (centre), Mary (right), Allan (front). The other girl is unidentified. (1905)

PLATE 7. The interior of John MacLean's house, with bannocks cooking, as described by the photographer Robert Adam. (1905)

PLATE 8. John Sinclair's house on the road south of the village (which lies below the ridge in the middle distance). Beyond is MacPhee's Hill. (1905)

PLATE 9. A crofter and cattle above the village. The mill can be seen in the valley bottom on the right. (1905)

PLATE 10. The graveyard, where countless generations are at rest. It is the site of the medieval Chapel of St Columba. (1922)

PLATE 11. Peat gatherers on Carnan. (1905)

PLATE 12. Malcolm MacPhee building a peat stack on the slopes of Carnan. He apparently blinked during the exposure. (1905)

PLATE 13. Men preparing to launch a boat into an exceptionally calm sea. The boat, *The Provider*, was owned by Donald MacPhee (Dòmhnall Bàn), fourth from left. (1905)

PLATE 14. The derrick, erected in 1901. The jib, seen resting above the steps, swung out to hoist loads from boats. It was an ill-conceived scheme and was practically useless. (1905)

PLATE 15. The Chapel House, built in 1898. The upper floor was St Columba's Chapel; the lower, the visiting priest's quarters (1905). The building collapsed in 1996.

PLATE 16. St Columba's Chapel. The former positions of the altar and other furnishings can be seen as marks on the wall. (1987)

PLATE 17. The schoolroom, built by Barra School Board in 1881. The school-house, behind, was added in 1894. (2000)

PLATE 18. The school buildings, about 1932.

PLATE 19. The croftlands inland from the village. On the right, the rounded bulk of Carnan; on the left, Hecla. (1922)

PLATE 20. Roderick MacNeil, painted in 1871 by J.F. Campbell, who called him 'Rory Rum the storyman'.

PLATE 21. One of eight spinning wheels made in 1859 by Donald MacKinnon from a single piece of oak driftwood.

PLATE 22. The ancient landscape of Skipisdale: three clusters of ruins of Iron Age and later buildings can be seen. Berneray, with the lighthouse of Barra Head, is across the sound. (1998)

PLATE 23. Sarah MacShane, the teacher, and her remaining pupils outside the school-house in August 1909. The three children closest to her are her own.

PLATE 24. Mingulay men in Vatersay in August 1909. Left to right: Hector MacNeil, Angus MacNeil (Beag), John MacKinnon, the joiner, Michael MacNeil (an Rìgh).

PLATE 25. Mingulay Village in decay in August 1909. Most of the people had left for Vatersay by this time.

PLATE 26. Houses in the northern half of the village in August 1909. The half-hidden house was occupied by Michael MacNeil (an Rìgh), the last to leave Mingulay in 1912.

PLATE 27. Berneray: Mary Campbell, right, outside her house above the road to the lighthouse, August 1909. The man may be Angus MacNeil (Beag) from Mingulay.

PLATE 28. Berneray: the giant's house. Peter Sinclair raised the roof at one end so that he could stand up! In the foreground, the road to the lighthouse; beyond, Pabbay. (1995)

PLATE 29. Berneray: the graveyard enclosure and site of the medieval Chapel of St Mary. Beyond lies Mingulay and the islands to the north. (2000)

PLATE 30. Pabbay: the settlement. The hillock between the gabled house and other houses (centre) is the graveyard 'Christ's Graveyard' and site of a medieval chapel. (1998)

PLATE 31. Pabbay: the graveyard, from the southwest, in a desert-like landscape in 1895.

PLATE 32. Pabbay: cross-incised memorial stone in the graveyard, dating to the sixth to ninth centuries. (1998)

salary would be raised by the people, and that about 70 children would attend', most of whom would have come from Mingulay, as Berneray's population was much smaller. A benefactor, William MacKerrell of Great Malvern, promised £20 per year for the first three years (in fact, his support continued for many years; in later years George Corran supported the school). Lack of accommodation and the remoteness of the island prevented the school being opened the following year, and by early 1859 it was too late:

> The light keeper, expecting to be removed, withdrew his offer of aid, and most of the people were in the adjacent island of Mingalay, where nobody could be found to make any preparation for the teacher, or to promise to encourage or to aid him. It was felt to be a very perilous and difficult experiment to send a young man to so remote a place where nobody could read, and all were Roman Catholics ... however, a young man being found willing to make the trial, he was sent in May, and was so well received, that in a few weeks he had a flourishing school of about sixty scholars, was lodged by the people as comfortably as they could, and in August, when the barn was required in which the school had been taught, they offered to build a new house if a little aid could be given them for timber for the roof and windows, for which they had to send a boat to Fort William. Stormy weather, and the exposed situation of the island prevented anyone from visiting the school; but the progress the children have made has been very encouraging, and this arduous enterprise has hitherto succeeded beyond the most sanguine expectations.

The pupils included 'full-grown men, and children from adjacent islands, boarded there on purpose to enjoy the advantage of the school'. The people said that 'there has been no school from the creation of the world till now'.

According to a tradition current in Barra, the teacher, John Finlayson, was destined for Berneray and was taken there by an islander, Duncan Sinclair, who would have been among those calling for a teacher. However, on the journey from Barra a storm blew up and they had to seek shelter at Mingulay, where Finlayson saw that there were many more children than in Berneray, and so he decided to establish the school there.

Finlayson's early days cannot have been easy: he was the first outsider known to have lived there, and brought with him the values of the outside world and a foreign religion. Muir speculated on his task on his arrival:

> The labour of breaking in even so merely a handful of utterly uncultivated homespuns must have been dreadful. It is supposed that [Finlayson] went forth to the task sufficiently apprised of the material upon which he was to operate; but if not, his earliest encounter with his sucklings-elect must have somewhat suddenly perfected his knowledge. Upon his landing in Mingula, the tiny vagrants crowded round to see the school they had been told they were going to have. They thought he had it with him packed up in his trunk!

The school was visited, and the children examined, at intervals by supporters of the Association. The first of these, in 1860, reported that the thirty-three pupils 'showed considerable acquaintance with Scripture, and had made good progress in acquiring English, though, like the other Barra schools, the work was elementary'. Three years later twenty-four children could read the Bible, and could write letters to their teacher during his periods of study at college in Edinburgh. The intelligence and ability of the children impressed the visitors, such as a Mr Ross in 1868:

The Bible lesson was remarkably well read by every one of the eighteen who were present, and they translated the chapter, verse by verse, with the utmost ease into Gaelic. The examination upon the lesson was conducted in English, and as readily answered by the pupils in English also. They repeated portions of the Psalms in both languages, and their spelling and translation from English into Gaelic, and vice versa, was well done. The writing was wonderfully good, and to appearance bore no trace of having been spoiled by the steel pen. Many of the children were this year able to write letters to friends absent for work in the south and east. A number of them performed sums in the advanced rules of arithmetic. [In 1865 there were] seventeen boys and ten girls; the latter were tolerably well dressed, for our visit was expected. The boys were very quaint in their rags – petticoats or sacks. One piece of dress was thought sufficient for a child, and the feet were all bare.

The Bible, reading, writing, English and arithmetic are the only subjects mentioned, but others may have been taught; in Barra these included history, geography, Latin, grammar. The children had books, and the London Tract Society was so impressed by the reports of 1865 that it donated a number of books, including a Gaelic translation of The Pilgrim's Progress, to the school. John Finlayson was much commended; his work must have been helped enormously by his knowledge of Gaelic, a facility that not all teachers had, but it was to be used only as an aid to learning English. The Association had high hopes of Finlayson: John Cowan, on his departure from his visit in 1865, 'commended him to the care of Him who has strengthened him, in the midst of much discouragement, to do what I believe will be a great work for Him'.

The first school building was situated on its own on the northern edge of the village, overlooking it.[5] It was, said Muir

Muir's sketch of the school, seen end-on from the west, in 1866.

in 1866, 'externally in no way distinguished, excepting in length, from the neighbouring huts'. The folklorist Alexander Carmichael, visiting in 1867 described the building as 30 by 13 feet (9 by 4 metres), 18 feet (5.5 metres) being the schoolroom, the remainder, Finlayson's accommodation: 'It was built by the natives and is most rude and primitive . . . floor in ruts and hollows and the roof just sufficiently high to allow a tall man to stand upright without touching the centre rafters.'[6] In 1865 'there was no glass in the windows and many crevices in the roof through which the sun's rays slanted, helping to lighten up the room' (and let in the rain?).

Muir described the interior as 'a rather sparingly-illuminated apartment of some length, furnished with a few desks and forms', an improvement on 1860 when 'writing was performed on a plank or seat, the children kneeling in the sand'. The children normally wrote in copy-books, but in 1865 these had not arrived, so roof slates saved from a wreck were used, the children writing with stalks of pipes instead of pencils.

Muir was horrified by Finlayson's own accommodation:

> [Finlayson] led us to the lower end of the apartment, and there, pushing aside a suspended curtain, ushered us into what was at once his sleeping room and parlour. Jacques's 'O knowledge ill-inhabited! worse than Jove in a thatched house!' came into my head as I looked around the solitary magister's ultra-economised sanctum – its earthen floor, deal chair or two, chest, and low roughly fashioned bedstead, covering fully one-half of the area. How it was that anyone at all smoothly brought up could stand out such a life of privation, I could not comprehend. Perhaps, as a Highlander, the poor probationer was in some measure to the manner born; and most likely Hope, the blessed partner of the downcast, soothed him o' nights with visions of vacant pulpits, into some one of which at no distant day or night he might peradventure happily be lifted; but for all that the good ladies should, I thought . . . have gone the length of at least making his lonely cell somewhat roomy and comfortable.

Carmichael noted Finlayson's books: 'Dunbar's Greek-English Lexicon, Confessions of Faith, Virgil and Tacitus in the original.'[7]

Finlayson's spartan accommodation must have seemed like luxury to him, for at the time of the 1861 census he was lodging with Donald MacKinnon, the constable, and his family of eight children.

In terms of its educational function, 'The teacher and school are highly appreciated by the people,' wrote Ross in 1868. So were the visitors, such as one in 1865 whose 'distribution of comfits and toys gave great joy, and a few of the parents who

were present cast on us looks of wonder and gratitude'. But
the missionary function of the school must not be forgotten.
The 1859 report reads: 'The success of this school proving,
as it does, that a wide and effectual door is open for diffusing
gospel light in all parts of Scotland where Popish darkness still
prevails, Christians will surely be stimulated to remove what is
indeed a reproach – the fact that there are districts in our land
which the Reformation never reached.' A visitor to the Barra
school in 1857 described 'the young in that benighted spot'
as 'a crooked and perverse generation'. Given such attitudes,
and the Free Church's strict austerity and condemnation of all
forms of entertainment and other aspects of culture, conflict
was inevitable. In the early years, the Association was content
with religious instruction during school hours, but in time it
wanted more than that. The 1864 report says:

> It is necessary to be very cautious in giving any re-
> port of the work of the Association in the Popish
> islands of Barra and Mingalay. The school in the
> latter island is as well attended as formerly, the priest
> offering no opposition to the day-school, but rather
> encouraging the children to go. It is otherwise, how-
> ever, with the Sabbath-school, where proselytizing
> is feared. But 'we have need of patience' . . . The
> people have been warned that unless attendance is
> secured on Sabbath as well as week-days the school
> may not be continued.

This 'caution' was repeated in 1866, with a rather sinister
reference to 'direct cases of conversion' in the Catholic islands;
but it was not until 1871 that the threat to close the school
was carried out, as we learn from the report of that year:

> In some of the work in the Popish districts there has
> been much interest, and some hopeful promises of
> success, whilst in other places faith and patience

have been tried by bitter disappointment. The school
in the island of Mingalay . . . was found lately in
so unsatisfactory a state that the Committee were
advised to drop it for a time, perhaps to be resumed
at a future period under a new labourer. It cannot be
said to have been useless, when all the young people
in the island, none of whom knew a letter before,
can now read the Word of God both in Gaelic and
English; but the influence for good on the population has not been what the Committee fondly hoped
to see.

Viewed in isolation, it is hard to be certain exactly what the
writer of these words was getting at, apart from pointing a
finger at Finlayson. But, considering previous and sometimes
equally nebulous comments, it is likely that the refusal of the
people to accept the Sunday school, or to be converted, were
the main reasons for the Association's decision. For this one
can only blame the Association's own naivety in thinking
these aims could be achieved in such a close-knit Catholic
community; Mingulay was not directly comparable with
Barra, where Sunday schools were accepted, and where there
were a few Protestants. The implicit criticism of Finlayson
therefore seems unfair, but there may be more to it than the
Association let on. So what about Finlayson?

John Finlayson was born in 1830 in Lochcarron, Ross-
shire. His father, Finlay, was a tailor who joined the Free
Church on its formation, and was keen to see a son of his
'wag his head in the pulpit'. [8] His grandfather was a Catholic.
He attended Edinburgh University, but never graduated.[9]
His appointment to Mingulay was his first with the Ladies'
Highland Association, who must have considered him equal
to perhaps their toughest post. He was a shy, scholarly man
– not, one would have thought, a proselytising type – and
a conscientious teacher. A witty uncle once referred to him
as 'the Philosopher at Patmos',[10] likening him to the Apostle

John who was exiled to that Aegean island; to the islanders he was known – in later life – as an Sgoilear Glas, 'the Grey-Haired Teacher'.

Originally the schools were intended to operate for only half the year, as the teachers were expected to spend the winter months at Free Church College in Edinburgh as part of their training for the ministry. Finlayson managed to do this some years, such as in 1863, when there was uncertainty as to whether he would return; the islanders offered to repair the school roof as an inducement. Other winters he remained, with no contact with the outside world. John Cowan wrote of his meeting with Finlayson on the former's visit in 1865:

> As we gained the sandy beach, a solitary figure was seen approaching, accompanied by his dog. It was your teacher, our friend Mr Finlayson, and our meeting was one that touched his heart and ours, for words we had few, but we warmly pressed each other's hands. It was like Robinson Crusoe visited for the first time after his solitary residence in his island.

If it was Finlayson's original intention to become a minister in the Free Church, it was not to be his destiny, for he spent the rest of his life in this remote Catholic community. In November 1871 he married an islander, Jane Campbell (Sìne Dhòmhnaill Nèill), and it is very likely that this was the cause of the school's closure. The marriage would have been unacceptable to the Association, being incompatible with their religious mission, and Finlayson's position would have become impossible. He may also have been criticised for not producing results in the narrow sense of converts. He decided on marriage and Mingulay rather than ministry, and the wedding took place not long after the closure of the school – if we assume that he was no longer in post at the time of his marriage – for the school was still open in July 1871.[11] The wedding was held, unusually, in Mingulay, and was a

Catholic ceremony. He was then forty-one, she forty-five; they had no children, but later brought up a great-niece of hers, Maria Campbell (Màiri Dhòmhnaill Chaluim), born in 1878. It was not unusual for childless couples who could afford it to offer to bring up a child of less well-off relatives. Finlayson was not alone in not 'finishing the course', for over the years only a quarter of the teachers reached the pulpit.[12] Finlayson's younger brother, Alexander, also began the training, but later gave it up to study medicine.[13]

The Association did not resume the school, perhaps because it discovered, in time, that a government school was planned there. But the story does not end here: ten years later, long after the new school had opened, the Association expressed a willingness to take over its running, as it had agreed to close its school at Northbay, where Barra School Board wanted to have its own school. Nothing came of the suggestion, and the Association's presence in Barra finally came to an end.[14]

It is hard to assess the school's success or impact, though the reports suggest that a great deal was achieved. One indicator is the ability of the people to write their own names, shown by the requirement to sign an entry in a register of birth, marriage or death (in the case of the first and last, as an informant). The first such signature was in 1868, and rarely after that; but one has to allow for the lapse of time between acquiring the ability and having an opportunity of using it before losing it through lack of use. This must partly explain Finlayson's comment in his first entry in the logbook of the subsequent Board School, four years later, that none of the pupils knew the alphabet. As he must have taught some of the same pupils before, it cannot have been quite true. On a broader level, there is no doubt that the school served to introduce the people to the ways and values of the outside world, which they were to relate to increasingly; and the school must have made the work of its successor much easier.

11

Mingulay Public School

The Education (Scotland) Act of 1872 brought education under state control for the first time, and made it compulsory for all children between the ages of five and thirteen (later raised to fourteen). On the local level, it was administered by school boards which appointed school 'managers' – like governors today – and the school staff. Schools received an annual grant according to attendance, the qualifications of the teacher, and the quality of the teaching, as perceived by the inspector on his annual visit. In poor districts such as Barra, school fees were not charged; education was funded out of local rates and from central government.[1]

Barra School Board was duly formed, and opened four 'public' schools initially – three in Barra, and the Mingulay school, much the smallest, which opened in November 1875. The school was intended to serve all four islands south of Vatersay. John Finlayson was appointed teacher, a choice which, although an obvious one, would not have been universally welcome in the Catholic islands of Barra and South Uist. Finlayson and all the other teachers in the islands were Protestant, and this was resented by the Catholic majority, which wanted religious instruction in schools. This paradox was no accident; it was deliberately engineered by those in power, a tiny Protestant minority headed by the factor (estate manager), and is an example of the discrimination Catholics still suffered. In theory the school boards, which made the appointments, were freely elected by the ratepayers, but in practice the estate authorities ensured, by devious means such as the threat of eviction from their crofts, that they always had a Protestant majority.[2] This injustice was redressed only when the Crofters Act of 1886 gave tenants security of tenure, and removed the fear of eviction for voting as they wished.

The affairs of the school are documented in the school logbook,[3] in which the teacher was required to make weekly entries, and the book also contains the inspectors' annual reports, copied in laboriously, and no doubt reluctantly in the case of critical ones, by the teacher. In his first entry Finlayson wrote: 'The children, 30 in number, are all beginners, not one of them knowing the alphabet.' As already indicated, this cannot have been strictly true, since some of them must have attended the Ladies' School which closed four years earlier; indeed, it is almost a negation of his past labours, though he may have wanted to give the impression that all were starting from scratch. The children were willing and made rapid progress in reading and writing. In the fifth week Finlayson started dividing the pupils into classes, to study at different stages in a scale of up to six 'standards' using set books. Once the school was established, the children were examined in the first standard at the age of seven or eight, and in subsequent ones at approximately yearly intervals. Pupils progressed from one standard to another on the basis of ability, assessed by the inspector at the annual examination. Only a few pupils reached the sixth standard, the next stage being 'intermediate'. This was the last stage offered in any of the Barra schools, so if this was passed, pupils had to go to Glasgow to continue. However, this was impossible financially for most families, bursaries being unavailable, and although a few Mingulay pupils did pass, none went any further.

Subjects taught in Mingulay were basic: reading, writing (on slate and paper), English (with much emphasis, in true Victorian style, on grammar), arithmetic, history, geography, singing, and, from 1885, Gaelic. Religion was not taught; it was left to school boards to decide whether to include it or not, and Barra decided against.[4] For the boys there was navigation, and for the girls sewing, for which a 'sewing mistress' was employed. For some years this was Finlayson's wife Jane, and later a Miss Glancy was employed. She was presumably one of the Barra Glancys, for she paid only short and occasional visits, as a result of which she was replaced by Mary Campbell of Mingulay.

Instruction was supposed to be in English, the existence of Gaelic being ignored by the original Act. (Gaelic was regarded as having no future, not only by the government, but by many parents as well. Emigration was still on the agenda, and Gaelic was useless to emigrants; it was also useless for work on the mainland. Gaelic as a school subject was subsequently permitted, as a result of campaigning by concerned organisations.)[5] Finlayson's use of Gaelic was, however, tolerated by the inspectors, though they gave him conflicting instructions as to how much he should use it.

School ran from Monday to Friday, and there were two sessions per day. The pupils sat on benches, infants at the front. The system of one teacher trying to teach pupils ranging in age from four to fourteen or more in one room cannot have been conducive to learning.

Finlayson and the inspectors were generally complimentary about the children's ability and progress. William Jolly, the inspector in the 1870s, found them 'bright, willing, and wonderfully intelligent, earnest to perspiration point and shy to a fault'. The inspection and examination were held in the summer, and heralded the annual holiday of between four and seven weeks. The first examination, in 1876, took place in Barra, with Barra pupils. Inspector Jolly described it:

> On turning round into the valley of Borve, where
> the school is, my attention was arrested by a group
> of bonnetless bairns, romping on the banks of the

stream which enters the sea close by. These were the Minglay children, both boys and girls, who had been brought by their teacher in an open boat, over the dangerous seas between, to be examined. The shock-headed creatures acquitted themselves surprisingly, beating with ease their Barra comperes.

Subsequently, the Board took the more logical step of sending the inspector to the pupils, although in 1877 bad weather prevented his visit altogether.

The inspectors would also have examined the attendance register and admissions register. During the years 1889 to 1894, for which an admissions register survives, numbers enrolled annually varied between thirty-eight and forty-eight, the age range was four to fourteen, and there were more girls than boys. One of the pupils came from Berneray, where there had been a 'sub school' in the 1880s, and another, though from Mingulay, had attended that school (Flora Sinclair, who would have stayed with relatives in Berneray). Two were from Pabbay, the children of John Campbell, originally of Mingulay. Four had previously attended Castlebay school, and the parents of one of them still lived in Castlebay. Two children, James and Annie Murphie, were born in Glasgow and lived with their Mingulay grandmother, Anne MacNeil (the midwife). James was nearly seven when he was admitted to the school in 1890, which may be when he arrived in Mingulay, as he had not attended a previous school.

The performance of the children at the examination was not only of interest in itself; it was regarded as a measure of the performance of the teacher, which partly determined the amount of the annual grant awarded by the Board. Attendance was also taken into consideration. Irregular attendance was an obstacle to progress, and an exasperation to Finlayson and his successors. Its main cause was the withdrawing of children by their parents for croft work in the summer months, and in the early years it fell to Finlayson to remind parents that their children's attendance was compulsory. In later years he was relieved of this irksome duty by the Board's 'compulsory officer'. Other causes of irregular attendance were bad weather (even though the school was no distance from the houses, the children had no adequate protective clothing) and the occasional epidemic, the worst of which was a measles outbreak in 1898, when the school was closed for three months. There were a total of twenty religious holidays throughout the year. In 1886 the Board reduced the grant merely because a small mistake by Finlayson in the attendance register had cast doubt on their accuracy and led to accusations of fiddling. Finlayson was then subjected to the humiliation of more frequent checks by the school managers, such as Father James Chisholm of Castlebay, who looked in during pastoral visits.

The first six years of the school's life were spent, in Inspector Robertson's words, 'in a hovel with appliances more in harmony with the premises than with present requirements'. In 1878 it was on the same site as the earlier school, where it had probably been since it opened (although an entry in the logbook in 1877 mentions a change of schoolroom; perhaps a rearrangement was meant). William Jolly described it:

> Their old school at Church Bay was one of the small thatched huts of the island. It consisted of a thick wall of rude stones five feet in height, and the low entrance was formed of the door of a ship's cabin, floated in from some wreck. The interior was dimly lighted by two small windows, and was open to the sloping rafters. The floor was covered by a layer of light-coloured sand from the adjacent shore. The walls showed the rough stones of which they were built, and were quite bare except where a newspaper was hung, on examination day, behind the inspector's seat. The whole apartment was, however, beautified by various natural gifts from sea and land. Every crevice had a wild flower inserted in

it, and these united their varied hues with pleasing effect, and shed a refreshing odour through the close, little hut. The window sills also were stuck full of coloured shells, while a string of seabirds' eggs hung in graceful curve from side to side of the room. The seats were formed of ships' planks resting on stones set all round the walls, and the only two desks consisted of flat boards nailed to uprights driven into the ground.

This delightful account says much for Finlayson's love of nature and imagination, and for the broad-mindedness of the inspector, who clearly appreciated it. The school had two wooden privies (quaintly termed 'offices' in Scotland at the time), which must have been a great curiosity to the islanders when they were installed.

The 'hovel' was replaced by a fine new building on a new site, next to the road between the village and the landing place (plate 17). It opened on 19 September 1881. The building, the first modern one in Mingulay, was a single rectangular room built of dressed stone and mortar, with a slate roof. It was designed by Alexander Ross of Inverness, the architect for twenty-three schools built at this time in the Western Isles (excluding Lewis).[6] The stone was quarried, using drills and wedges, from rock outcrops to the west. It had large windows high up in the walls, fitted with blinds, and was lined internally with match boarding (linoleum was later placed on the walls, which the children enjoyed drawing on). Heating was provided by a coal-burning stove. The furnishings were desks and forms, and a desk and blackboard for the teacher. The school was designed to accommodate an average of thirty pupils'[7] but when numbers rose later they must have been rather squashed. The original grant for building the schoolroom and the planned schoolhouse was £494, but only the former was built at first. This was presumably because John Finlayson was already living in Mingulay, but it seems unfair on him as he was denied the standard of living provided to teachers at other schools. The new facilities must have transformed the process of education in the island and increased the regard in which it was held.

The building sits within a generous enclosure, 150 by145 feet (45.7 by 44.1 metres), defined by a stone wall. This was probably built at the same time as the school, as stipulated by the terms of the feu charter, and defines the area sold to the school board.[8] The enclosed area was the playground. At a later date a magnificent set of three privies was erected against the west wall of the enclosure.

In 1894 a modest teacher's house was added at right angles to the schoolroom on its western side. It was presumably built in anticipation of John Finlayson's retirement and the need for suitable accommodation for his replacement. It provided a standard of living previously unknown on the island. The builder was Alexander MacLean of Borve, Barra.

John Finlayson retired in June 1897. He was sixty-six, and may not have been in good health; illness had kept him off work twice in the previous few years. The logbook and visitors' accounts show him to have been a gentle and con-scientious teacher, rarely critical of the pupils; but the inspec-tors' reports were not on the whole very flattering, and he cannot have got much satisfaction from them. He seems to have lost heart somewhat in later years, as his entries in the logbook tail off into one-liners. But he was undoubtedly a good teacher, and he contributed to the islanders becoming articulate participants in the modern world; it was he who taught most of those who fought, and eventually won, the battle for better living conditions.

Finlayson was regarded with respect and affection by the islanders, and that is how tradition remembers him; and one would expect, from one who had married into the commu-nity and devoted his working life to it, that the feelings were mutual. But they do not appear to have been, in later years at least. Letters he wrote to his friend J.A. Harvie-Brown, the naturalist, show little sympathy for the crofters' values, aspirations for better living conditions, and religion; and it is hard to believe that, although a retiring person, he kept his feelings secret from all but his distant friend. Perhaps he knew Harvie-Brown would have been receptive to such comments, and thus his emphasis on them may not be a fully accurate reflection of his attitudes. So what drew him to Mingulay and kept him there? The answer lies in his letters: it was the fishing 'and the sport it afforded that fascinated me about Mingulay, not the people';[9] also the birds, the plants, and the isolation.

Finlayson's correspondence with Harvie-Brown began before the naturalist visited Mingulay for the second time, in 1887, in the course of gathering material for his book on the fauna of the Outer Hebrides. Harvie-Brown clearly regarded Finlayson as a valuable informant on the island's birdlife, and quoted extracts from the early letters in his book. Finlayson, in turn, valued Harvie-Brown as a real friend, confidant, and fellow bird enthusiast, something he seems to have missed on Mingulay. Finlayson expressed his views on human affairs on Mingulay, as we saw in chapter 4, and also in the wider world, in which he maintained a lively interest through the *Scotsman*; his comments reveal his political views to have been Conservative. A strong sense of humour comes across in the letters, and Father Allan McDonald of Eriskay, who knew Finlayson in his later years, wrote that he was 'entertaining and sociable',[10] while Harvie-Brown appreciated his 'good companionship and genial conversation'. These are not quite the impressions one has of him from other sources, but in the company of the rare visitors, especially fellow intellectuals, this is how he appeared.

Finlayson enjoyed his retirement: 'I have nothing to do now but play and admire nature,' he wrote in 1899, adding, 'I am now master of 100 flowering plants. Last year I had the assistance of Miss Freer from London.'[11] She wrote of him: 'He has books, and is quite an accomplished botanist, having observed and classified the flora of the island without knowing the names of a dozen flowers.' She also noted that 'his one luxury is tea – which he imports – of the very best'. Finlayson spent several winters on the Earl of Dunmore's estates in Harris as a gamekeeper. He had been going there since 1878, and had supplied information on the local wild-life to Harvie-Brown.[12] He didn't want his double life to be public knowledge, however, and in his book Harvie-Brown acknowledges him as an informant as two different people!

Finlayson died in March 1904, and Harvie-Brown was informed by his grief-stricken adoptive daughter, Morag Campbell Finlayson, as she signed herself.[13] She mentioned that she and Finlayson's widow Jane (who died the following year) were in touch with his younger brother Alexander, who was a doctor in Munlochy, Ross and Cromarty. Being a Protestant, he could not be buried in the islanders' graveyard, and so his body was taken to Barra. This is a translation of the account Ealasaid Chaimbeul wrote of his final journey in her Gaelic autobiography:

> With great sorrow and sadness, the brave men departed with the Grey-Haired Teacher's remains bound for burial at the old graveyard at Cuithir in Barra, beside the people of his own religion. It is un-derstood that the weather got so wild on the way to Castlebay that they were forced to lash the coffin in a vertical position to the mast – otherwise it would have been swept out to sea – and because of this, even on his last journey, the mortal remains of the fine man looked over those to whom he had given their first knowledge of education.[14]

The story is told that the party arrived at Castlebay too late to continue on foot to Cuithir. The only place they found to leave the body overnight was the bank, so they left him there as a 'bank deposit' until the following morning.

Finlayson was succeeded by John Johnston, an Sgoilear Bàn, 'the Fair-Haired Teacher', aged nineteen. He was born in Mingulay but was brought up in Barra, and had been a 'pupil teacher' for all of four weeks at Castlebay school. The appointment of a Catholic at last should have satisfied everyone, the more so as he was a local man. Johnston's performance during his four years' service was considered satisfactory in difficult circumstances, which included epidemics of measles, mumps, and influenza. The 'epidemic of mumps', recorded Johnston in October 1899, 'aggravated by an epidemic of harvest work reduced attendance' However, Barra School Board felt he needed more supervision, and in September 1901, only two months into the school year, he was transferred to Barra. Exactly what supervision was needed was not elaborated, but he is known to have visited Castlebay frequently. He had his own boat, and the story is told that one evening he started rowing home to Mingulay only to wake up next morning to find the boat still tied to Castlebay pier! The Barra storyteller, the Coddy, told a story about how Johnston once fell overboard on his way back to Mingulay, and on getting back in, had to strip and dry his clothes before arriving in the bay.[15] When he was away during the week, he would open the school on an equivalent number of Saturdays to make up. This was not approved of by everybody – Malcolm MacLean (Cadaidh), for instance, thought croft work was more important. Johnston was interested in navigation, which he studied while in Mingulay; but he remained a teacher, firstly in Barra, and then in some of the Inner Hebridean islands before returning to teach in Barra, where he is remembered with great respect.

The Board now wanted a woman teacher, and in October 1901 appointed Miss Margaret Haggerty from Liverpool. Miss Haggerty earned a high grant (from central government) for the school by virtue of her teaching qualifications, and saved the Board money by virtue of her sex: women teachers' salaries were appreciably lower than men's. Her entries in the logbook and the inspectors' reports show her to have been very professional, and she must have been very able, for she presumably had no Gaelic. She faced an outbreak of scarlet fever in 1902. She sent the children home but was unaware that a boat was leaving for Castlebay which would have allowed her to inform the Board and the doctor. Her entry in the logbook, 'no one from whom to ask advice' illustrates the remoteness she felt not only from the outside world, but also from the islanders.

Miss Haggerty resigned in December 1903, and the following month Mrs Sarah MacShane, a qualified teacher and a Catholic, took over as the last teacher. She was born Sarah Tinney in Beauly, Inverness-shire, about 1873, but the family later moved to Barrhead, near Glasgow, where she trained as a teacher. She married Edward MacShane, a railway worker, in 1898, and their first child, Peter, was born about 1902. In Mingulay, Peter was looked after by local 'childminders' while his mother was at work. He was a naughty child, and when the women told his mother, in Gaelic, how he had behaved, Peter, who had picked up some Gaelic, would 'translate' these bad reports into glowing ones. Mrs MacShane was musical and a good needlewoman, and these helped her to be accepted by the islanders.[16] She introduced the novelty of 'concerts with a charitable purpose' performed by the children, and balls, in the schoolroom. On one of these occasions, Mary Campbell said, one of the Barra Head lightkeepers brought a gramophone, the first one seen on the island. Malcolm MacLean (Cadaidh) thought that anything that sang like a person must be the devil's work, and refused to listen to it.[17] Mrs MacShane gave prizes for best attendance, and gave Christmas cards to the children. The inspectors' reports show that she performed satisfactorily, though they had become very brief by then. She was a strong-willed woman, as her determination to work at the same time as raising a family, unusual at that time, shows. She could also be quite formidable: in her attempts to get a croft on Vatersay, where the family moved in 1910, she wrote

to the Secretary for Scotland, Lord Pentland when she had no
success with local officials of the Congested Districts Board,
but still got nowhere.[18]

A visitor in June 1905 wrote of her:

> The schoolmistress is an active, energetic capable
> person doing good work on £60 a year and house.
> Her husband, who lives with her, was a moulder up
> by Hamilton. Fancy a moulder on one of the lone-
> liest of the islands of the Hebrides! I asked my native
> guide what the moulder did. 'Oh, he just digs the
> garden, carries peats, and attends on his lady. What
> else would you have him do?' What else indeed! The
> ladies are up-to-date in Mingulay.[19]

Mrs MacShane gave birth to five children during her
years in Mingulay and Vatersay. Two of these were born in
Mingulay, Eleanor in November 1906 and John in October
1908, John's being the last birth ever to take place in the
island (the last native islander, Marion Sinclair, Mòrag Iagan
Iain, was born in August 1907). She described herself in the
logbook as 'ill' around the time of Eleanor's birth, but didn't
take a single day off for John's. She asked Donald Martin, the
Castlebay priest and future Bishop of Argyll and the Isles, to
be Eleanor's godfather. Eleanor later became a teacher. Mrs
MacShane's husband, Edward, took on two crofts which became vacant when their tenants left the island and were not
required by other islanders.

In 1907, just as families began to leave for Vatersay, Mr
Coats of Paisley donated a library of books to the school (and
later, a school bag for each child), as he did to many others. The
lending register shows that there were various English classics,
such as *Robinson Crusoe, The Arabian Nights, The Pickwick
Papers*; but, with the exception of Maggie MacMillan, who
borrowed practically everything, not many children made
use of them, even when they moved to Vatersay. A book on

electricity was not amongst the more popular titles. One book was 'returned in a disgraceful condition'.

A curious incident occurred in October 1909. A bull was 'interfering' with children on their way to and from school, and their parents threatened to keep them away. Mrs MacShane reported the business to the police, and a policeman came from Barra. This seems to be a rather odd way of dealing with a situation which, one would have thought, the islanders could have solved themselves; but of course there must have been more to this story than Mrs MacShane recorded in the logbook!

The school's decline set in when the emigrations to Vatersay began in 1907, reducing the school roll from twenty-five in 1906 (as it had been in 1901) to just seven at the end of 1908. Despite this, the school struggled on with a handful of pupils – the number varied, as there was a lot of coming and going between Mingulay and Vatersay and Sandray – until Barra School Board decided that its operations should be transferred to Vatersay. It finally closed on 27 April 1910, when there were nine pupils, and Mrs MacShane was on duty when its successor opened in Vatersay – initially in Vatersay House – two months later. Some of the Mingulay children had missed three years of school by then.

As in the case of the Ladies' School, it is hard to assess the impact of the Board School, especially as so many other changes were taking place in the islands at the same time. Mary Campbell said they learned to read and write, but didn't learn much otherwise.[20] As to the ability to sign their own names, it is surprising how few people did so in the registers of births, marriages and deaths even in the last years when most people would have been to school. Many of the 'signatures' on the petition for improved landing facilities in 1896, and the deed of agreement concerning the derrick in 1901, were clearly written by other hands. Regarding knowledge of English, a potential indicator recorded in the censuses from 1881 is of limited use. People who were 'in the habit of making colloquial use of the Gaelic language' were recorded in 1881; not surprisingly, all but four were in this category, which reveals nothing of actual ability in English. The censuses of 1891 and 1901 recorded whether only Gaelic, or Gaelic and English, were spoken; again, not very revealing. The 1891 figure for the latter category was five, including John Finlayson and the two children from Glasgow. The 1901 figure was seventy-seven, but it is impossible to evaluate its significance or to compare it directly with the previous one. The school inspector in 1899 recognised that 'The teacher has unusual difficulties to contend with in imparting instruction to children who never speak a word of English.' When John Johnston arrived he found that 'after reading a paragraph fluently they have little idea of the meaning'.

On a broader level, education was one factor in that inevitable process, the islanders' growing contact with, and knowledge of, the outside world. The story of the desertion might well have been different without it; education was a factor in the desertion, and in that sense the school contributed to its own redundancy. On the negative side, education contributed to the loss of their culture: as J.L. Campbell wrote of Barra in 1936, those people who had grown up before the 1872 Education Act came into effect retained more of their culture than younger people.[21] Mrs Murray's prophecy of 1888, that Finlayson was 'busy with his English standards and methodical training to turn this remote and interesting island into as commonplace a village as any in our own neighbourhood' (Cardross, on the Clyde), was not to be fulfilled.

12

A 'most devout group of Catholics'

> The population of Miulaidh [Mingulay] . . . was the
> most devout group of Catholics 1 have ever known.

This was written by Donald Buchanan, a native of Barra who
had spent many years in other parts of Britain, in 1942, and
shows the strength of the islanders' faith, a faith that was
fundamental to their lives.

The early history of Christianity in the Barra Isles has already been discussed. When Sir Donald Monro, archdeacon of
the Diocese of the Isles, visited the area in 1549, he found the
Church apparently flourishing, with chapels in many of the
islands, and he gave no hint of the impending Reformation.
Over most of Scotland this momentous upheaval, culminating
in 1560, brought to an end a thousand years of Catholicism,
first the Celtic monastic tradition, latterly the Roman diocesan system. The southern Outer Hebrides were among the
few places where the old religion lived on.

In the decades after the Reformation, there was a general
breakdown in church organisation; although the isolation
of the islands preserved them from the ravages of Protestant
persecutions, priests could no longer operate. The Catholic
Church was curiously slow to respond to the threat of its
total annihilation in the Highlands and Islands, and it was

not until the 1630s that Irish Franciscans were sent there to 'reconcile' people to the old religion and perform marriages and baptisms. In 1636 Father Cornelius Ward 'spent a month working in the isles of Barra, Feray [?Fiaray] and Barnaray . . . though the people of the Hebrides may be rough and uninstructed, they have not entirely forgotten the traditions of their fathers, as they always show great affection for the mass.' The following year he worked 'in the Bishops' Isles . . . where no priest had set foot since the Reformation'.[1] In 1654 another priest, Dermot Duggan, arrived in Barra, where he found 'a people so devout and anxious to learn that I was astonished. It was enough to teach one child in each village the Pater, Ave and Credo; in two days the whole village knew them – children and adults.'[2]

The conditions under which these early missionaries laboured were tough but must have been rewarding. Father Duggan described his work in the islands:

> I have to employ two men; one helps me to row when I travel from island to island, and carries my Mass-box and my scanty luggage overland . . . the other man helps me to teach the Pater, Ave, and Credo, and serves my mass . . . we take only one meal a day, of barley bread and oaten bread with some cheese or salt butter. Sometimes we spend whole days without a meal because we cannot procure anything.

He called for 'good apostolic workers acquainted with the language and prepared to bear with hunger and thirst and sleeping on the ground'.[3]

Father Duggan spent five years in the islands, and had reconciled people as far north as Benbecula, when he died. The islanders have remained steadfast to this day, despite discrimination and attempts at conversion such as we saw in the last chapter. One happy by-product of the survival of

Roman Catholicism was, as related in chapter 3, the survival
of traditional culture, which in the northern Outer Hebrides
was oppressed by the more austere Protestantism.

A later worker, Father Francis MacDonel, complained of
the difficulty of working in the Barra Isles:

> The Sacred Congregation only gave me one vest-
> ment, when two were very necessary, for the journey
> has often to be made from island to island, and there
> is great danger and difficulty in taking vestments
> between the five islands where there are Catholics.
> Indeed there should be one set of vestments in each
> island.[4]

Whether Mingulay's medieval chapel was in use at this
time is uncertain. Bishop Nicolson, writing of Barra in 1700,
reported that there were 'six other inhabited islands, and there
is a chapel in each'. Mingulay must have been one of these,
but there is no indication as to whether the chapels were in use
or intact. Nicolson said of Cille Bharra, Barra, that there were
the ruins of 'two or three churches and a priory'; St Barr's
chapel was in ruins in 1625, but was still used for worship.[5]
There is no subsequent reference to the chapel in Mingulay
(or any of the other southern islands), and it was not until
the end of the nineteenth century that another one was built.
Mingulay's other site that had religious associations, Crois an
t-Suidheachain, has already been mentioned.

By degrees a continuous succession of priests was established
in Barra, which survived even the renewed persecutions of
Catholics after the 1745 Jacobite uprising, and the conversion
to the reformed faith of the MacNeil chiefs themselves. The
MacNeils had been forced into this by the anti-Catholic legislation passed after the uprising. A story about James Grant,
Barra priest at the time of the uprising, is given in chapter 4.

The Barra priest served the southern islands, which he visited, according to MacQueen in 1794, 'twice a year, unless by

a particular call to visit the sick, and to administer extreme unction' (the last rites). The priest also baptised children on his visits, including children who had already been baptised by a member of the community;[6] this was done if the child's survival was in doubt, to ensure it did not enter the state of 'limbo' in the event of its death. Marriages generally took place in Barra. There were occasional confirmation ceremonies in Barra, at which hundreds of young people from all over the parish were confirmed. At one of these, in 1884, twenty-one youngsters from Mingulay were confirmed by Bishop Allan MacDonald.[7] Confirmations accompanied the opening of Mingulay's new chapel, as we will see. In 1819 a Mingulay man was paying an annual amount for seats in Craigstone church.[8] This is curious, as it must have been rare for Mingulay people to attend the church. People in Pabbay and Sandray also paid these 'dues', as well as Barra people, which was how the Church was, and still is, funded; there was no state funding for the Catholic Church as there was for the Church of Scotland. Seats for two usually cost 2s 6d (12½p); marriages and christenings were also charged for, at 5s and 1s respectively.

The pattern of once or twice yearly visits continued for most of the nineteenth century, but by the early 1900s the visits had become monthly in summer, and less often in winter.[9] The servicing of the islands could have taken weeks, or not happened at all, if the weather was bad; we have seen how Father Allan McDonald was once stormbound on Mingulay for seven weeks. In the absence of a chapel, Muir was told in 1866, 'The people always meet on Sundays and fast days to hear prayers at one of the elders' houses.' How this was accomplished when the population was over 150 is hard to imagine. Individuals would lead the prayers; in the last years this was Donald MacPhee (Dòmhnall Bàn).

In 1804 Bishop John Chisholm wrote: 'Those in the Western Islands and especially in the islands around Barra are splendid Catholics, who in the innocence of their lives and the firmness of their faith resemble the early Christians, and have the greatest horror of heresy.'[10] The strength of the Mingulay people's faith is underlined by the complete failure of the (Free Church) Ladies' Highland Association to get them to attend Sunday school, let alone be converted; and the tolerance they showed by accepting the school contrasts with the intolerance of their beliefs by their 'benefactors'. Families prayed together at night, as was the case in Barra. One member would lead the prayer; there were Gaelic prayer books in Catherine MacNeil's house, which her mother read.[11] The islanders' faith also had its own characteristics which differed from that of the Barra people, due to their isolation and having to take most services themselves: they held prayer meetings on weekday evenings, with one person leading, a practice not found in Barra, and their faith could be considered to have been *god-fearing* rather than *god-loving,* which is a characteristic of that of Barra. It could be suggested that the Free Church school had some influence, but the school was open for only twelve years, there was no Sunday school, and the teacher, John Finlayson, does not seem to have been a zealot. Furthermore, the schools in Barra operated for much longer and Sunday school and other prayer meetings were held.

Mary Campbell told the story of a catechist who was sent to Mingulay to try to convert the people to Protestantism. He asked Ruairidh Dhòmhnaill (the storyteller, Roderick MacNeil) if he knew what kind of a place Hell was. The reply was (in translation) 'Hell, a deep place, you can't measure it, and if you continue in the direction you're going in, you'll get to the bottom!'[12] The people were spared the endless stream of fanatical Calvinist missionaries which the St Kildans were subjected to in their last two centuries.

The lack of a chapel, and of accommodation for the visiting priest, was remedied at last in 1898, when a building fulfilling both needs was erected (see plate 15). The Chapel House was built in a prominent position overlooking the humble cottages of the village, as if symbolising the role of

the church in the lives of its inhabitants. Its design was unlike
that of any chapel in Barra or the Hebrides generally, being
domestic rather than ecclesiastical. The only outward sign of
its function was a concrete cross on the top of the central
dormer window on the front of the building. It was also very
unusual, and possibly unique, in that the chapel and priest's
quarters (presbytery) were arranged one above the other
rather than next to each other.[13] It was a plain building but
what it lacked in architectural inspiration, it made up for in
scale – 45 feet (13.7 metres) long by 25 feet (7.6 metres) wide,
it was large even by Barra standards, and in a small island
it was truly incongruous. It was solidly built from blocks of
local stone, probably quarried from outcrops nearby at the
foot of MacPhee's Hill. It was roofed with Ballachulish slates
and it was well appointed internally and externally. It was
designed and built by John MacIntyre (Iain Mogach) of Barra
(who built a smaller version for himself, as a house, in his
home village, Earsary).

The ground floor was for the use of the visiting priest
and his housekeeper; there was never intended to be a resident priest. It consisted of five rooms opening off a central
hall, with fine woodwork and plastered walls and ceilings
throughout. This may seem unnecessarily spacious, but it was
determined by the size of the chapel on the first floor. This
was dedicated to St Columba, like its medieval predecessor.
It was a single room, reached by an external stairway, lit by
three windows on each side and lined with matchboarding.
The altar and altar rail were made in Mingulay by John
MacKinnon the joiner. The fourteen stations of the cross were
hung on the walls. It is not known if there were benches; there
is no memory of their existence, and the benches of Vatersay
church, which was built in 1913, were made in Vatersay (by
John MacKinnon). In the last years there was a large bell,
thought to have hung somewhere above the chapel steps, but
there is no sign of it in plate 15. The bell survives; it was made
in Glasgow in 1875, and may have been a ship's bell. Neil

MacPhee (Niall Chaluim Dhòmhnaill) made a small sundial on a nearby rock outcrop, by levelling a small area on its top and erecting the pointer in a hole in the middle.

The building of the chapel must have been a huge undertaking, for apart from the stone, and sand for cement and plaster, everything down to the last nail had to be imported. The materials would have been landed on the beach on rafts and carried up to the site, perhaps by ponies. The main structure of the building was complete by the summer of 1898; work had probably begun the year before, as the lease between the estate and the diocese for the land was dated Whitsunday 1897.[14] The plot of land was precisely 140 feet (42.6 metres) square, and this was defined by a drystone wall. In the lease the building(s) to be erected were referred to as 'Mission House and Chapel'.

In hindsight the timing of this enterprise, so soon before the people left, seems inopportune. It can be explained partly in the context of the creation of the See of Argyll and the Isles in 1878, a re-creation, in a sense, of the pre-Reformation Diocese of the Isles.[15] Hitherto the region had been a remote and neglected part of a much larger see which included Glasgow.

The early years of the new see witnessed a programme of church building and the appointment of more priests. James Chisholm, appointed to Barra in 1883, was responsible for building the Church of Our Lady, Star of the Sea at Castlebay, which opened in 1888. It was funded by Neil MacNeil of Berneray. Chisholm's next project was Mingulay, which he must have decided was in need of a church. Evacuation had already been mooted by then, in 1883, so it may be that the provision of a chapel for these devout islanders was an attempt to encourage them to stay. Another suggestion is that Tady Glancy, the Castlebay merchant who put up the £600 building costs,[16] saw the chapel as a memorial to himself or to his wife.

One cannot help wondering whether the islanders were involved in the decision, or whether they would have preferred money to have been spent on improving conditions in a practical rather than a spiritual way. From as early as 1890 they were appealing for improved landing facilities, and the derrick they eventually got cost only £200. The chapel building itself could have been simpler and cheaper. But such considerations, had they arisen, would have been academic; the will and the funds were there. There is no doubt that the people would have welcomed the new chapel and more visits from the priest, though they would have preferred him to have stayed. The priest was the most important figure in their lives, and their isolation from him was one of the many reasons for the evacuation.

The first mass in the new chapel was said on Sunday 19 June 1898 by Father Allan McDonald of Eriskay. He noted in his diary: 'Altar and chapel decorated with wild flowers. Natives pleased and no wonder. House and Chapel so appropriate. Communicated infirm woman and heard confirmands' confessions till 10.30.[17]

The next day:

> Mass and Communion. Communicated 2 infirm old women. Wet and wildish. Bishop, Fr Chisholm, MacKenzie, Saville, and company arrived per puffer about 1pm. Confirmation preceded by a clerical rendering of the Veni Creator and an English Instruction by the Bishop. 44 confirmed – more than one third of them Campbells.

The Bishop was George Smith, Bishop of Argyll and the Isles, and MacKenzie and Saville were priests. It seems strange that McDonald, rather than Chisholm, the parish priest and the chapel's founder, said the first mass. Perhaps the plan was that he and the bishop would do so but they may have been delayed; McDonald may have been asked to go in case of such an eventuality. He arrived on the 13th and 'stayed with Finlayson for food but slept in chapel on improvised bedstead'. Finlayson was the retired teacher who lived in the nearest village house to the chapel. McDonald spent the night of the 18th in the kitchen of the priest's quarters in the new building. On the 16th, which he described as a hot day, he said mass in the schoolhouse, and the same day Chisholm visited. Apart from his spiritual duties, McDonald indulged his antiquarian interests, as described in chapter 2.

An early visitor to the chapel was Ada Goodrich-Freer, who went to Mingulay in August 1898 with her companion Constance Moore, together with, according to her, three priests and a doctor. She wrote of her visit:

> We made our headquarters in some rooms under the new chapel in process of building. It was bright August weather, and the scanty furniture was quite sufficient for our needs. There was a bedstead and bedding, which, with the aid of a lavish loan of clean home-spun blankets, we were enabled to distribute into three separate rooms; there was a board and trestles left behind by the workmen, and a good cooking stove, with a pot and kettle as part of its fittings. Within an hour of our arrival we were supplied with chairs, cups, plates, the inevitable teapot ... Our companions, the men, both of religion and medicine, found plenty of occupation, for the people naturally took advantage of their visit to supply their needs spiritual and bodily.
>
> At an early hour next morning Mass was said in the little unfinished chapel, with such fittings as could be arranged. There were no seats, but we were glad to bring up our four chairs for the very old and infirm. Almost every adult in the island was present, except a retired Presbyterian schoolmaster, and outside, a little group of awe-stricken children silently awaited the dispersion of such a gathering as they had never beheld.

Fortunately, this is not the only record of the event, for, as related in chapter 1, Goodrich-Freer's testimony is not entirely reliable. Her companions were not three priests and a doctor, but one priest, Father Allan McDonald, together with Everard Fielding, a member of the Society for Psychical Research, and Walter Blaikie, who was interested in traditions of the 1745 uprising.[18] It is no coincidence that two of the three stories Goodrich-Freer quotes concern the uprising; it is very likely that Blaikie got McDonald to ask the people for such stories at the time of their visit.[19] Goodrich-Freer had been in contact with McDonald before, because he recorded in his diary on 9 June , before his visit to Mingulay 'I meant to have set to the task Miss Freer gave me today . . . I feel unfit for it with all the will in the world.'

The Chapel House, as it is called today, had less than nine years of use before the people it had been built to serve started leaving Mingulay. How quickly things changed; and how ironic that Donald Martin, who had succeeded the chapel's founder as Castlebay priest, was to encourage the people to leave, as we will see in the next chapter. The priest's monthly visits in summer continued to the end of 1909, when they became occasional only.[20]

The people used St Columba's well, mentioned in chapter 9, as a source of holy water. Goodrich-Freer wrote:

> In Mingulay is a well, known as the well of Columcille [St Columba], which the people regard with such special reverence that, left often for months together without any religious privileges, or any means of consecrating water for devotional purposes, they use the well as 'holy water', and will cross themselves with it as they go by, and carry it in the prow of their boat, as is the pious custom of the fishermen.

The holy water was carried in stone bottles, according to Alexander Carmichael.

13

The 'Impossible Place'

> We spend the winter months lonely and dull but I
> hope summer shall get us relief as we shall be like
> prisoners during the bad weather . . . I am hoping to
> leave Mingulay soon.

So wrote Morag Campbell Finlayson, John Finlayson's adoptive daughter, in April 1905; two months later she was in
Kentangaval, Barra.[1] No doubt her sentiments were shared by
others, as Roderick MacNeil said there had been talk of evacuation long before it started.[2] The community was already in
decline by this time: at least two roofless houses can be seen
in Robert Adam's photographs taken in June 1905, and the
corn mill had been abandoned. Only a year and a half later,
in 1907, the emigration to Vatersay began. This process was
well documented, as government departments were involved,
and there was a trial which was reported in the newspapers,
so we know a good deal about some aspects of the Mingulay
community's last years.

This was not the first time people had considered leaving;
a few moved to Barra in or before 1883, and others had
applied for holdings there. Thereafter, the islanders seem to
have been confident of their future in Mingulay, and were
even prosperous, for they built improved houses and a mill,

THE 'IMPOSSIBLE PLACE'   177

and acquired two large herring fishing boats; and a chapel and landing derrick were provided.

Despite these positive signs, conditions in Mingulay were deteriorating. Neil MacPhee (Niall Dhòmhnaill Dhòmhnaill), interviewed in Vatersay in 1907, complained of the problem of access, the lack of land for a house and croft of his own, and the lack of seaweed for fertiliser; instead of seaweed, he had to get fish guts from Castlebay and spread them on the land, all during the fishing season when time was most precious.[3] The difficulty of access – getting to and from Mingulay, landing and loading people and goods, landing and launching boats – was the principal cause of hardship for the islanders. It prevented their taking full advantage of the fishing potential, and made landing of supplies difficult; getting a doctor or priest in an emergency was often impossible. The provision of the derrick in 1901 seems to have done little to ease the problem. The people had been shaken by the loss of the Pabbay fishing boat with all hands in 1897. Living conditions had become crowded and insanitary as the population grew, and there were epidemics of disease. The only remunerative employment was fishing, but, as dependence on cash to buy food and other necessities grew, it was not enough. Some of the men were forced to work away during the winter; in November 1899 it was reported that 'most of the men are absent at present in Glasgow',[4] where they worked in the shipyards and gas works.[5] There was nothing new about this, though more men were doing it; a visitor to the school in 1868 had reported that some of the children were able to write letters to friends absent for work in the south and east. The community, which had once been largely self-sufficient and had even exported various commodities, had become increasingly dependent on the outside world.

The inhabitants of Mingulay were not alone in the Barra Isles in suffering overcrowding and land hunger; the townships around Castlebay were amongst the most congested in the Hebrides. Landless cottars from these townships had been trying for some time to get land on Vatersay, and no doubt the Mingulay people followed these attempts with interest. Vatersay was then run as a single farm, occupied by the tenant farmer and his workers; it had been crofted before 1850, when the people were evicted,[6] and had been designated as suitable for crofting by a government commission in 1894.[7] It is easy to understand the attraction of Vatersay to cottars living in squalor – some of them in wooden huts, as they were not allowed to build houses – around Castlebay: there was ample land for house building, grazing for animals, cultivation, and a good harbour and many landing places. Its northern coast is only 2.5 kilometres (1 mile) from Castlebay. Some of the cottars from Barra were descended from the former inhabitants, and had continued to bury their dead in the graveyard at the south end of Vatersay.[8]

In 1883, forty-five Barra cottars, living in wretched conditions and eking out a meagre existence by fishing, applied for holdings on Vatersay, but were turned down by the landowner, Lady Gordon Cathcart. Her reasons were that, based on her experience of Mingulay, there was no guarantee that tenants in Vatersay would pay rent; there would be huge expense in settling crofters there, the water supply was inadequate, and she had recently improved Castlebay pier for fishermen.[9] The tenant farmer of Vatersay, Donald MacDonald, however, allowed the cottars to use some land at Caolas for growing potatoes. Further appeals to Lady Gordon Cathcart failed, including one from Barra Parish Council, and the men grew desperate. Then, in September 1900, emboldened by the success of cottars raiding (illegally squatting on) the farms at Northbay and Eoligarry in Barra (later bought by the Congested Districts Board for crofting), the men raided Vatersay, though they subsequently withdrew. In 1903 the Board bought land on Vatersay – the eastern end of the Uidh peninsula – for potato growing, but the cottars claimed this was unsuitable, and requested the Board to buy more land.[10]

The cottars again appealed for holdings in 1905 when the tenant farmer's lease of Vatersay expired, but they were again ignored and the farmer's lease was renewed.[11] In February 1906 forty-three cottars from Barra stepped up their campaign and raided Vatersay, marking out symbolic crofts. The following July three Mingulay men joined thirty-seven Barra men in the most determined raid yet, in which some of the Barra men started to rebuild a ruined part of the farm steading as temporary dwellings, and others selected sites for wooden huts, in the area which became Vatersay Village. The Mingulay men were John Sinclair (Iagan Iain Dhunnchaidh), Hugh MacLean (Eòghann Chaluim Iain) and Donald MacPhee (Dòmhnall Iain Dhòmhnaill), part of the crew of the *Snowbird* owned by MacPhee.[12] Michael Campbell (Teac) from Mingulay decided to be a bit different and in early August started building a 30-foot (9-metre) wooden hut at Ledaig, on the east side of Castlebay. He had relatives there, which probably explains why he chose to build there instead of Vatersay. Perhaps he was unsure about joining in with the Barra men; he may have felt different being from Mingulay. The Mingulay people were regarded in Barra as being self-contained and a little reserved.

Campbell stopped building when requested to do so by local crofters, and in November he and his nephew, Duncan Sinclair (Dunnchadh Anndra Dhunnchaidh), also from Mingulay, started building his hut on Vatersay, near those of the raiders from Barra. In January 1907 they took up residence in the hut, becoming the pioneers among the Mingulay people in seeking better lives. They were joined by Catherine Sinclair (Catrìona Nèill Eachainn), Campbell's widowed sister and Duncan's mother, closely followed by the brothers Hector, Michael and Neil MacPhee (mic Dhòmhnaill Dhòmhnaill), Donald MacNeil, Hugh MacLean and John Sinclair.[13] At first they all crowded into Michael Campbell's hut, but later they built others; they brought their cattle over and proceeded to cultivate ground for potatoes.[14] Despite appeals and warnings from the estate factor and the farmer, Donald MacDonald,

the raiders refused to leave; they knew they were breaking
the law but were desperate. In April 1907, therefore, Lady
Gordon Cathcart brought an interdict (injunction) against ten
raiders, ordering them to leave; four were from Mingulay –
Michael Campbell, the cousins Duncan and John Sinclair, and
Hector MacPhee – and six from Barra – Donald MacIntyre,
John Campbell, William Boyd, Roderick MacNeil, John
MacDougall – including their overall leader, Duncan
Campbell.[15] Neil MacPhee of Mingulay (mac Dhòmhnaill)
should have been on the list but the court official who jour-
neyed to Vatersay to serve the papers personally couldn't find
him, so the case against him was dropped.[16] They ignored the
interdict, and the stream of settlers continued. Although the
first raiders from Mingulay were all cottars, they were soon
joined by crofters; as we have seen, the land issue was only
one of many causes of the evacuation. The Barra settlers, on
the other hand, were all cottars.

The government was alarmed, and in May 1907 sent a
judge, Sheriff John Wilson, to investigate and persuade the
men to leave. He was unsuccessful, but his report was sympathetic to the raiders.[17] He described them as 'respectable
men, and except in their views as to their right to get land
and to take it if need be, they appeared to me to be both
intelligent and reasonable. They were not only courteous, but
kindly.' He found that there was a 'considerable body of local
opinion to the effect that Lady Gordon Cathcart had not fully
appreciated her duty as landowner, and that long indifference
to the necessities of the cottars had gone far to drive them to
exasperation'. He quoted Neil MacPhee (mac Dhòmhnaill) as
saying that he had 'grown sick of waiting and would prefer
imprisonment rather than go back to Mingulay to starve or be
driven to the US'. Having been convinced by the seriousness
of the raiders' case, Wilson recommended that the government buy all or part of Vatersay for crofting use. It was most
unusual for a judge to support law-breakers in this way, and
this must have been a great boost to the raiders.

Vatersay was not the only destination of raiders: in November 1907 six Mingulay men sailed to Sandray to select sites for houses, and by January they had built two houses of stone and thatch at Sheader. Sandray was then part of the grazing of Vatersay farm and was uninhabited, the last shepherd having died in 1904. The raiders brought their cattle and cultivated ground; they carried on lobster fishing, which was easier there than from Mingulay, as there was a sheltered beach for landing on, they got better bait there, and Castlebay was much nearer.[18] In October 1908 five of the six raiders wrote to the Board applying for holdings on Sandray:

> We are satisfied that it is a most suitable place for us as lobster fishing to make a fairly decent living and we will be very thankful if we are given holdings here instead of the impossible place of Mingulay where hitherto we have been trying to make a living among such dangerous surroundings.[19]

The Sandray raiders were John Gillies (Iain Nèill Eòghainn), John MacNeil (Iain Sheumais Iain), and Donald MacNeil (Dòmhnall Iain Mhìcheil), John MacKinnon the joiner and his brother Alexander (of whom it was earlier said 'There is no woman in the house, they act as if they were steamboat stewards'), and Michael MacNeil (an Rìgh) and his aunt Flora MacNeil. The first three of these had children, and there were twenty-seven people altogether in November 1908, each family in a separate house.[20] The ruins of the houses, joined together in an irregular 'terrace' facing the beach can be seen at Sheader. They were built in traditional style using stones from the houses of the people who lived there before the clearance of 1835. They had fireplaces and chimneys but no windows in the walls. One of the houses was excavated by Sheffield University archaeologists in 1995.

Meanwhile, the Vatersay raiders were conducting a lively correspondence with various politicians who were concerned in the case or whose support might be enlisted. The letters were written by Neil MacPhee (Niall Chaluim Dhòmhnaill, cousin of the above Neil MacPhee) of Mingulay, whose eloquence, command of English, and grasp of the wider political dimensions of the affair were quite remarkable for someone whose opportunities in life had been so limited.

The Vatersay affair, highlighting as it did a widespread problem throughout the crofting areas of Scotland, was debated in both Houses of Parliament. It illustrated a major failing of the Crofters Act, the passing of which more than twenty years before had been intended to solve the land question once and for all: it had made no provision for the creation of new crofts. The affair was a challenge for the Liberal government, elected in 1906 and pro-land reform (and even pro-raider, as an unwise comment from the Lord Advocate expressing sympathy for the raiders revealed). The government and police were criticised for failing to take action against the raiders, as previous governments had done in similar cases, thereby encouraging raiding elsewhere.[21] 'The Scotch Office and the Government', commented the *Glasgow Herald,* 'have been landed by Vatersay in a bog.'[22] The Congested Districts Board had repeatedly declined Lady Gordon Cathcart's offers to sell Vatersay, on the grounds that such a purchase would be against government policy and that the issue of compensation to the tenant farmer was not their concern.

In the absence of an agreement, Lady Gordon Cathcart pressed on with her legal action against the raiders. Having given the raiders plenty of time to leave, in January 1908 she served a complaint for breach of interdict against them, and an order to serve answers; their answers made it clear that they would not leave Vatersay. The raiders, therefore, were summonsed to appear in person before the Court of Session in Edinburgh on 2 June 1908.[23]

There were elements of farce to the raiders' journey to Edinburgh by steamer and train. To begin with, they had to ask their adversary, Lady Cathcart, for their fares. They were inexperienced rail travellers; it is unlikely that any of them had been on a train before. A reception party of 300 had gathered to meet the train at Edinburgh – testament to the publicity surrounding the case and the level of public sympathy for the raiders – but when the train arrived, there were no raiders. The *Edinburgh Evening News* of 2 June reported:

> The men had got into the wrong portion of the train at Larbert and had been carried to the Waverley Station. Mr Donald Shaw, their law agent, and several members of the committee formed to look after the interests of the Barra men immediately repaired to the Waverley Station to welcome the squatters. Few persons were in the station, but a cheer was raised as the blueclad fishermen made for their quarters in High Street.

At the trial the next day,

> the proceedings excited a considerable amount of public interest. The courtroom was packed to overflowing . . . Counsel for Lady Cathcart stated that the men had breached the interdict served on them by the court, had continued to occupy the land, and intended to continue to do so. The only previous case where a respondent for breach of interdict had taken up that position was in 1887, and this led to his imprisonment.
>
> Counsel for the men, Arthur Dewar, stated that they admitted that they had gone to Vatersay without the authority of the complainer, and that they had failed to obey the order of the court . . . they had been driven by the system and circumstances they were powerless to control into disobedience. The disobedience was not due to disrespect, but entirely to their environment.

The court regarded the background as irrelevant, and sentenced the men to two months in prison. Before beginning their sentences, they posed for press photographers outside the court. They sit or stand, impassive but dignified, in the suits hired for them for the photoshoot, not betraying the incongruity of their circumstances.[24]

The case aroused enormous public interest and sympathy; people were intrigued by such goings-on in a remote and little known area, and because the trial took place in the capital, it was widely reported in the press. Petitions for the men's release were sent from all over Scotland, including Barra (written by Neil MacPhee),[25] and a relief fund for the raiders' families was launched by the *Edinburgh Evening News*. Memories were revived of previous (mostly pre-Crofters' Act) land raids in the Hebrides, when there were pitched battles between raiders and police sent to clear them off land they had occupied. The *Glasgow Herald* clarified the situation:

> An impression has got abroad that the Barra raider is a fiercely rebellious fellow. As a matter of fact, he is rather phlegmatic. He is surely the mildest mannered person who ever set a country's laws at defiance . . . the raiders of Barra have not in them the stuff of the true rebel . . . The talk of gunboats in these waters or a force of Glasgow policemen on the islands to protect the interests of landlordism may be dismissed as the idlest of rhetoric . . . And yet one wonders why anybody should choose to live on Vatersay or Sandray, still less on Mingulay. The raiders in Edinburgh doubtless find the barriers of the Calton jail irksome enough, yet they choose to return to islands often veritably imprisoned by the sea.[26]

The publicity surrounding the case and the desire of both the Congested Districts Board and Lady Gordon Cathcart not to lose face must have given negotiations a renewed urgency, for on 18 July the Board announced that agreement had been reached on creating crofts in Vatersay, and the men were immediately released, two weeks early.[27]

The *Oban Times* said of their return to Barra:

> At Castlebay they were met by large crowds of the inhabitants . . . flags and bunting and stirring pipe music gave the occasion a gala aspect. The general feeling is one of relief and thankfulness that the hope that the government and Lady Gordon Cathcart would come to terms has not been disappointed.[28]

By August 1908 there were thirty-four families in Vatersay, of which fourteen were from Mingulay.[29] Six families, totalling about twenty-six people, remained in Mingulay, and all were planning to leave.[30] John MacLean (Barnaidh) had already been to Vatersay and started building a hut but had stopped when asked to. John Sinclair, one of the original raiders, had also been asked to stop building a hut; he had been staying with other raiders, and his family remained in Mingulay. John MacLean wrote a letter of application for a croft in Vatersay at this time, in which he said: 'I am in possession of a holding in Mingulay but as the people have deserted this island I cannot remain there.'[31] The others were adults living with parents, brothers or sisters. A seventh family was that of the teacher, Sarah MacShane; they must have been very uncertain of their future. By November there were thirty-seven families in Vatersay, eighteen of which were from Mingulay, and the five in Sandray.[32]

Vatersay was finally purchased by the Congested Districts Board in March 1909 for the sum of £6,250 and fifty-eight crofts were created. However, the jubilation over the apparent success of the raiders' campaign turned sour over the acrimonious process of allocating the crofts. The Board invited applications for the crofts, for which a ballot was held;

eighty-two applications were received. The Board said that no account would be taken of whether or not applicants were already resident; and priority was given to applicants who had assets in terms of livestock or fishing boats and gear and could demonstrate an ability to manage, and pay rent for, a croft. By definition, some of the original raiders could not meet these desirables, and there was uproar when the names of the successful applicants were announced, excluding some of them, but including some applicants from Barra with no assets, crofting experience or families to support, who had not even settled on Vatersay. Many of the unsuccessful applicants, some of whom had been living there for over two years, refused to leave, so the Board began legal proceedings to evict them.[33]

Neil MacPhee fired off a letter to Lord Pentland, Secretary for Scotland and Chairman of the Congested Districts Board, on behalf of rejected applicants:

> We have been in possession for over two years and we are the lawful heirs of those evicted from this island sixty years ago ... while others from the mainland of Barra are accepted to dispossess us. We know it, My Lord, it is the Board's dastardly attempt to compel us to go back to the barren island of Mingulay. It shall never never be, My Lord, it is better a thousand times to die here than to go through the same hardships which were our lot on that island.[34]

MacPhee also expressed the suspicion – probably correct, as the documents demonstrate – that the Board deliberately excluded some of the raiders because they were regarded as troublemakers. The ballot also revealed divisions among the settlers: there was resentment among cottars from Barra who were unsuccessful against crofters from Mingulay, some of whom were comparatively well off, who were successful. The

MacPhees (that is, Neil mac Chaluim, the raiders' PR man, and his cousin Hector, who was imprisoned, and Hector's brother Neil) were an example of the latter; a Board official wrote that Neil MacPhee (mac Chaluim) had fenced off a large part of Mingulay, where he had a lot of livestock, and his cousins had earned £500 in the last fishing season, and 'they should be sent back to Mingulay. They have no sympathy among the general body of settlers.' The official described the MacPhees and Duncan Campbell, as the 'ringleaders' in stirring up dissent. Neil MacPhee (mac Chaluim) in particular made himself unpopular with the Board and some of the settlers when he claimed that details of the croft agreements tenants were given to sign were contrary to the Crofters' Act, and tried to dissuade tenants from signing them.[35]

There was further resentment when another ballot was held to allocate crofts within the four crofting townships of Vatersay, Caolas, Uidh, and Eorisdail. Some settlers who had established themselves in one place were allotted crofts elsewhere.

It would have been ironic and grossly unjust if those who had led the battle for land, and had gone to prison for it, were now, at the last minute, about to be deprived of it. However, as some crofts were not taken up by the people to whom they had been allotted, nearly everyone who wanted a croft got one in the end. About a third of the crofts were taken by Mingulay people, including three of the Sandray raiders: John Gillies, Donald MacNeil and John MacNeil. These three were still in Sandray in March 1909 when the Congested Districts Board ordered them to leave; the island was not considered suitable for settlement, and was to be used as grazing by the southern townships of Vatersay. Despite the order, John Gillies remained there as he had initially failed to get a croft on Vatersay, but he was eventually given one at Caolas, and moved there in early 1911.[36]

Even after the 'official' settling of Vatersay a handful of people hung on in Mingulay where, in December 1909, there was a 'state of anarchy reigning on the island . . . the King's writ has no application' according to the estate factor, John MacDonald, in a letter to Sarah MacShane, the teacher. She had written to him informing him that certain people were keeping far more livestock than they were entitled to. As a result of her letter, MacDonald wrote to Donald MacKinnon, the constable (landlord's representative):

> Matters on Mingulay have now reached a climax, and unless the tenants there are prepared to pay up out they must go. For many years, I have had occasion to suspect that you and one or two others have taken more than your fair share of the island . . . keeping more stock than you are entitled to . . . you have realised a considerable sum of money from the sale of surplus stock. Unless I receive a substantial sum, and certainly nothing under £10, before the 31st of this month, I shall take such action against you as will compel you to hand over your stock and clear out of your holding. You have occupied the position of servant of Lady Cathcart for many years and your past actions have been most irregular and you must accept this warning as final.

MacDonald, in his letter to MacShane speculated that people from Mingulay, whose applications for crofts on Vatersay had failed, might return to Mingulay. Photographs taken in August 1909 (plates 25 and 26) show the village in decay, with weeds growing on the roofs of abandoned houses. Fishing continued; twelve fishermen and boys were recorded in 1909, 1910 and 1911.[37] A few families with children, such as John MacLean's, may have stayed because of the school; there was no school in Vatersay until June 1910, two months after the closure of its predecessor in Mingulay. But eleven people were still there in April 1911 when the Congested Districts Board heard of a rumour that Lady Cathcart has let, as from Whitsunday, the Islands of Pabbay, Berneray, and Mingulay to one grazing tenant, and that notice has been served on the people resident on these islands that they are to leave, and that their stock if not cleared off will be seized.[38]

The tenant referred to was Jonathan MacLean (Eoin Mòr), a Castlebay hotel-keeper and merchant. He was married to Mary MacNeil, daughter of Neil MacNeil, Castlebay fish-curer and merchant, who was originally from Berneray. MacLean was known by the Board to be interested in the islands for grazing as early as 1908.[39] He had gained a foot-hold on the islands in 1910, when he took over a croft on Berneray; by the following year he was the tenant of most of the crofts on all three islands, and by 1915 he was sole occupier. Four years later he completed his empire when he became owner of the three islands.[40]

The Board detailed the inhabitants of Mingulay at this time (April 1911):[41] eleven adults, in six families. Four families were the same as in August 1908; in addition there were the MacKinnon brothers, and Michael MacNeil, all of whom were last heard of in Sandray. Seven people, in two families, remained in Pabbay, but none in Berneray. All the islanders were said to be 'anxious to leave' (as they had been three years before!). The Board seems to have taken the rumours seriously, for, keen to avoid those islanders who had nowhere else to go being forced to squat illegally on Vatersay, it found them holdings there. However, the rumoured evictions did not take place, as some people remained. In August (1911) Neil MacPhee (mac Chaluim) wrote to the estate asking for a holding on Mingulay, having been refused one on Berneray.[42] He said he did not intend to live on the holding, but wanted it for grazing purposes; he had tried to get another holding on Vatersay for grazing.[43] The estate must have been keeping all the land in reserve for Jonathan MacLean, a policy the Congested Districts Board would have approved of.

By August 1911 only four of the above eight families remained. The Board's 'policy of fetching the Mingulay islanders nearer civilisation' was not completed until the following summer, 1912, when Michael MacNeil (an Rìgh) was finally accommodated in Vatersay.[44] One of the ten fishermen based in Mingulay during the summer of 1912[45] may have been John MacLean who moved to Vatersay in 1910,[46] but who was said by Robert Adam to have left in 1912.[47] 1912 was, therefore, the year that Mingulay was finally deserted by its native human population.

It was ironic in the end that after most of the inhabitants had left of their own accord, the remainder were threatened with eviction in favour of sheep. But this was merely the 'last straw'; the people wanted to go, the Congested Districts Board wanted them to go, and Lady Gordon Cathcart would not have further risked her reputation by being involved in evicting tenants (could this have been done legally anyway?) without knowing there was somewhere for them to go.

There are few details of the physical processes of the desertion, as it happened over a number of years. Large items of furniture that could not be transported, such as looms (which were made largely redundant anyway, because imported woollen cloth was now available) were left behind,[48] and many things that would have been of no use to their owners in their new lives were probably abandoned. Getting full-grown cattle and ponies into boats must have been quite a problem: perhaps the derrick really was useful here, if the animals could have reached the platform.

What was it like leaving Mingulay? A relief in many ways, no doubt, although the first few years, before people got their crofts and could build proper houses, must have been hard. Although most of the islanders settled in Vatersay, the move spelled the end of the community as an entity, as they were scattered between different townships. There was no longer a need for many of their traditional communal activities, such as waulking cloth, cutting peat, hauling in boats, and holding church services on their own; ceilidhing practically ceased. There was certainly no Home Rule here. Because of their former isolation, the Mingulay people didn't find it easy to fit in with the Barra settlers, and kept themselves to themselves. At least one family opted for Glasgow in preference to Vatersay. Mary Campbell always preferred Mingulay to Vatersay: it was wild in the winter, but people were friendlier and more content; they changed a lot when they moved to Vatersay.[49]

This leads on to another question: how unanimous had the cry for evacuation been? Not everyone wanted to go; John MacLean (Barnaidh), for instance, was doing well with his fishing, but he would have known that he could stay only if several other fishermen did too. A certain minimum number of people would have been needed to make life possible in Mingulay, if only to launch and land boats. MacLean may also have been concerned about his children's education, for he left Mingulay at the time the school closed. Mary Campbell (Màiri Dhòmhnaill Eachainn), who, with her sister Elizabeth, was one of the last to go, is also said to have been reluctant to do so. There were probably a good many people who didn't actually want to go, but knew they had to.

Another consideration is the role of the Castlebay priest, Donald Martin. Despite the recent building of the chapel in Mingulay, he is thought to have encouraged the people to leave (he was said to be 'not dissuading' the raiders from Barra in 1907),[50] perhaps for their own good, or, it has been suggested, because he didn't like going there and didn't get much in the collecting box. He is also known to have been friendly with Jonathan MacLean, the new tenant, though whether there is any significance in this is impossible to say.

The process of evacuation had lasted five years, starting with the islanders joining illegal land-grabbing, and ending with the government (eventually) giving them all they wanted and actively settling the last 'stragglers' in Vatersay. It happened this way only because the sheer numbers of people from Barra and Mingulay raiding Vatersay in search of better conditions forced the landowner and the government to act. Land reform was on the political agenda anyway, with the election in 1906 of a Liberal government under Sir Hugh Campbell-Bannerman of Glasgow, after twenty years of Conservative government;[51] and the public outcry at the sentences had ensured high-level attention. Just as the Vatersay raiders had been spurred on by the success of previous land raiding in Barra, so people in other crofting areas were encouraged by the Vatersay raiders. The case illustrates the change of attitude to the problems of the islands; not many decades before, emigration was seen as the solution, but now it was recognised that these issues should be faced and solved at home.

The Scottish Office and the Congested Districts Board seem to have encouraged the evacuation of the small islands in the end, because they were keen to avoid the risk of anyone remaining there squatting on Vatersay at a later date. Having made a commitment to the majority by giving them Vatersay, they may have felt a responsibility for the remainder. Having a few people scattered about in remote islands who might have needed services such as health and education would have been inconvenient and expensive. The state was taking an increasing role in island life, but there were limits to the size of communities on small islands it was considered economic to support. Hence the decision not to settle any crofters on Sandray, largely because providing a school would have been expensive. Such considerations were also behind the willingness to fund the evacuation of St Kilda in 1930, for example. The eventual desertion of Mingulay was inevitable because of its remoteness and the lack of a landing place; its exposure to the Atlantic and the nature of its coast meant that it would never have been possible to create an adequate landing place. The First World War would have been disastrous to Mingulay, as the fishing industry collapsed almost completely, most of the men being away in the merchant navy if not in the services.

Depopulation has been a feature of Scotland's islands for two centuries. In the Barra Isles, 27 per cent of the population lived on seven of the smaller islands in 1764. By 1841 the percentage was nineteen (on eight islands), in 1901, eight (on six islands). In Scotland as a whole, over a hundred of the islands described by Monro in 1549, or inhabited since, have since been deserted. Over half of these had fewer than twenty people at the time of their desertion, showing that small numbers were the least viable, and only nine, including Mingulay, had over a hundred.[52] Some of the smaller islands were settled only temporarily by people evicted from elsewhere; and some, like Mingulay, had their populations swelled by such people. Apart from those communities which were evicted, the reasons for their desertion were in most cases similar: the values and living standards of the outside world were rapidly catching up on the islands, and were becoming known to the people through education and travel to the mainland for work. Life on small islands had become an unacceptable struggle.

It is ironic that Vatersay, a Promised Land for the raiders, was itself in danger of being deserted by the 1980s, because of the lack of facilities on the island and the inadequate ferry service to Barra. The community was saved by the opening of a causeway from Barra in 1991. Since then, all the remaining inhabited small islands in the Outer Hebrides have been connected by bridges or causeways to their larger neighbours, Eriskay being the last in 2001.

What if . . . the population had not been swelled by evictees from other islands in the nineteenth century? Adequate landing facilities had been provided? There had not been an empty island to raid? The raiders had not been allowed to stay? . . . One can speculate endlessly along these lines. Possibly a dwindling number would have struggled on, but the basic fact remains: Mingulay had become an 'impossible place', as the Sandray raiders described it, in the changing social and economic climate around the turn of the century.

14

The Deserted Island

The departure of the last inhabitants from Mingulay in the summer of 1912 gave Jonathan MacLean, the new tenant, a free hand to turn it into a grazing island. To guard against anyone returning, he dismantled the derrick, using some of its wooden parts as corner posts for fencing (so *he* must have thought it had been useful, even if the islanders didn't, though not useful enough for him to keep). He is reputed to have cut up the rafters of the houses as fence posts, and burnt the thatch. The houses would have been in a sorry state by then. In April 1911, five houses were still occupied and another seven were said to have been 'uninhabited'.[1] If this meant empty though habitable, all the rest were presumably deteriorating; thatched roofs have to be maintained regularly. Certainly, by 1922, when Robert Adam returned to take photographs, only walls remained.

MacLean stocked Mingulay, Pabbay and Berneray with sheep, and the first two with calves as well. He and his successor, John Russell, built small sheep pens, for a milking ewe and lamb, wherever stone – usually the remains of earlier structures – was available. He made the school buildings the centre of his activities, accommodating his shepherds who were to live on the island during the spring and summer in the schoolhouse, and using the schoolroom as a store. He built a sheep dip next to the schoolhouse and made use of the school enclosure when rounding up the sheep. The school buildings were much more convenient than the Chapel House, being near the landing place and having a view of the route followed by the approaching boat from Castlebay. Because of the problems of landing and launching boats, the shepherds did not keep a boat at Mingulay; the successive owners of the island kept their boat at Castlebay. Their main lifeline, however, was the lighthouse boat which came down weekly in summer, fortnightly in winter, calling in with supplies and mail.

MacLean was advertising trips by motorboat to see the birds on the cliffs of Mingulay and Berneray as early as 1912. Robert Adam noted that visitors to Mingulay, including himself in 1922, were put up in the Chapel House.[2]

MacLean rented the islands until 1919, when he bought them (and the small tidal island of Orosay on the east side of Catlebay, Barra) from Lady Gordon Cathcart for £1,000.[3] This was the first time this trio of islands came under separate ownership from the other islands. In 1929 he sold them (but not Orosay) to John Harold Russell, for £2,000, and 800 ewes already on them also for £2,000, an interesting indication of the relative values of land and stock at that time.[4] Russell, originally from East Sussex, had sailed to America at the age of sixteen in 1894, found work on a sheep ranch, and later set up his own ranch on the border of Montana and Canada. He became a US citizen. After the First World War he lived in Australia and New Zealand. In 1929, on a visit to South Uist he heard that the three islands were on the market and bought them. Russell lived on Mingulay all year round, in the schoolhouse, alone except in the spring and summer when he was joined by his two shepherds. The folklorist Margaret Fay Shaw, then living in South Uist, described a visit she made to Russell in the early 1930s:

> The coal stove had an oven, which was sometimes
> hot enough for baking. A whisky bottle was the

rolling pin for my oatcakes and there was plenty
of milk from the two nanny goats. The eggs were
from the cliffs – from gulls, guillemots and razorbills
– good for custards and omelettes but never to be
boiled, when the taste would be of foul fish. Spam
was made interesting in many ways and then we had
rabbits which were caught by a pair of ferrets, the
treasured friends of Mr. Russell who could pet and
handle their wild jumping play as though they were
harmless pussies. I was with the shepherds in not
daring to touch them. [Russell also kept 'harmless
pussies' – five of them.]

The goats were probably housed in one of the house ruins to
the west, adapted for them.

Russell put the islands on the market in 1935, and in 1936
sold them to Miss Bowen-Colthurst, later Mrs Greer, an Essex
farmer, for £2,500. She paid only occasional visits to the
islands, leaving them in the care of shepherds from Barra. She
fenced off large parts of the cliffy coastline to prevent sheep
clambering along the cliff ledges in search of grass, getting
stuck, and falling off. In 1948 she imported a small motor
plough to plough the potato field, previously used by Russell,
next to the road alongside the village. Potatoes were stored
in the Chapel House. This building had remained church
property until 1936[6] but the church furnishings were removed earlier in the 1930s, during the time of Father Donald
Campbell of Castlebay. The altar, made by John MacKinnon,
was taken to the church in Castlebay, where it became the
side altar; the altar rail and other fittings were taken to the
church in Vatersay, where they remained in use until the
1980s. In about 1946 the schoolroom was gutted by fire,
and has remained a roofless ruin. Mrs Greer tried to sell the
three islands in 1951, but couldn't find a buyer she considered
suitable for several years; in the meantime she let them to
two graziers from Harris.[7] In 1955 the islands were bought

for £7,000 by the Barra Head Isles Sheepstock Company, a syndicate of Barra crofters. With motorboats being by then in common use, making the islands more accessible, it was no longer necessary for shepherds to live there for long periods; shearing, dipping, taking off lambs could usually be done in a day. However, the schoolhouse continued to be used for overnight stays and as a store, and in 1986 it was reroofed in corrugated iron; at the same time the roof line was changed at its western end, from hip-ended to gable-ended.[8] From 1996 to 2011 the artist, Julie Brook, spent long periods living in the house and using it as a studio while painting the cliffs on the west side, focussing mainly on Biulacraig, on paper and large canvases. She also constructed sculptural works in the landscape such as Stone Bowl near the school and Pierced Wall on the west coast.

The Chapel House remained unused. In 1960 a visiting architect reported it to be in excellent condition,[5] but only five years later it was described as semi-ruinous.[9] By this time groups of campers had begun to stay on the island, and it was also used for a survival course by the British army, during which the schoolhouse was broken into. (Dun Mingulay was also used by the US navy for a training exercise at some point, during which metal supports for a high wire, one on each side of the neck of the peninsula, were put up.) Campers continued to rob the woodwork of the house for firewood, and a hole in the roof may have been made deliberately.

In 1975 Colin Archer, a teacher of English working over-seas, bought the building as a holiday home following a visit to Mingulay. He had doors and windows put in, and had the roof repaired temporarily, pending more permanent work. Archer tried, unsuccessfully, to interest organisations who might make use of the building, for example as a hostel for small groups. Attempts to get the essential work on the roof done failed, and it continued to deteriorate. The front wall began to bulge outwards, and in November 1996 the building collapsed in a storm. The front wall and the roof fell forwards, the back of the roof ending up on the chapel floor, which withstood the impact. The ground floor rooms remained intact for many years, and one could enter and wander from room to room as if nothing had happened. It is a sad story; the building, made to last for ever, served as a church for hardly more than ten years, after which it stood empty and useless for more than sixty years. The work done on it subsequently gave it only a temporary reprieve from eventual dereliction.

Mingulay remained in the hearts of the islanders after they left, despite the hardships they had suffered there, and the strong words some, such as Neil MacPhee, had had for it. MacPhee was able to look back with longing and romance many years later, as his song (Appendix 2) shows. There used to be annual pilgrimages to Mingulay from Vatersay, but these had become irregular by the 1970s. In 1975 some descendants of islanders held a final service in the chapel before it was sold. There was another gathering to mark the centenary of the opening of the chapel. On 19 June 1998 Father Donald MacKay, the Castlebay priest, celebrated mass outside the ruin.

After the desertion, Mingulay and its neighbours continued to attract ornithologists and botanists. The importance of the natural heritage of Mingulay and Berneray was recognised by their being created a Site of Special Scientific Interest in 1983, and a Special Protection Area, as regards the seabirds, in 1994. The cultural heritage has also been recognised: the main settlement areas of Mingulay and Pabbay have been scheduled under the Ancient Monuments Act, the former in 1997.

The growth of leisure and the interest of individuals and groups in such areas for recreation or study meant an increasing number of people visiting Mingulay in the later decades of the twentieth century. Unfortunately not all the visitors treated the island with respect, and the village suffered from people knocking stones off walls, even heaving massive lintels off doorways; crosses in the graveyard were broken, as were quern stones. Attempts were made to remove ancient objects such as quern stones. Sheep clambering on walls eating grass, and burrowing rabbits (originally introduced as a source of food by the shepherds after the desertion), contributed to the deterioration of the village.

The turn of the millennium saw a new dawn for Mingulay and its two neighbours. In 1998 the three islands were put on the market for the first time since 1955. Falling prices of sheep made sheep farming on the islands uneconomic. The sheep on Mingulay were removed to be sold, and the islands were put up for sale in November 1998 with an asking price of £1m. Within a few months the National Trust for Scotland made an offer of £400,000, based on land valuations, but it was not accepted. A community buy-out was considered, but in May 2000 the islands were sold to the National Trust for Scotland for £450,000. Most of the funding came from a bequest from Jean Fawcitt of Harrogate, which stipulated that it should be used to secure remote and uninhabited areas. There were additional contributions from an anonymous member of the Trust, from Scottish Natural Heritage, and from the Chris Brasher Trust.

Trevor Croft, Director of the Trust, said of the purchase of the islands: 'They really are exceptional in terms of their heritage and value to the people of Scotland. The Trust has the ability to ensure their careful management to protect their unique characteristics. We will be working closely with the people of Barra and Vatersay, whose connections with the islands go back generations.'[10]

The Trust seeks to conserve the natural and cultural heritage of the three islands while enabling responsible public access. The purchase by the Trust coincided with the 'discovery' of Mingulay and Pabbay by rock climbers. In the early years of the Trust's ownership, there were concerns among the people of Barra and Vatersay about large groups of climbers camping near the settlement ruins on Mingulay and Pabbay; stones had been removed from ruins to use as fire surrounds and weights for tent pegs, and litter was left. Leaflets (in Gaelic and English) giving visitors information on the islands and guidance on, for example, responsible camping were produced and there have been few problems since.

Since 2005 the islands have been managed by the Western Isles Area Manager. A part-time ranger, a resident of Barra, was appointed in 2010. He spends 3–4 days a week on Mingulay during the summer months when climbers and other campers are there, also day visitors from Barra. There are between 700 and 1,000 visitors annually. The ranger also organises work parties of volunteers from Barra and Vatersay.

The Trust initiated research into the cultural and natural heritage of the islands. It carried out archaeological surveys in partnership with the Royal Commission on the Ancient and Historical Monuments of Scotland (RCAHMS), and gathered historical information from local people. It has carried out surveys and monitoring of the seabirds, mammals, and vegetation. A seasonal seabird ranger has been employed since 2013. Vegetation changes are being monitored. There have been changes in the relative abundance of some species as a result of the removal of the sheep. Nearly all of them were taken off in 1998, but a few stragglers which escaped the round-up remained until 2007. The vegetation is becoming quite dense and rank in places, although rabbits are keeping the grasses down on the formerly cultivated land around the village.

It has been suggested that Mingulay could be used to support a satellite flock of Soay sheep, the wild sheep of St Kilda. Under current regulations, the flock on St Kilda is considered wild, but if any were to be moved elsewhere they would be considered domestic and thus subject to the same regulations, including needing to be managed, as domestic sheep. It was for these reasons that the Trust removed the remaining black-face sheep on the islands.[11]

The Trust has researched the two principal buildings on Mingulay, the schoolroom/schoolhouse and the Chapel House. Research into the history of the schoolroom, built in 1881, and the schoolhouse, built onto it in 1894, was in advance of the restoration of the latter in 2012–13. The corrugated iron roofing of 1986 was repaired and painted, and the windows and front door were replaced in the style of the originals. Interior woodwork needed replacing. The schoolroom ruin was consolidated.[12] The schoolhouse is used as a base for the ranger, work parties and researchers. In 2013 a small wind turbine and two solar panels were installed to provide power for recharging batteries and laptops, enabling internet access via satellite for half an hour a day. A revolution for Mingulay!

The ruin of the Chapel House was acquired from the owner, Colin Archer, in 2004. With only three standing walls it was a safety hazard and it was fenced off. In January 2005 the upper part of the south gable fell in a storm; the Trust took down the upper part of the north gable in 2014 and the remaining walls were consolidated. As part of this work, research into the building and its history was undertaken, for the first time; ironically, this had never happened when the building was intact.

Measures have been taken to reduce the rate of decay of the remains of the buildings of the last inhabitants. The rabbits are being controlled; they cause havoc with the ruins of the houses as they burrow into the sand under the walls and between the internal and external stone faces of the walls. Streams that threaten to undermine walls have been kept away from them and original drainage ditches dug out. The spread of bracken in the village is being controlled. Volunteers have assisted with all the above varied tasks, and have also removed old wire fencing dating from the grazing era.

Mingulay and its neighbours have not so far been found to have strategic value in the defence of the nation, and have been spared the fate of St Kilda, where the British army built a base as part of the missile-testing station on South Uist in 1957. Sandray has been threatened with a different kind of development: as a nuclear waste dump.[13] It is to be hoped that the conservation designations and their ownership by a conservation organisation, will protect the islands from such uses.

15

Berneray

Berneray is the most southerly of the Outer Hebrides, and is also known as Barra Head, the name of its southernmost point (see maps 1 and 4). It is the smallest of the three islands, being 3 kilometres (1¾ miles) long, and 1.3 kilometres (¾ mile) across. It resembles a tilted wedge in form, the land rising from the east and north coasts to a central ridge, Mullach a' Lusgan, the southern and western flanks of which plunge down to the sea, in cliffs up to 190 metres (625 feet) high. The cliffs reach to within three metres of the summit of the island at Sotan, and the lighthouse perches on the cliff edge near this point. The power of the sea and wind during times of storm is so great here that the lighthouse compound is deluged with salt spray, and small fish have even found their way up. As on Mingulay the cliffs are the breeding ground of seabirds which were caught for food by the islanders. A visitor to Berneray in 1868, Captain Elwes, wrote:

> It was the grandest sight I ever experienced, to look out of the window of the lighthouse on a very stormy day, and see oneself hanging, as it were, over the ocean, surrounded on three sides by a fearful chasm in which the air was so thickly crowded with birds as to produce the appearance of a heavy snowstorm, whilst the cries of these myriads, mingled with the

roar of the ocean and the howling of the tremendous
gusts of wind coming up from below as if forced
through a blast pipe, made it almost impossible to
hear a person speak.

Apart from its cliffs, Berneray is less varied and interesting than
the other islands; there is no glen, bay, or beach, and the few
streams are very small. The only relatively flat area is around
the northeast coast, where settlement was concentrated.

Berneray was surveyed archaeologically for the first time
in 1992, by archaeologists from Sheffield University and from
Prague; about 90 sites and buildings of all periods were recorded.[1] The most recent fieldwork by the Royal Commission
on the Ancient and Historical Monuments of Scotland
(RCAHMS) was in 2010. There is a possible Neolithic chambered tomb on the north coast at Leac a'Langaich west of the
landing place,[2] and there are other stone settings that could be
early burial monuments.

The Iron Age is represented by the most prominent ancient
site – the dun, Dùn Sròn an Dùin, dramatically situated on the
cliff-bound promontory west of the lighthouse. It attracted
attention as early as 1695, when Martin Martin wrote: 'There
is an old Fort in this Island, having a Vacuity round the Walls,
divided in little Apartments.' It was also mentioned in 1768
and 1794, and was described by visitors and antiquarians in
the nineteenth century.[3]

The dun is a wall built approximately north–south across
the neck of the promontory, most of which is now occupied
by the quarry which supplied stone for the lighthouse. It is
now about 20.1 metres (66 feet) long, and curves slightly
towards the landward side (east). The wall is galleried, that
is, it originally consisted of an inner and an outer wall separated by the 'gallery', just over a metre wide, between; it
was originally two 'storeys' high, joined at first floor level
by massive transverse lintel stones forming the floor of the
upper gallery. It is thus built in the style of the brochs. Only

the outer wall survives, to a height of up to 2.45 metres (8 feet).

The wall has been used as the western wall of a compound associated with the lighthouse, and it is clear that it has been extensively modified, probably during and after the building of the lighthouse. Most of the wall is built of massive blocks, but there is an abrupt change to much smaller stones at its northern end, where there is an entrance passage, paved and lintelled. The entrance must have been rebuilt, because all the stone for the lighthouse buildings would have been hauled from the quarry by this route, and in its present form it is far too narrow for this to have been possible. However, it includes some original features such as a bar hole, so parts of the original may remain, or the builders were careful to rebuild it authentically, thus deluding later observers.

There has been much discussion and speculation about the original form of the monument. MacQueen's 1794 description of the dun as being 'more entire' than any of the duns in the Barra Isles, for which, he believed, it had served 'as a pharos or watch tower', suggests a circular structure, like the other duns in the islands. In September 1830, just before construction of the lighthouse began, the dun was described by fifteen-year-old David Stevenson, son of Robert, the lighthouse engineer. He wrote of 'Dune Bernera . . . the remains of one of the old Pictish Douns Burghs or Pictish castles . . . it is shaped like a segment of a circle, its walls, which where highest do not exceed 20 feet, contain hollow compartments like the Pictish buildings of Shetland.' In 1863 Isabella Bird wrote: 'This singular enigma . . . is about 30 feet high . . . under the circumstances, the act which demolished a part of it in order to give a full view of the light from the westward must be considered a necessity rather than vandalism, but it is disgusting to an antiquary.' The extent of the rebuilding of the northern end of the wall and the entrance is uncertain. Bird's sketch and her estimate of its height are probably exaggerated: Alexander Carmichael records the height of the wall at

the door as 14 feet (4.2 metres) in 1867. By the late nineteenth
century the wall was lower, and there has been deterioration
since 1915 when the RCAHMS recorded it. New walling
has also appeared since then, presumably built by lighthouse
keepers, on the cliff top west of the northern terminus.

It is highly unlikely that the surviving remains were ever
part of a larger structure: although the quarry west of it has
removed any evidence there might have been, the wall is not
sufficiently curved to indicate this, and at the southern end
it tapers in thickness and curves inward suggesting this was
its terminus. Large-scale cliff erosion can be discounted as
erosion rates of the gneiss are very slow. Sites of this type are
known elsewhere, such as Dùn Grugaig and Rudh an Dunain,
both in Skye, and at Clickhimin, Shetland, where there was a
curved galleried wall; the latter two may date to the sixth or
seventh centuries BC.

According to a local tradition, the dun was used as a refuge
by an outlawed laird of Barra.[4] It is hard to imagine that it
was ever occupied for long periods.

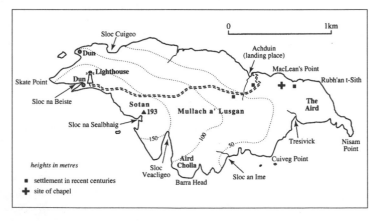

Map 4. Berneray

A romanticised view of the dun and Barra Head lighthouse, Berneray
(from Bird, 1866). The height of the dun is exaggerated.

North of the lighthouse, there is another cliff-bound promontory with a single wall, not galleried, stretching across its
neck. It is known as Dùn Briste, and is also assumed to be
Iron Age in date, but is unlikely to have been defensive. The
wall consists of two rows of stone slabs set on edge, the space
between having been filled with earth and stones; it cannot
have been very high. It was marked on a map of 1861–3 as an
'ancient burial ground'.[5]

Evidence of Norse presence is in the form of many of
the island's place names; the name Berneray itself (Gaelic
Beàrnaraigh) comes from the Old Norse Bjarnaray, 'Bjorn's
Isle'.

In medieval times there was a chapel, and the last reference
to it was in 1700. Its traditional site is in the graveyard in
the settlement, near MacLean's Point.[6] The graveyard enclosure is a complex multi-period site. The graveyard itself
is a low mound, now turf-covered, but under the turf there
are beach cobbles. There are a number of upright stones,
presumably grave markers, on it. The mound lies in the

eastern part of an irregular oval drystone enclosure, divided
into two by a north–south wall. Buildings have been built
over parts of the mound and of the enclosure wall and the
dividing wall. Some of these are houses of relatively recent
date. None of the buildings is clearly identifiable as a chapel;
in 1867, Carmichael, the only source of information about
it, was told that it was small, a few feet square, in a corner
of the graveyard, and it was dedicated to Naomh Moire
(St Mary).[7] Carmichael was also informed that 'the hut in
which the bishop dwelt was very small. There was a square
stone at one end on which he rested his book . . . Latter people
used to put into the hut young cattle but never one of them
came out alive . . . the end of the bishop's house was up till
lately.'[8] No more information about this bishop is given, but
Berneray was referred to as the Bishop's Isle (Beàrnaraigh an
Easbaig) in 1794,[9] which could refer to a particular bishop, or
to the former connection of all five southern islands with the
Bishop of the Isles; or the bishop connection may have been
added simply to distinguish it from other Bernerays in the
Outer Hebrides.

There may have been a chapel in Early Christian times,
for there is a stone slab with a simple incised cross in the
graveyard, possibly dating to between the sixth and ninth centuries.[10] Another stone in the graveyard has two hollows in
it, perhaps used for grinding up shellfish for bait. Carmichael
mentioned that there was a stone 'font' in the graveyard which
was regarded as having special powers, and that people who
were afraid would go and stroke it.[11] He also described such
stones in Mingulay and Pabbay.

The graveyard area seems to have been a focus of settlement for a long period, and there are traces of a field system
earlier than the present one.[12] A map surveyed in 1829, before
the landing slip and road to the lighthouse were built, shows
eight buildings in a tight cluster around the west side of the
enclosure.[13] Later, houses were built both to the west, nearer
the landing slip and road, and to the east.

Carmichael was told an intriguing story about a stone pillar which 'had some writing upon it. No person was ever able to read the rude letters but one priest who was here, Mr Alein Donullach [Alan MacDonald]. He could speak twelve languages. A crew of fishermen were one day in Berneray. They could not get out to fish so they amused themselves by shaking the carradh pillar to and fro. They threw it down and over the precipice so the pillar which stood the storm of ages was broken in three "halves"'.[14] The priest could have been Allan MacDonell, who served in Barra from 1779–84.

Berneray was inhabited in Monro's time, 1549, and it was one of the islands where Cornelius Ward, the Irish Franciscan, worked in 1636. In 1764 its population was twenty (paying £6 rent) and thirty years later there were three families. In 1811 there were four tenants each paying £5 5s. In records of the lighthouse, four families were recorded in 1828, eight in 1830 (matching the eight houses on the 1829 map) and nine in 1833. If these latter two figures are accurate it is possible that, in the turmoil of the Barra estate at the time, there was an influx of people evicted from other islands. There was movement the other way too: in 1830 it was reported that 'Eoin MacNeil formerly at Bernary is living or about to live at Pabbay'. Four people emigrated to Canada between 1821 and 1826.[15]

As described in chapter 4, the islanders were themselves evicted in 1834 and forced to work at MacNeil's kelp factory in Barra for three or four years. By the time of the 1841 census there were twenty-one people, the highest figure of twenty-eight, being reached in 1851 (in four families in both years). It is possible that these people were evicted temporarily later in 1851, because Gordon of Cluny, the proprietor of the islands since 1840, threatened that he would do so and let the island to a grazing tenant. In November 1850 Duncan Sinclair, one of three crofters, who was employed as Occasional Assistant Lightkeeper, informed his bosses of the threat and suggested that they rent the whole island from Gordon and keep the current tenants; it was in their interest that the island remained inhabited. The Commissioners wrote to Gordon to ascertain the position, and in reply he said that:

> during the last four years I have had to pay more for supplies of food with public and parochial burdens [rates] effecting that island than the returns from it would cover. When my factor wished the tenants to give stock to meet part of their arrears of rent, they immediately boated what they had to the Island of Mull and sold them there on purpose to defraud me.[16]

The Commissioners decided against renting the island on the terms Gordon demanded, and there is no further mention of a new grazing tenant, or of the threatened evictions actually being carried out.

Between 1861 and 1891 population figures varied between seventeen and twenty-one, in two or three families. These figures exclude the lighthouse keepers and, from 1871, fishermen staying temporarily on the island. By 1901 there were ten people in three families, and the last of these left about 1910. This stability of population contrasts with Mingulay and shows that the figures were about right for the island to support. There remained four tenants: four were recorded in 1836, each paying £5.[17] Between 1843 and 1889 one of the crofts was rented by the lighthouse keepers who kept livestock and grew crops.

The main family names in the nineteenth century included MacNeil, MacLean, Campbell, MacIntyre, and Sinclair. The MacLeans are believed to have come from Mull originally. John MacNeil from Tangusdale, Barra, and his wife Ann MacIntyre moved to Berneray from Glen sometime between 1835 and 1841, perhaps when the island was resettled after the clearance. Two of their sons, Michael and Neil, became prosperous merchants and fish curers in Castlebay when the village was developing as a fishing port in the 1870s and 80s.[18] Neil (1842–86) left £800 in his will for the building of a Roman Catholic church in Castlebay, and the Church of Our Lady, Star of the Sea opened in 1888.[19] He also built the house which became the Craigard Hotel, and the house and shop which became the bank. Another brother, Allan, was an Assistant Occasional Lightkeeper at the lighthouse from 1875 to 1879, when rheumatism obliged him to give up work and he moved to Tangusdale. The brothers were educated: it is recorded that Michael, the eldest, attended the Ladies' School in Mingulay (although he was twenty-four when the school opened in 1859) and passed on his knowledge to his brothers. Michael engaged Dòmhnall Ruadh Sgoileir (Donald Sinclair) to teach his own children in Berneray before the family moved to Castlebay in about 1889 (although the children are also re-corded as having attended the Mingulay school). His son John (1882–1958) was ordained and served as a priest in Eriskay and the Small Isles; he was an army chaplain during the First World War, and became a Canon in the Catholic Church at Morar. The MacNeil house was the L-shaped building later used as a sheep fank, east of the graveyard.

The Sinclairs were the family of Duncan, originally from Argyll, and Mary, who settled in Berneray in the 1840s (see chapter 3). Duncan was also an Assistant Occasional Lightkeeper. He and his sons were fishermen; they had a fishing boat which they kept at Castlebay, it being too big to haul up at Berneray, and, before Castlebay became a fishing port, took their fish to Lough Swilly, Donegal, to sell. Most of his children settled in neighbouring islands, but one of his sons, Peter, remained in Berneray. He was a huge man, known as Pàdraig Mòr, 'Big Peter', or the 'Barra Giant'. The antiquary T.S. Muir put his tape measure to unusual use on his visit in 1866; Peter, then seventeen, was 6 feet 8 inches tall. He reached 7 feet (2.13 metres), and attracted attention in national newspapers. In 1891 he gave evidence on crofting, rents and living conditions to the Crofters Commission at Castlebay, and the *Aberdeen Journal* of 26 September reported, under the heading 'A giant at the Crofters' Commission' – 'One of the crofters known as The Berneray Giant was of an extraordinary size. He gave his height as seven feet, and he was stout in proportion. He had been south for nine months and had been making 37s a week, but he had not paid his rent since 1883.' In 1905 he was described as the tallest man in the postal service, being postman for the southern isles.[20] The family home, in the later years anyway, was close to the landing place, and it was a traditional style house with the walls the same height all the way round. Peter was the last of his family to live in it and he modified it in an unusual way and for an unusual reason: to enable him to stand up! He raised the height of the eastern end wall and created a flat roof which sloped towards the end of the former house. He joined a travelling show for a time, but disliked the publicity and returned to the islands. He used to bring his cattle to Castlebay in the summer months and run a dairy, returning to his distant home in the winter.[21] Peter and his wife Ann (Anna Chaluim), were the last inhabitants of Berneray, probably leaving in late 1910.

Alexander Carmichael was told an extraordinary story about Duncan Sinclair in the 1860s.[22] He relates that Sinclair lived for a year on Gearuim Mòr, the cliff-bound islet off the south coast of Mingulay. 'There was a sort of machinery for drawing up a boat. Lime was used in building the house where this mach[inery is]. On the top of the island are the remains of an old fort. Was this the place where lived Sinclair? Gearuim was also called Eilean an Each (Horse Island). The story is too detailed to be dismissed out of hand. It is told as if it had happened long before, but Sinclair was still living and it must have happened within the previous twenty years so everybody would have known about it; however no other references to it are known. Walker in 1869 calls the islet Sinclair's Rock, suggesting an association. Why would anybody choose to live there? Could it have been when the Berneray people were evicted or threatened with eviction? A possible time was the threatened eviction in 1850. The story is preceded by an anecdote which is told in the context of atrocities committed in Mingulay by soldiers at the time of the 1745 uprising (see chapter 4), about how the Berneray people, on seeing a strange sail approaching their island three or four years previously (i.e. 1863–4), fled to the hills with their blankets. The only exception was Duncan Sinclair. This anecdote is rather hard to believe, since by that time the lighthouse had been operating for more than 30 years, so a lot of strange sails must have approached.

The people lived, like their neighbours in Mingulay, by crofting, fishing and fowling. They grew barley, oats, potatoes, turnips and cabbages when Muir visited in 1866; and kept cattle, sheep and ponies. The ponies may have been bred for sale, as there was no peat for them to carry. Miss Bird recorded goats in 1863, kept by the lighthouse keepers. In 1828 there were forty black cattle and 100 sheep; in 1883 there were no ponies, forty cattle, almost all of them calves which would have been sold, and twenty-one sheep.[23] Berneray's common grazing included the above-mentioned islet of Gearuim Mòr. Although not high like Mingulay's stacks, it was accessible only in exceptional weather. It was still being used as late as 1907, when Robert Adam accompanied five men and five dogs in rounding up just seven sheep, the survivors of twelve which had been landed the year before.[24] Agriculture on Berneray was limited, as there is little naturally fertile land, and lazy-beds had to be made. These can be seen around the settlement area and on the Aird peninsula to the east, and on the southern slopes of Mullach a' Lusgan east of Barra Head.[25]

Berneray had peat, which was cut for fuel, and twenty-four peat stack platforms, similar to those on Mingulay, have been identified by RCAHMS investigators. One of these overlies formerly cultivated land. However, by 1828, when David Stevenson visited, usable peat had been worked out and the islanders had to cross to Mingulay for it. This must have been an enormous undertaking, and was one reason why, Muir said in 1866, Duncan Sinclair reckoned the Mingulay people to be much better off than he and his neighbours were. They would have cut peat within reach of the landing place at Skipisdale, the nearest one to Berneray.

Berneray was an easier place to fish from than Mingulay, on account of its superior landing places. There are sheltered creeks on the northeast coast, and there is a tiny beach of boulders and (sometimes) sand at Achduin[26] where the landing slip was built for the use of the lighthouse. Boats could be dragged up here, and there is a pair of boat shelters or noosts, as on Mingulay. In the late nineteenth century the islanders had only one boat, which was used mainly for catching white fish such as ling and cod. In 1903 this was owned by Peter Sinclair, and called *The Three Brothers*.[27] In the late nineteenth century, Berneray was used as a base by fishermen from Mingulay, Pabbay and Barra exploiting the rich stocks of white fish around Barra Head. The population censuses, taken in early April when the season had begun, show these fishermen in Berneray. In 1871 the practice was beginning, perhaps because of the recent development of Castlebay as a fishing port, and seven fishermen were lodging with crofters. In 1881 twenty fishermen were living in four temporary huts, and ten years later, there were eleven in two huts; none were recorded in 1901. The fishermen cured fish there; Donald MacPhee (Dòmhnall Bàn) of Mingulay said that the above Neil MacNeil had a curing station on the island.[28]

The seabirds nesting on the cliffs provided the islanders with an important item of food, and feathers and eggs for sale. An early visitor to Berneray mentions the use of birds and their eggs. William MacGillivray, professor of Natural History at Aberdeen University, and a landowner in Harris, wrote in 1818:

> On reaching Berneray we landed and soon after betook ourselves to a hut which we found cleared for our reception. We dined on roasted mutton, wild-fowls' eggs, bread, butter and whisky. The goodman [head] of the house came home with a basketful of

eggs from the rocks, and some birds which he had caught.

An account of fowling using the pole method, *stearradh*, appeared in the *Edinburgh Evening Courant* on 20 August 1829:

The natives of the island derive a plentiful supply of excellent food from the nests of these birds, first robbing some of them of their eggs, and others afterwards of their young. They also procure abundance of puffins by dragging them from the holes in which they breed at the summits of the cliffs. . .When the wind blows strongly from the south or southeast some of the birds, especially the puffins, are carried inland over the summit, when they wheel about and regain their nests . . . a man lays himself upon his back, close to the edge of the cliff, with his head to the sea and having in his hands a stout fishing rod or light spar, which is directed over his head towards the sea. He remains patiently in this state until a bird, driven over him by the wind, comes within reach, when he suddenly raises the rod and dextrously hits it. The bird falls, and is immediately secured. This method of procuring birds is practised only in the island of Berneray, none of the other breeding places being so constructed as to admit of it.

In 1845, the *Inverness Courier* tells us, feathers were 'reckoned of greater value than even the St Kilda down, as they possess none of the oily flavour of the latter . . . their eggs have lately become an article of commerce and the people of the island send boats laden with them to Glasgow and Greenock.' In 1868 Captain Elwes noted that the islanders were supplying birds to the crews of fishing boats from Islay; he also noted that a fowler caught 600 birds in six to eight hours, using the pole method.

In 1829 Berneray was chosen as the site for a lighthouse, and a number of descriptions of the island by visitors to the lighthouse are known. David Stevenson wrote of his visit on 3 September 1830:

> The island was inhabited when I landed there 2 years ago, by 8 families* who have of late had the company of the work men employed at the Lighthouse works but who have profited little by it as I can see very little difference on them, they are very ignorant and cannot speak a word of English, none of them can read a word in their own language, and wonderful to say in this islet of the British dominions there is not among the natives a single leaf of a printed book, they are all Roman Catholics, and the priest pays them a visit once a year. Most of their houses consist of holes dug in the earth, perhaps 3 feet in depth, a wall of 3 feet is then built round the hole, and over it there is a covering of thatch. We went into one of them where we found several women and a number of children all squatting on the ground round a fire of peats on the floor. The house was without a chimney and excepting a few cooking utensils we saw no other articles of furniture whatever. In the other apartment there was a large box bed and a weavers loom of very rude construction and we were shewn a part of the floor on which 5 or 6 of the family made their bed of straw, with only a single plaid to cover them. The women and children had a cleaner appearance than might have been expected. The small quantity of corn which they require to grind, is prepared with the quern or ancient hand-mill which we saw them use with great adroitness, accompanying the operation with one of their native airs, we saw them also at the churning, a small barrel which in a sitting posture they rock, till the butter comes.[29]

[*in his own account of the 1828 visit he recorded
four families.]

The description of the construction of the houses is intriguing,
being reminiscent of techniques used in sandy areas of the
Outer Hebrides over thousands of years – although the soil at
that spot is not sandy – but not known to have been used as
late as this period.

Another visitor was Isabella Bird, who travelled the world
and wrote prolifically about her adventures. She landed in
1863 from the *Shamrock*, under the charge of Captain Otter,
who was engaged in mapping the islands for the Admiralty.
She described the landing place as a

> shelving table of rock at the foot of a rent in the cliff,
> and this is only available in calm weather and in cer-
> tain winds. As it was, we had to watch our oppor-
> tunity when the boat went in on the top of a wave,
> and spring ashore. The shelving rock was steep to
> climb, and so slippery with fish scales and fish oil
> that one of the officers fell on his face. At the top
> of this inhospitable pier there were several trays full
> of dogfish and skate lying in brine . . . Long poles,
> with which the natives kill the sea-fowl, were lying
> about. Above the ledge of rock on which we landed,
> the whole island population was congregated. We
> received an outrageous welcome; everybody shook
> hands with somebody, all the people poured out
> torrents of words in the vernacular, and a few made
> the most of some very lame sentences in English, re-
> sorting to patting and stroking to make them more
> emphatic. There was something only half civilised
> about the whole affair, and I doubt not that strings of
> beads, and looking-glasses, would have been as glee-
> fully received as in Central Africa. Yet these people
> were all well-dressed, cleanly, and healthy looking,

and most anxious to take us to their abodes. We
spent some time in one of them, and were regaled
with delicious cream, in large, clean, wooden bowls.

This was the lightest, cleanest, best appointed
Highland hut I ever entered. Its inmates seemed entirely dependent on their own resources; tobacco and
tea, and the last used not as a beverage, but as a luxury,
appeared the only exotic articles. The garments were
all made of homespun wool, and the striped winceys
of the women, woven by themselves, would not
have disgraced Aberdeen. Crinoline had penetrated
even to Bernera, but it too was home-manufactured,
out of hoops of barrels thrown up from a wreck.
Two buxom girls had never seen 'ladies' before, and
occupied themselves with a minute but surreptitious
scrutiny of the garments of those of our party. The
hut was furnished with tables, benches, boxes, beds
and stools of driftwood. The guidman [Duncan
Sinclair] was the only native Protestant on the island,
and as if in proof of a fact no doubt of considerable
importance in this little insular world, he bought a
Bible, paying for it in the currency of Bernera – dried
skate. His son, a fine boy of ten years [Duncan], has
the distinction of being the scholar of the island, and,
after diving from the top of a rock and swimming
out to see the 'Shamrock', he returned, ruddy and
dripping, to read a lesson in English, a tongue of
which he evidently comprehended not one word.

After receiving us thus hospitably, the whole population set off in their great boat to the 'Shamrock',
where curiosity and bargaining kept them for three
hours chaffering with the cook and sailors, paying for
their purchases in fish. To their credit be it recorded
that they seemed more disposed to give than to take
. . . It seemed they were never weary of the sight of the
black cook, whom at first they had taken for the devil!

Far out in the Atlantic, exposed to its fullest fury, and generally inaccessible, [Bernera] yet has nursed a population before, rather than behind, those of the other Hebrides. Without any advantages or other religious ordinances than are supplied by the annual visit of a priest from Barra, these very interesting people thirst for education, and would make considerable sacrifices to obtain it.

Another visitor who was moved to write about Berneray was William Chambers, a Commissioner of Northern Lighthouses, after a tour of lighthouses in 1866:

The road slanted across the open hillside, which was devoted chiefly to the pasturage of a few cattle and sheep. Here and there were small patches of barley and oats, enclosed with fences of turf; but so meagre were the crops and so plentifully interspersed with tall dock weeds, that there was promise of but an insignificant harvest.

Where the road crossed the stream which enters the sea at the landing place, Chambers noticed

a low building which appeared to be a mill of some kind, with a wheel at one end . . . The mill is entirely the handiwork of an ingenious assistant lighthouse keeper (a Fife man), who diverted his leisure hours in its construction. He erected the building, covered it with a tarpaulin roof, and fabricated the whole of the grinding apparatus. The most difficult part of the undertaking was accomplished by adapting an old cart-wheel. The idea of erecting a mill was suggested by the absence from the island of all means of grinding except for a primitive species of hand-querns. Glad of the opportunity of so easily transforming their corn into meal, the crofters besought the privilege of using it, which was of course allowed; and the multure was arranged on the convenient footing of giving a lamb for a grist, be the quantity much or little ... The interior of the mill ... [is] about eight feet square; adjoining is a kiln, equally diminutive, made from a piece of old sheet-iron, for drying the grain.

I afterwards visited two thatched dwellings, poor lowly biggings with no attempt at neatness or cleanliness in their miserable surroundings ... A leading feature consists in a twisted orifice in the roof to let out the smoke from the peat fire in the middle of the clay floor ... I had learned, from various knowing hints and looks of a Commissioner, that it was not advisable to enter any of the dwellings ... In the first hut there was an old woman barefooted, who could speak only a few words of English, but seemed anxious to be hospitable, and set a chair for me beside the peat fire. The cottage contained a loom in one corner, in which was a web of dark woollen cloth, for the clothing of the family. In the other hut was an old woman carding wool, and her daughter neatly dressed in tartan, who spoke English tolerably. Here also was a loom ... The husband and sons connected with these families occupy their time partly as fishermen, and take cargoes of cured fish to Portrush on the northern coast of Ireland, or sell them to Glasgow traders.

The mill was built on the vertical principle, and can only have worked after heavy rain swelled the tiny stream, and the roadside ditch, which powered it. It was one of only two mills marked on maps of the Barra Isles in 1861–3 and 1878,[30] and without Chambers's account it would be hard to explain, the native population being so small. The builder was very probably James Oswald, from St Monans, Fife, who served an exceptionally long time, from 1851 to 1875, as Assistant Occasional Lightkeeper, so he would have had plenty of spare time. At the time, the lighthouse keepers were growing their own food on the island, including barley, which would have needed grinding, so they would have used the mill themselves as well as allowed the locals to use it. The mill eventually fell into disuse, perhaps after Oswald left, or after 1889 when the keepers stopped growing their own food. John MacKinnon of Mingulay built a copy of the mill, and may have used some of its parts.

Isabella Bird mentioned the people's 'thirst for education'. This was not the first time the people had tried to get a teacher; as related in chapter 10, they nearly got one in 1859, but the teacher went to Mingulay instead. Earlier, in the 1851 census, several of Duncan Sinclair's children were described as 'scholars at home', and in the 1861 census Allan MacDonald, 'Ladies' Association teacher' was recorded as a visitor in the house of John MacNeil. Some Berneray children attended the Ladies' School on Mingulay. In October 1883 the islanders petitioned Barra School Board for an itinerant teacher, and the Board agreed to establish a school there, as a 'sub school' of the Mingulay school.[31] Michael Campbell of Mingulay (probably the 'Teac' who was later prominent in the raiding of Vatersay) was appointed, but he seems to have left as a result of an unspecified 'misunderstanding' between parents and teacher recorded in 1884. In 1884 Michael MacNeil promised, on behalf of the parents, to provide accommodation for the school, board and lodging for the teacher, and £10 a year towards the teacher's salary. S. MacPhee was teacher then, and the following year it was Donald MacNeil. The school was mentioned briefly in the log book of its parent between 1884 and 1887, when it closed.[32] It cannot have had many pupils, for there were fewer than ten children on the island in 1881 and in 1891. The children were examined with their Mingulay neighbours, and the inspectors' comments were complimentary. It is not known where schooling took place, but in 1886 a building that had been begun as a school was completed as a 'refuge' for the lighthouse boatmen.[33] On the school's closure, some of these children, and presumably others before and after, attended the Board school in Mingulay, perhaps as weekly boarders. The children of Michael MacNeil did so, lodging with relatives, the family of Angus MacNeil (Aonghas Dhòmhnaill Ruairidh). Eight 'scholars', including a daughter of a lighthouse keeper, were recorded in the 1891 census, but only one of these appears in the admission register of Mingulay school, so in what sense the others were scholars is unclear.

There is a story about one of the teachers at Berneray, a woman from London who applied for the advertised job without any idea where the school was. She was appointed, and on arrival at Oban asked for a cab to take her to the school. She was informed that she would have to take a steamer to Castlebay; on arrival there she again asked for a cab, only to be told that she would have to take a boat. She was taken over in August, but had to wait until May of the following year before she could return to Barra, whereupon she boarded the steamer back to Oban and no more was ever heard of her.[34] One can imagine what the experience would have been like for a Londoner unaware of what she was letting herself in for.

Berneray was deserted in 1910 or early 1911, after many years of dwindling numbers. Donald Campbell (Dòmhnall Dhòmhnaill) built a shed in Vatersay in spring 1908, and Michael Campbell and his mother were there by October 1908.[35] Catherine Campbell had gone by the end of 1909.[36] Peter Sinclair applied at least three times for a croft in Vatersay in 1909 and 1910 – the last application being in September 1910 – but he was unsuccessful.[37] He was the last to leave Berneray. Nobody was there in April 1911[38] and in July Neil MacPhee (mac Chaluim), formerly of Mingulay, asked to rent Sinclair's and the other two crofts, in order to keep stock on them.[39] In September 1911 one of the lighthouse keepers

fell ill but there was no way to summon help because all the
islanders had left. Peter Sinclair received a stern letter from
the estate factor in August 1912 criticising him for removing
his roof (presumably in order to use the materials on his
new house in Castlebay), saying it was the property of Lady
Gordon Cathcart, and he had informed the police![40] The grazier, Jonathan MacLean, had taken over Catherine Campbell's
croft in 1910, and by 1914 he had the whole island.

Berneray's most prominent monument is the lighthouse,
known as the Barra Head Lighthouse. Situated at the very top
of the island, it is by far the highest lighthouse in Britain. It was
built by the Commissioners of Northern Lighthouses (later
the Northern Lighthouse Board) as part of a programme to
improve navigation and safety for shipping on the west coast
of Scotland, informed by reports by Robert Stevenson of the
engineering family in 1828 and 1829. Barra Head was chosen
because it is the southern point of the Outer Hebrides, and
at the entrance to the Minch, and, being visible from almost
every direction, would assist coastal shipping as well as shipping heading for, or approaching from, the Atlantic. It was the
second lighthouse to be erected in the Outer Hebrides, the first
having been built at Eilean Glas, Scalpay, Harris, in 1789.[41]

MacNeil of Barra, the landowner, who was heavily in debt,
demanded a price for the lease of the land which the commissioners regarded as 'exhorbitant'. MacNeil claimed that the
land was valuable 'owing to the proximity to the best fishing
banks and its value as a most excellent grazing'. In a cynical
display of mock sensitivity to the islanders, he requested that
no buildings should be built within fifty yards of the edges of
cliffs where birds bred, 'for such of my tenants as follow the
occupation of taking these Birds. . .the feathers of which are
a source of considerable profit', however, he had to relent on
that demand.[42]

Robert Stevenson designed the lighthouse, and the building
contractor was James Smith of Inverness.[43] Construction
began in 1830, and the following year forty-eight workers

were employed at the site. The invasion of the technology of the outside world, and of dozens of strangers, must have been bewildering, if not traumatic, for the islanders.

Robert Stevenson wrote of the conditions for the builders in 1831:

> Such is the violence of the wind in this station that the temporary buildings occupied by the artificers were repeatedly unroofed. On the face of the precipitous cliffs the winds and seas acquire a force which the reporter has never experienced elsewhere. It is not indeed uncommon to be actually struck down by the more violent and sudden gusts of wind, while the seas remove incredible masses of rock. The artificers are often reduced to the necessity of passing the most exposed places on their knees clinging with their hands to the ground in going to and from their barracks.

And in 1833:

> In one of these storms the lighthouse cart and horse overturned by the force of the wind. Both shafts were broken and the body of the cart was disengaged and carried into the air 15 or 20 ft while the wheels ran down the sloping bank for some distance. It is remarkable that the horse sustained no injury.

The lighthouse and two elegant single-storey keepers' cottages, all within a paved courtyard, together with storehouses, enclosure walls, and a substantial byre for the keepers' cattle, were built from stone quarried from the nearby promontory. Everything else, however, had to be imported. Landing everything, especially bulk materials, such as sand for cement (which Stevenson planned would come from Mingulay), and sheet lead for roofs, was a laborious and hazardous process only possible in calm weather. Materials were transferred from large boats to small ones for landing at the landing slip at the other end of the island, and hauled up the road built for the purpose, by horse and cart. A 'boat creek' was constructed for the attending boat, based at Castlebay, to shelter in. The first one, made by adapting natural rock ledges, was destroyed by heavy seas shortly after it was finished in 1834 and another was built, possibly in the next rocky inlet along the coast east of the landing place, where there are the remains of a quay. Much later, boats were hauled out of the water on rails by means of a windlass (winch). A derrick similar to Mingulay's was later provided to ease the landing of supplies. A store-house was built near the landing place.

The lighthouse itself was built of bolted and clamped blocks of stone, with a roof of sheet lead. It is not high, only 18 metres (60 feet), being already 190 metres (625 feet) above the sea. Indeed, it was criticised, even ridiculed, at an early stage for its lofty situation, as the light was often invisible because of cloud. In clear weather, the light could be seen from a distance of 53 kilometres (33 miles). The light, first lit on 15 October 1833, was fired by oil and was fitted with an ingenious mechanism to obscure it intermittently; the cycle was rather long, two and a half minutes on, half a minute obscured (changed in 1881 to half a minute on, half a minute obscured). The total building costs were £12,000, amongst the highest of any lighthouse built at the time, on account of its remoteness and inaccessibility, and the severe weather conditions and landing conditions.

There were special challenges due to the violence of the wind and weather. On its north side the lighthouse teeters near the edge of a huge chasm, facing west, acting like a funnel for wind and spray. A short distance away on its south side is another sheer cliff. In storms the panes of glass of the lightroom were pelted with small stones picked up from the cliffs, and salt spray containing an oily substance derived from the guano of seabirds smeared the glass. The glass had to be heated in winter to combat condensation. The ash pits where the keepers threw the ash from their domestic coal fires had to have covers made for them as the ash was whipped up and blown onto the glass of the lightroom. Smoke from the fires would fill the houses in certain conditions when the wind blew down the chimneys. The water supply for the keepers and their cattle was intended to be rainwater collected from the flat lead-covered roofs of their houses, but in stormy weather salt spray constantly contaminated the water, so a well was sunk near the road at its eastern end. The lighthouse horse and cart thus had a lot of extra work to do, hauling up water as well as coal, oil and other supplies for the lighthouse. A well was later provided closer to the lighthouse.

At first there were two lighthouse keepers at Barra Head, but within a year the keepers were deprived of the means of communicating with Barra in an emergency when the island's inhabitants were evicted, and it was recorded that 'the duties of the keepers at Barrahead are perhaps the most severe in the lighthouse service' on account of their distance from the nearest church, in Barra, and nearest market town, Tobermory, Mull. So a third keeper was recruited. His services were dispensed with when the islanders returned, but one of them (unnamed) was trained as an Occasional Assistant Lightkeeper. Duncan Sinclair held this post in 1850 when he informed the Commissioners of the eviction threat. In response to this threat, the Commissioners, expecting Sinclair to be evicted with the other tenants, appointed James Oswald from Fife. He was in post by the time the population census was taken in April 1851, but the eviction threat had not been carried out by then, if it ever was. Oswald had not worked in the lighthouse service before, but he must have taken a liking to the job, for he stayed for twenty-four years. Another keeper who seems to have enjoyed being there was George MacLachlan who was interested in the bird life, and became very knowledgeable during his stay in the 1860s. He supplied information to the naturalist J.A. Harvie-Brown. He was presumably the 'Mac' who accompanied the Walker brothers on cliff-scaling excursions on their visit in 1869, and who collected seabirds' eggs for his own consumption.

For most of the men, life as a keeper at Barra Head must have been a somewhat grim existence, particularly in winter, idling away their shifts in the lightroom with little to do but make sure the machinery kept going; however, they were better off than their colleagues in lighthouses on mere rocks in the sea. They served four or five years, and in the early decades would not have left the island during that time; it was too risky to leave as there was no knowing when you would be able to return. In their spare time they cultivated the croft they shared. Their croft was at the eastern end of the island near the islanders' crofts. Originally, the keepers were expected to keep their own cattle in the 35 acres (14 hectares) of ground surrounding the lighthouse; however, they found that, being blasted by salt-laden winds, the land was only usable as summer grazing and it would not provide a hay crop for winter fodder. So in about 1843 the Commissioners took on one of the four crofts at the other end of the island, on which the keepers grew food crops for themselves, and hay. One year, 1860, there was a violent autumn storm and all the hay, which had been neatly stacked, was blown away. In 1889 a Board official complained that 'farming not lightkeeping was the mens' first consideration' and the croft was given up. In 1851 one of the keepers requested compensation of £8 for the loss of two cows over the cliffs, and a third in a ditch. He was granted £5.

There must have been tensions between keepers cooped up together for years on end. One incident was so serious that it was discussed, and minuted, at a meeting of the commissioners in 1855. Principal Lightkeeper James Brown Scott committed a 'gross outrage' against his subordinate James Oswald in a dispute over the lighthouse horse, or rather, mare, which was in foal. Scott had used the mare to plough his part of the light-house croft, which was against the rules as the beast was kept solely for the purpose of hauling supplies for the lighthouse in the lighthouse cart; he had even lent the mare to local crofter Donald MacIntyre in return for borrowing the latter's horse. Oswald, who was responsible for the mare, raised the matter with his superior, who was abusive. The last straw was when Oswald saw Scott's son 'driving the animal at a furious pace' on the croft. Oswald took the mare from the boy, shook the boy who ran to his father, who punched Oswald in the chest so hard that he was in bed for a week.

In another recorded incident, in 1866, Principal Lightkeeper William Kirk was accused of the rape of the sister of the Assistant Lightkeeper. He was sent for trial at the High Court of Justiciary in Edinburgh, an indication of the gravity of the offence. The *Caledonian Mercury* of 12 June reported that he was 'charged with committing a rape upon Agnes Ferrier . . . the accused pleaded not guilty . . . the jury found the prisoner guilty of an assault with intent to ravish.' He was sentenced to six months imprisonment, and dismissed from the service.

Life must have been hard for the families of the keepers. Some of the families were large: their total population in 1851 was sixteen. They came from all over the coastal parts of Scotland, including Orkney and Shetland. Two keepers and their families would have shared one of the lighthouse cottages until 1882, when a third cottage was created by infilling the house-sized gap which had thoughtfully been left between the two original cottages. In the early decades there was no medical provision and it is not surprising that some children died. A sad legacy of this is the little cemetery, enclosed by a neat oval stone wall, near the cliff top not far from the lighthouse. It contains the graves of four children of lightkeepers who died on the island in the 1830s and 40s, and one lightkeeper, John Ross, who had fallen to his death from the cliffs while gathering eggs in 1840. The keepers were nearly all Protestant, so their dead could not be buried in the Roman Catholic burial ground on the island, and the nearest Church of Scotland church and cemetery was in Barra (Cuier) which was in practice virtually impossible to get to because of the long sea journey, long walk at the other end, and the uncertainties of getting back. For these reasons there was no question of attending the church on Sundays; the minister visited Barra Head annually or less frequently, and a missionary did a tour of lighthouses every year or two. Otherwise, the principal lightkeeper would take Sunday service.

Nor was there any educational provision in the early decades; the children were home-schooled. As we have seen, in 1859 a lighthouse keeper tried to get a teacher for his own and some local children, but he was transferred to another lighthouse, and the teacher went to Mingulay instead. In 1865 a teacher was provided, apparently by the Commissioners, for the large family of the Principal Lightkeeper, and ten years later a keeper was allowed to transfer to a less remote lighthouse so that his children could attend school. In 1886, two years after Barra School Board opened a school on the island, the Northern Lighthouse Board began to build a schoolroom, only to abandon it when it decided to appoint only unmarried keepers to lighthouses where there was no school within reach.

Two cases of mental illness, or insanity as it was referred to in those days, were recorded in 1863–4. The Board tried to deal with both in a sympathetic way. In one case, the wife of a lightkeeper was insane and the Board eventually agreed to her husband's request to be transferred to a less remote lighthouse where there was an asylum nearby. The lightkeeper's replacement, Mr Craib, had an adult son who was, according to a visitor in a letter to the Board, 'out of his mind . . . and when his mind was affected everyone was in terror of their lives'. Duncan Sinclair and the other islanders were moved to write to the Board in the son's defence, claiming he was 'civil to all' and that a previous lightkeeper had been spreading rumours about the family out of spite. Craib was ordered to remove his son; he was sent to Oban, but got no further than Mingulay where he stayed and attended the school there, but he was obliged to leave there as well.

A comically romanticised view of Berneray (from Bird, 1866)

The keepers kept in regular touch with Castlebay by means
of the mail/relief boat which was based there. In the later
nineteenth century the boat came once a week in summer,
once a fortnight in winter, though conditions often made the
intervals much longer. Before 1855, when Barra finally got a
postal service, the boat took mail to, and brought mail from,
Tobermory, Mull. If the sea conditions forced the boat crew
to stay overnight in Berneray, James Oswald was required to
put them up and feed them in a room in one of the lighthouse
cottages. In 1855 Oswald complained that the crew were 'in
a state of starvation, and ate so greedily during their stay that
the Board's allowance did not compensate him. . .and that
they were so extremely filthy in their persons that each visit
left the house in such a state with vermin as to be almost
intolerable.' Thereafter the Board instructed the boatmen to
find their own accommodation among the crofters, and no
doubt this business opportunity was taken up. In 1886, as we
have seen, the Board built a 'refuge' for the boatmen to stay
in in case they were stranded by bad weather, a simple gabled
house built on the site of the former mill at the junction of the
stream and the road.

In the early years three of the boatmen employed by the Board were drowned in accidents at sea, and on several occasions boats were swept away while sheltering at the landing place or even drawn up on the rocks. In 1870, following the drowning of Roderick MacPhee, the Board considered having the boat based in Berneray rather than in Castlebay, but decided against. Malcolm MacAulay from Barra, a Protestant incomer, was appointed boatman. This did not go down very well with members of the Sinclair and MacNeil families, who had applied for the post. MacAulay was succeeded by his son Donald in 1906. (The Sinclair brothers' father, Duncan, had himself been a Protestant incomer once!)

While Berneray was inhabited, the keepers could summon help from Barra in case of emergency, but in 1911, after the last inhabitants left, the Board started experimenting with a system of visual signals between the lighthouse and Castlebay, Barra. Donald MacAulay, the boatman, who lived on the east side of Castlebay, undertook to look out for signals from the lighthouse between 10am and 11am every morning, but the signals were rarely visible. In 1914 the Board tried wireless telegraphy, and this was successful. A radio-telephone link was established by 1925, and a wireless beacon was installed in 1936. There were other advances: the lighthouse boat was fitted with an engine in 1914, and a motor lorry replaced the horse in 1930. Later in the twentieth century a tractor and trailer were used. A concrete landing slip was built at the landing place, with a derrick for landing supplies. The road to the lighthouse was tarred in 1976.

During the Second World War a Blenheim bomber crashed into the cliffs near the lighthouse, but this must have happened during a storm, for no one heard it. Its remains were discovered many years later by a climber on the cliffs.

The lighthouse was finally automated in October 1980.[44] The main optic is an acetylene operated Dalen revolving pedestal. The rotating Fresnel lens equipment rotates at one revolution every thirty seconds, and flashes every fifteen seconds.

It has a mantle exchanger (gas) and it incorporates duplicate gas pressure operated devices. The equipment is automatically started and shut down by a sunvalve. Apart from the main optic, the equipment is electrically powered by batteries which are automatically recharged by diesel alternator.

The lighthouse is visited regularly by maintenance crews, who nowadays stay in fibreglass accommodation units rather than the old cottages. Since 1997 all goods and personnel have been brought in by helicopter from the mainland.

After the islanders left in 1910 Berneray was used for grazing, and has had the same owners as Mingulay. The National Trust for Scotland removed the remaining sheep in 2009. It has plans to convert the old tractor garage near the pier into a simple bothy for visiting staff, researchers and volunteers.

16

Pabbay

Pabbay lies roughly midway between Mingulay and Sandray. It is smaller than both, the main body of the island being a rough rectangle about 2 kilometres (1¼ miles) long, and 1.5 kilometres (1 mile) wide. A long finger-like peninsula, Rosinish, springs from the northeast corner of the island in a southeasterly direction, enclosing a sheltered bay. Rosinish (Gaelic Roisinis, from the Norse for 'Horse Headland') is now a tidal island, being separated from the main island by a narrow channel covered by the sea at high tide; this channel appears to have originated from the collapse of the natural arch marked on the early Ordnance Survey maps.

Like its southern neighbours, Pabbay slopes up from the east to the west. Its highest point is An Tobha (The Hoe), 171 metres (564 feet) high, the southern and western slopes of which descend steeply to the sea. In places there are cliffs up to about 120 metres (400 feet) high, but they are not extensive and are not used by breeding seabirds as in Mingulay and Berneray. This is thought to be because of the wide shelf separating their base from the sea.[1] Pabbay does not have the nature conservation designations of its southern neighbours.

There is a curious depression in the middle of the island formed where several igneous dykes intersect and have been eroded away. Its sides are steep, occupied in places by eared willow growing up to 1.2 metres (4 feet) high,[2] and its floor

is a marshy peat bog, fed by small streams and draining out
to the east. According to the map of 1861–3 it was cultivated
at that time. It is a rather sinister place, contrasting with the
pleasant green slopes of the small, intimate glen occupied by
the former settlement area, between it and the bay.

Bàgh Bàn ('White Bay') on the east of the island is more
sheltered than Mingulay's bay, and is backed by a beach of
dazzling white sand. Behind the beach is a rampart of dunes
which developed during the twentieth century; these are now
stabilised by marram grass, but the sandy soil continues for a
long way inland.[3] The sand is rich in lime from seashells, and
in places it has solidified into a form of impure limestone. As
on Mingulay, drifting sand has been a feature for thousands
of years, and no doubt has overwhelmed formerly fertile land;
'This island is greatly spoiled by the Sand Drift,' wrote Walker
in 1764.

Pabbay was surveyed archaeologically for the first time
between 1992 and 1998, by archaeologists from Sheffield
University who also carried out the first excavations[4]. Over
130 man-made structures of all periods were recorded, and,
as on Mingulay and Berneray, many sites are of uncertain
date and function. The two ancient sites recorded in the nineteenth century were the broch, Dùnan Ruadh, and the site
of a chapel on the mound occupied by the graveyard. There
are cairns of various kinds, although whether any are Bronze
Age is uncertain: some are relatively recent marker cairns
or sighting cairns. The folklorist and antiquarian Alexander
Carmichael found worked flint flakes in what he called an
'immense subterranean natural cave' in 1872, but he didn't
elaborate on the location of this intriguing feature, which has
not been recorded since.[5]

In the grassy area north of the cemetery mound, there are a
number of clusters of large stones protruding from the sandy
soil. Sheffield archaeologists investigated one of these and
found a multi-cellular building which had been created by
digging into the sand and lining the excavation with drystone

walling. The structure consisted of two sub-circular 'chambers' linked by a passage, off which there was an entrance. One of the chambers had three offshoots or cells. The floor of the structure was about a metre (3 feet) below current ground level, which seems to have been the original ground level. The structure had been roofed in places by large lintel stones. Large slabs had also been used inside, in a vertical position, and in one place, three were placed in a row to make, in the words of the report, an 'arcade'. Pottery of probable late Bronze Age or early Iron Age date (c.1000–200 BC), and some charcoal and sheep bones, were found on the floor of one of the chambers. It had probably been a dwelling, and other stone clusters visible on the surface in the vicinity may be similar structures; similar sites from this period, also sunk into sand, have been found at Cladh Hallan in South Uist.

In the Iron Age a dun, Dùnan Ruadh, the 'Red Dun', was built on a low rocky promontory, a naturally defensible site, on the north coast near the neck of Rosinish. Originally it was probably a broch, or round tower, consisting of an inner and outer drystone wall with a passage, or gallery, between. All that survived before it was excavated in 1996–7, however, was an arc of outer and inner walls, approximately 15.8 metres (52 feet) long and 3.3 metres (10 feet) wide on the higher, landward side of the promontory; the remainder had been washed off the smooth promontory surface by the sea. This had happened by 1878, when it was first described.[6] The surviving arc indicated that the diameter of the broch had been about 19 meters (62 feet). The excavations were undertaken by Sheffield University in order to recover information before any more of the site was lost to erosion.

The excavators found that the broch was probably built in the first century AD and was occupied until about the fourth century. It had been a dwelling rather than a refuge, and it would have been roofed. Parts of the walls survived to a height of about a metre (3 feet) in places. Up to a metre of occupation debris also survived, including various floor levels.

The gallery between the walls was narrow and irregular and at the west end it had been modified to form two corbelled chambers.

Hebridean Iron Age pottery, typical of finds from sites of the period in Mingulay, Sandray, Barra and the Uists were found. Many of the sherds were from cooking vessels. Large quantities of animal bones, the remains of meals, had been discarded within the living space of the broch and indicate the diet of the inhabitants. Nearly all the bones of domesticated animals were of sheep, most of which had been killed when under a year old – during the winter when there was not enough grazing to maintain them. There were a few bones of cattle, also very young, and a very few of pig. These findings are similar to other excavated sites although the proportion of sheep was higher. There were a few bones of juvenile Common and Atlantic (Grey) seals, which could have been caught on the beach or on rocks or from boats. There were a very few bones of deer, probably imported as joints of meat or as bone for making tools; antler was also imported for this purpose. Bones of many species of inshore fish were found, all of which could have been caught from the shore or by small boat. There were bones of various species of seabirds, the most common being shag. Animal bones had also been used to make a variety of tools and domestic items such as needles and a toggle. Barley grains were found, also rubbing stones used for grinding grain in stone querns.

Other finds indicate that metalworking was going on: iron slag either from smelting or from reworking ready-formed metal, and a crucible for melting copper alloy. In each case the raw materials would have been imported. Spindle whorls used in spinning wool show that adult sheep were kept for their wool and perhaps for milk.

The broch was abandoned for a century or two and the site was reoccupied in the sixth century until about the ninth, the Pictish period. By this time the broch walls had been lowered by collapse, or by reusing the stone, to approximately their present height; midden material from this period had been dumped on the wall top, spilling onto the collapsed roof rubble of one of the wall chambers. A cellular building was constructed in the interior of the broch at this time, using stone from the Iron Age walls, athough very little of this building actually survived. The inhabitants had a similar economy to their predecessors. The most interesting find was a copper alloy pin, 71mm (2¾ in) long, found in the rubbish on the wall-top mentioned above. It has a decorated head made in two parts, each made in a mould, as was the shaft. By analogy with similar pins, it dates to the sixth or seventh century. A longer enamelled bronze pin of the late seventh century was acquired by the antiquary Erskine Beveridge in 1895 and donated to the National Museum of Antiquities in Edinburgh.[7] Wedderspoon, writing in 1912, said that 'one of the islanders produced a bronze pin about six inches in length', probably also from this period. Such pins are not common, and three from one small island is exceptional.

Four memorial stones in the graveyard on the northeast side of the recent settlement also date from this period.[8] The graveyard occupies a prominent steep-sided hillock between 4.5 and 7.5 metres (15–25 feet) above the surrounding ground. It is exceptional in the islands, and, although modified by human activity, is probably an ancient sand dune in origin.[9] It is now grass-grown, but when Wedderspoon examined it there was

> very little grass on the mound except on the graves, which are neatly covered with turf . . . the top is narrow, affording space for one grave only. The sides are very steep, and it is difficult to know how interments can be made, but it is covered with graves from top to bottom, each marked at head and foot with an upright slab of native rock, from three to six feet in height. The interior consists principally of sand, bones, and shells of the edible mollusc

varieties. Among them were found a few horse teeth,
several large tusks, also teeth of the ox and a number
of bones of the tooth-pick pattern . . . there can be
no doubt that the mound occupies the site of a prehistoric midden.

Human bones are said to have been found scattered on the
mound, at its base, and in the bed of the stream curving round
its north and east sides. Carmichael described seeing 'human
remains surrounded by rows of carefully selected polished
pebbles from the strand and others by common moor stones
from the hill, bits of cinerary urns of different periods with
pins and needles of bone, bronze and brass'.[10] Two interesting
burials were recorded by Seton Gordon in 1950:

Through the action of water some of the bones
were exposed of a man of considerable stature. My
informant was born on Pabbay. His father was six
feet four inches in height, and the jaw-bone which
became exposed was so large that it 'fitted over his
jaw, and scarcely touched his whiskers.' In a stone
coffin was found a skeleton with a clam shell over
the face. Clam shells were used as drinking cups . . .
Father John MacMillan [of Barra] a grand singer of
the Oran Mor believes the composition of classical
pipe music Bodach na Sligean (Old Man of the Shell)
was composed on the finding of this skeleton.

If the shell was a scallop rather than a clam, it has been suggested that the occupant had been on pilgrimage to Santiago
de Compostella, in Spain.[11]
Two of the upright slabs, likely to be gravestones, have
crosses incised on them, and one of the slabs has a cross on
each side. Until recently there was a third incised slab, lying
loose on the top of the mound in two pieces, but it has disappeared. These crosses probably date from between the sixth

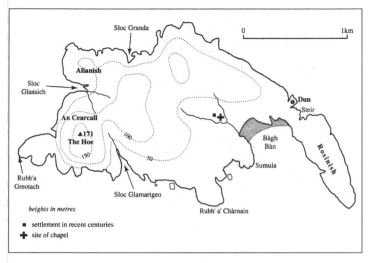

Map 5. Pabbay

and ninth centuries. The fourth and most important slab is
the Pictish symbol stone, one of only two known in the Outer
Hebrides.[12] It is an unshaped stone slab 1.1 metres (3 feet
6 inches) long, bearing incised symbols of Pictish type: a cres-
cent and V-rod, and a lily, and these date the stone to the eighth
century. These symbols are found on other stones, mainly in
the Pictish areas of eastern Scotland, and their meaning is unknown. A cross was subsequently added to the stone, perhaps
to represent the Christianising of the inhabitants, or simply to
turn it into a gravestone. The symbol stone was found in 1889
by Father Allan McDonald (of South Uist and Eriskay) where
it was lying on the southern flank of the mound, exposed by
shifting sand. He notified Joseph Anderson, Keeper of the
National Museum of Antiquities in Edinburgh, but it was six
years before Beveridge could get to the island to examine and
photograph the stone and the mound (plate 31).[13]

The Pictish symbol stone, Pabbay (from Anderson, 1897)

Wedderspoon described other signs of early occupation between the mound and the beach, revealed a few years before
when the inhabitants stripped off turf to burn as fuel (after
the peat ran out) and a depth of 6 feet (2 metres) of sand was
blown away These included 'small detached middens, each
with a broken down ring of stones bearing marks of fire', and
human and animal bone, teeth, hammerstones, and pottery.
The pin he was shown had been found here, and he was told
that 'many old things had been got and sold to Jew pedlars
at Castlebay'. An earlier episode of sand-blow was described
by Carmichael in 1870. The area inland from the beach was

> formerly covered with bent [marram] and other
> grasses but the surface breaks caused by the winter
> storms have been inattended to of late. The winter
> winds have swept away the sand to a great depth
> leaving studded over the valley high cone-like
> mounds. Cladh Chriost [the graveyard] is one of
> these mounds. It is about thirty feet high and com-
> posed of successive and distinctive layers of sand.[14]

Much of this area was subsequently covered by sand dunes, which have since been colonised and stabilised by vegetation. The dunes may have developed as a result of the stripping of the turf; there are no dunes in Beveridge's 1895 photographs of the symbol stone and the mound.[15]

The mound is also the traditional site of a medieval chapel. The remains of the stone-and-lime walls of a chapel were recorded by the Royal Commissioners in 1915 on the mound, measuring 31 x 14 feet (9.4 x 4.2 metres).[16] Although there are traces of what may be walling on the mound, it is not clear what they saw, and no building of these dimensions could fit on the summit as it is today. The casual nature of some of their work in the islands casts doubt on its reliability. However, it is likely that the mound has changed over the centuries and was once larger. The cross-incised slabs on its southern flank, however, seem to be in their original position. The dedication of the chapel is unknown, although Carmichael records the name of the graveyard as Cladh Chriost, Christ's Graveyard. Another cross-incised stone has been identified in a dyke near the sheep fank.[17]

Another clue to Pabbay's early inhabitants is provided by its name. Its Gaelic name, Pabaigh, derives from the Old Norse Papa-ey, 'Hermit's Isle', or 'Priest's Isle', a reference to the inhabitants of the island at the time of the Norse settlement of the Hebrides, which began in the ninth century. It is one of several Pabbays in the Hebrides, but the only one where physical remains from this period are known. Small monastic communities on isolated islands were common in Early Christian times, often associated with a 'mother' church, which in Pabbay's case may have been Cille Bharra in Barra. The hermitage, with chapel, if any, may have been on the mound. Remains of a conjoined pair of small round huts on a coastal shelf above the southwest coast may be the remains of another such eremitical community.[18] It is comparable to such a site on Canna, Sgurr Ban nan Naoimh. Taken together with the pins, the memorial stones and the symbol stone, all this evidence suggests that Pabbay was a very significant place in early medieval times. The importance of the mound and its monuments has been recognised by its being scheduled under the Ancient Monuments Act, the protected area including the adjacent recent settlement.

As on Mingulay many of the place names of Pabbay are Norse in origin, and indicate an intimate knowledge of the island by Norse speakers, who almost certainly inhabited it.

Carmichael collected a very interesting object from Pabbay. It is termed a 'font stone' being a stone with one surface hollowed out to form a basin or font. It is made from a lozenge-shaped local stone, with one end wider than the other. It is 51cm (20 inches) long, and the font is 6cm (2⅓ inches) deep. Carmichael wrote of it:

> Embedded in the grassy sandy summit of this disused and neglected burying ground, this simple font rested for ages. But having been lost to sight of late, a search was made for it two years ago, at my request which resulted in finding it in the bed of the stream beneath. This font was for centuries an object of credulous belief to the inhabitants of Pabbay and the other southern Isles of Barra. These simple people implicitly believed that the touch of this font like that of another stone in St. Mary's burying ground (Cladh Naomh Moire) in the neighbouring island of Berneray (Barra-Head) was efficacious in preventing and removing many mental and physical disorders incident to themselves and their flocks. The lixivium [mixture of sea spray and rain water] found in the font was considered doubly consecrated, firstly through contact with the already consecrated font, and secondly through the friendly agency of some invisible and mysterious power that presided over the scene. The virtues of this salinated water were deemed secondary only to those of the water consecrated by the priest.

The people rubbed their bodies and their cattle with the font and sprinkled themselves and their flocks with the water contained therein, for the cure of certain bodily ailments and for the prevention of specific acts of witchcraft. And when this ceremony was duly performed with the necessary amount of formality and with the necessary admixture of pagan and christian rites, the people firmly believed that creative spirits of the air, nor the witches of the earth, nor the mermaids of the deep surrounding sea could infuse or molest them.

For a number of years past the belief in the virtues of this charm has been falling into abeyance and now only two old men as far as I know can give an intelligible account of the faded glories of the primitive little font.[19]

The way this stone was used and regarded is reminiscent of the 'sort of stone with which the natives frequently rub their breasts by way of prevention' which Martin Martin mentioned in 1695 (chapter 9); since his account of the three southern islands is very muddled, it is equally possible that he was referring to this one as to the Berneray or Mingulay stones. Carmichael donated the stone to the National Museum of Antiquities in Edinburgh in 1870. It was wrongly recorded as being from Pabbay near Harris and this error has only recently been corrected.

Pabbay was inhabited, and had a chapel, in Monro's time, 1549. There are few subsequent references, and no visitors' accounts are known until Wedderspoon's in 1912. Martin Martin's comment of 1695 is hardly worth repeating: 'The Natives observe, that if six Sheep are put a-grazing in the little Island Pabbay, five of them still appear fat, but the sixth a poor Skeleton.' This is more likely to refer to one of the small islands or stacks off Mingulay. In 1764 Pabbay had sixteen inhabitants (paying a total of £5 rent), and in 1794, three families.[20] These figures remained similar right up until the island's desertion in 1911 or 1912, although the families did not remain constant. In 1810 there were three tenants: two John MacNeils and a Rory MacNeil, each paying £5 10s rent.[21] At least seven people emigrated to Canada between 1818 and 1828, and there may have been others. There was also immigration: as seen in the last chapter, Eoin MacNeil came from Berneray. In about 1835 the inhabitants of all the southern isles were evicted, as described in chapter 4. In 1836 there were two tenants, Neil MacNeil (who arrived from Greian in Barra at about that time) and Hector MacPhee, each paying £10. By 1845 there were three crofts, and in 1850, one croft.[22] At the time of the 1841 census there were twenty-five people, the maximum recorded, in three families, those of Hector MacPhee, tailor, John MacPhee, crofter, and Neil MacNeil, fisherman. The latter two featured in news-paper articles in 1847 for rather different reasons. MacNeil is listed as a donor to a fund for the 'Relief of Destitution in the Highlands and Islands' at the time of the potato famine.[23] He must have been doing alright, for he gave five shillings, and was the only donor in the islands south of Vatersay, apart from two lighthouse keepers at Barra Head. MacPhee, together with two other Pabbay residents, Angus MacNeil and Donald MacPherson, were imprisoned in Inverness, charged with theft from the *Helena* of Sonderburg (see chapter 4). In 1851 only Neil MacNeil, tenant, remained, now joined by the family of his daughter Flora, married to John MacLean of Mingulay.

By the time of the 1861 census the population had com-pletely changed – the island had been taken over by people from South Uist, the families of Donald Morrison, his son Alexander and his daughter Marion, married to John MacCormick. No one knows exactly why this happened. The Uist families had crofts at the south end of South Uist, but how they ended up in Pabbay is not known. It is hard to believe that they would have actually chosen to settle there, so far from home, where they would have had to depend on boats and fishing which they were not used to. The single holding remained a croft, Donald Morrison being the tenant, and the small increase in rent, from £16 to £18, was not necessarily related to the change in tenants. £16 was a very high rent for one croft in the islands at the time, so perhaps Neil MacNeil left for that reason. Whatever happened, the MacNeils and MacLeans left, the MacLeans settling in Mingulay. What is more certain is the date of the change. MacNeil was still tenant in 1856, and in April 1858 Flora MacLean gave birth to a daughter, Margaret, there. Alexander Morrison's family had arrived by May 1859, when his son Ronald was born there, and a year later Donald MacCormick, whose parents had married in South Uist in 1858, was born. The foreigners, as they would have been regarded, and felt themselves to be, were subsequently joined by cottar families from Berneray (Donald Sinclair) and Mingulay; three of the Uist women married Mingulay men and stayed in Pabbay. The Morrisons remained in Pabbay, but John MacCormick's family left for Barra in the 1880s.

The incomers are known today for their activities as illicit whisky distillers. They set up their still in Sloc Glansich, a precipitous inlet on the northwest coast, which the customs and excise men knew about but never found. Could this be a reason why they came to Pabbay? The whisky found a ready market in neighbouring islands. This was not the first still there, for tradition has it that an Irishman named Glancy, after whom the inlet was named, was engaged in similar business; the officers of the Ordnance Survey may not have got the whole story when they were told that Glancy had fallen over a cliff and drowned.[24] Another illicit activity the Uist men engaged in was concealing twenty-one timbers that had washed up on the beach. Donald and Alexander Morrison and John MacCormick were accused of burying in the sand timbers from the *Harmony*, which had been wrecked on the south coast of Vatersay in 1866. The men claimed that the timbers were not wreck (and therefore the property of the

Board of Trade) but the property of the man who had purchased the cargo of the *Harmony*. At their trial in 1869 the
Morrisons were fined £5 each and MacCormick, 10s.[25]

The people, natives and incomers alike, lived by crofting
and fishing. There was good land on the east of the island,
and the central valley was also cultivated. There were ten
acres of arable in 1891,[26] a surprisingly large area, perhaps big
enough to produce a surplus. From 1850 there was only one
croft, which meant that the single tenant had the whole of the
island as grazing except for the cultivated area. Considering
this, it is surprising that the grazing included the small island
of Outer Heisker, 2 kilometres (1¼ miles) into the Atlantic.[27]
The tenant, before and after 1859, seems to have sublet some
of his land and received income for it.[28] In 1856 the island
had one pony, one cow, and six sheep.[29] In 1883 it had one
pony, forty-six cattle – mostly calves, bred for sale – and thirty-seven sheep,[30] a huge increase in cattle and sheep, perhaps
explained by the fact that there were now four families rather
than one as in 1856. In 1820 tallow was being produced and
sold, as on the other islands.[31]

Pabbay provided some peat – one peat stack platform has
been identified[32] – but not enough: the people also cut peat on
the small island of Lingay to the north. At one time a pony was
kept there all year round to carry the peat cut inland to the
landing place.[33] The islanders also stripped turf for fuel near
their own houses, with, as seen above, devastating results.

Fishing was an important part of the economy of Pabbay, and
landing conditions were better than on Mingulay. One landing
place was at Steir, an inlet on the north side of the narrow neck
joining Rosinish to the main island. Another landing place, the
one used today, is a creek in the rocks at the south side of the
bay; boats were beached. In 1888 the islanders had a large
herring fishing boat, presumably kept at Castlebay, and three
smaller boats used for lobster fishing and line fishing.[34] The
herring boat is not recorded again, and numbers of the smaller
boats vary between one and three until 1897. On May Day of

that year disaster struck the community; their only boat was lost in a storm and its crew of five drowned.

Donald MacPhee of Mingulay (Dòmhnall Bàn, later, in Barra, known as Dòmhnall Bàn Eileanach) told the story of the disaster which had been foreseen by a Mingulay girl long before, to Seton Gordon fifty-three years later. He and the Pabbay men were lifting their fishing lines in the area known as Cuan a' Bhòcain, 'Sea of the Ghosts', about 8 kilometres (5 miles) south of Barra Head, when a southeasterly gale blew up, turning the sea wild. The boats made for home, but the Pabbay boat was never seen again.

> When they had fought their way to the neighbour-hood of Barra Head they reached, said Donald Mor, the abode of two great and terrible giants. These giants lived in the air currents which the gale for a time imprisoned in two high ravines, Sloc na Beiste (Ravine of the Monster), Berneray, and Sloc Dubh an Dùin (Black Ravine of the Fort), Mingulay. The wind currents, which for a time were held prisoner in the ravines, burst out from them with extraordinary violence, and contended with each other with extreme ferocity above the sound between Barra Head and Mingulay . . . by this time the wind had veered to the south-south-west, bringing in the full might of the Atlantic waves and making the task of the Pabbay boat still more formidable . . . their one chance was to have sailed across the Minch to Skye; Donald Mor Eileanach believes that the boat filled when attempting to reach Pabbay.[35]

Four of the five crew were from Pabbay: the brothers Ranald and Alexander Morrison (mic Alasdair Dhòmhnaill), Donald MacNeil (Dòmhnall Choinnich Mhìcheil, originally from Mingulay), and Ronald Campbell (Raghnall Iain Dhòmhnaill). The fifth was a visiting Barra man, John Gillies, whose sister, Catherine, was married to Alexander Morrison. Gillies is said to have been against going out that day. The boat was the *Lizzie*, owned by Alexander Morrison. The loss of the boat and of four breadwinners was a disaster for the community from which it never recovered fully. But it was not defeated; the people remained and, although Pabbay disappears from the fishing records, they must have had a boat and carried on fishing, as life would have been impossible otherwise. It is said that the disaster was seen by some as an act of God – a punishment for the islanders' whisky distilling activities. One of the bodies, that of John Gilles, was washed ashore on the coast of Ireland. He was identified as being from Barra by the design of his jersey.

Some curing of fish was done on the island. Near the south-western corner of the bay a large concrete 'box' sits on the rocks. This was used for storing salt used in the curing process, and the flat rocks in the area were used for laying out the fish.[36]

Pabbay's cliffs are not inhabited by seabirds in the breeding season, and so that resource was not available to the islanders. However, in 1820 Pabbay men were selling feathers, which they presumably got from Mingulay or Berneray. One huge consignment of 109 pounds (49 kilos) of feathers was sold in Greenock.[37] Later, in the 1880s, Pabbay men sailed to the stack of Liànamuil, off Mingulay, and could take 2,000 guillemots in a day, at a time when few Mingulay men were still fowling.[38]

The islanders' houses were huddled together in a sheltered spot near the stream which runs into the bay.[39] The surviving buildings, of the traditional thatched type, were joined together in a single complex. They are poorly preserved, largely because they were turned into a sheep pen and dip after the people left. Nearby is the shell of a fine gabled house of modern type, built of dressed stone and mortar with chimneys and windows. It was built in 1890–1 for Ranald Morrison, by Malcolm MacAulay of Castlebay, (the boatman for the Barra Head lighthouse).[40] He charged the princely sum of ten pounds five shillings and sixpence (£10.27.5p, equivalent to about £922 today), which included gunpowder to assist in the quarrying of the stone. Ranald Morrison drowned in the 1897 disaster. According to tradition, before the tragedy, noises like the surging of the sea were heard in the house. Although the noises stopped afterwards, Ranald's widow Ann moved out and Mary Ann MacNeil (MacCormick, also widowed in 1897) and her family moved in. After the island was deserted, fishermen from Vatersay sometimes used the house as a base while fishing and they too heard the strange noises. They called it Taigh nam Bochdan, the house of ghosts. The roof collapsed in a storm in 1939. Vatersay fishermen took the timbers and slates to Vatersay to be used for building byres, but they wouldn't use the materials in their houses for fear that the ghosts of Pabbay would follow them!

The lack of educational opportunities was a drawback to living in Pabbay, at least in the later decades when education became compulsory, and had been available in Mingulay since 1859. One of the families, that of Alexander Morrison, had a tutor living with them in 1871, a lad of fourteen from Barra. The children of John Campbell (Iain Dhòmhnaill) later attended the school in Mingulay, where they lived with his brother Roderick.

Visits from the priest were probably even less frequent than in Mingulay's case. In 1820 Lachlan MacNeil was paying an annual amount for seats in the church at Craigstone in Barra.[41]

The disaster of 1897 sounded the death-knell for the community, although some of the people stayed for another fourteen years. In 1901 the population was eleven, only two fewer than ten years previously, in three families; but the islanders must have known there was no future there, and when their neighbours in Mingulay began to leave, they joined them. In July 1907 John and Matilda Campbell, their son Donald and daughter Anne abandoned their home for Vatersay.[42] In 1910 nineteen year-old Kenneth MacNeil, left fatherless in 1897, applied (through the Castlebay priest, Hugh Cameron) for a croft in Vatersay.[43] The following April (1911) he and his sister were still in Pabbay, as was Annie Morrison, the tenant, widowed in 1897, with her three children and her brother-in-law.[44] Mrs Morrison was still there in November, and owed a lot of rent, despite being said to be well off and having a large stock.[45] They had all left for Vatersay by the following summer, 1912. Johnathan MacLean, the grazier, became tenant of some of Pabbay in 1911, and the following year rented the whole island.

Wedderspoon's visit, which he wrote about in 1912, probably took place in 1911 or in the preceding few years, at the time when the people were leaving. He wrote that he was 'accompanied by several officials, who intended to visit both Mingulay and Pabbay'. These may have been officials of the Congested Districts Board. He was himself an official, being 'Sanitary Inspector of the County', although he doesn't reveal whether he found time to undertake professional duties as well as to indulge his antiquarian interests.

Pabbay continued to be used for grazing for the rest of the twentieth century, and it has had the same owners as Mingulay and Berneray. It was rarely visited, but since 1998, when a BBC television programme about rock climbing on the cliffs was broadcast, it has been a popular location for climbers in the summer months.[46] In 2003 the National Trust for Scotland consolidated the ruin of the Morrison house, and in 2008 the Trust set the Pictish symbol stone in a concrete base after it was found to have been moved, perhaps in an attempt to steal it. The sheep were taken off in 2007.

Each of these three Barra isles has its own story to tell, but together they are representative of the group as a whole, and in a wider sense they illustrate many themes in the archaeology, history, economy, culture and society of the Highlands and Islands. They were inhabited over a period of around 5,000 years; but their physical nature, and the social and economic changes which led to their desertion, make it certain that they will never again be inhabited – by people living largely off their natural resources, at any rate.

Notes and References

Abbreviations

CEBB	Comunn Eachdraidh Bharraigh agus Bhatarsaigh
EUL	Edinburgh University Library
NLS	National Library of Scotland
NRS	National Records of Scotland
NTSA	National Trust for Scotland Archives
NTSCHA	National Trust for Scotland Canna House Archives
PP	Parliamentary Papers
RCAHMS	Royal Commission on the Ancient and Historical Monuments of Scotland
RMS	Royal Museum of Scotland
SAU	St Andrews University
SCR	Scots' College, Rome
SSS	School of Scottish Studies
SUEA	South Uist Estates Archive
TES	Tasglann nan Eilean Siar

Chapter 1: 'The Nearer St Kilda'

1. PP XXXIII, 1847–8, 65
2. Nicolson in J.L. Campbell (ed.) 1936, 191
3. NRS: RHP 44187. Harvie-Brown said that white-tailed eagles bred there until c.1850.
4. NRS: RH4/23/106
5. Carmichael 1884, 456
6. Campbell 2000, 110–12. The location of the leap is shown incorrectly on the map.
7. Dunn and Grant 2015
8. Boyd and Boyd 1990, 208
9. DEFRA
10. NRS: HH62/14
11. Gearuim Mòr was also known as Horse Island (NRS: RHP 44187) and Sinclair's Rock (T. Walker 1870). Wave incident

was recorded by Elwes (1869) and T. Walker. Rock incident: Geikie 1865

12. geology: Jehu and Craig 1925; Robertson 1964; Pleistocene geology: Gilbertson et al 1996, 64–9
13. botany: Ball 1976; NE Buxton 1987; Cheke and Reed 1987; Clark 1938
14. Pankhurst and Mullin 1991, 170
15. Ratcliffe 1977, I, 64; II, 43; Boyd and Boyd 1990, 208, 374–6
16. Harman 1997
17. MacGregor 1967, 161–2
18. RMS: Scottish Ethnological Archive. Adam photographs: SAU. Norrie also took 'Life on Mingulay', which has not been located (RMS: Norrie letter).
19. J.L. Campbell and Hall 1968
20. Buxton 1991

Chapter 2: Early Times

1. EUL: CW362 (letter to Capt. Thomas)
2. Branigan and Foster 2000; RCAHMS 2010 & Canmore; Hale 2004
3. Branigan and Foster 2000 & 2002
4. Branigan and Foster 2000,126
5. Ball 1976; Buxton 1981
6. RCAHMS Canmore site NL58SE 132; Branigan and Foster 2000, 98 (MY33)
7. RCAHMS Canmore site NL58SE 22; Branigan and Foster 2000, 119–20 (MY345)
8. RCAHMS Canmore site NL58SE 120; Branigan and Foster 2000, 120, 307–8 (MY346)
9. RCAHMS Canmore site NL58SE 115; Branigan and Foster 2000, 118–9 (MY344); sheep pen: personal information from John MacNeil (Iagan an Dollaich), former shepherd
10. RCAHMS 2010 & Canmore
11. Branigan and Foster 2000, 121–2, 291–306 (MY384); Branigan and Foster 2002, 87; RCAHMS Canmore site NL58SE 6; Buxton 1981. Possible EBA pottery identified in the excavated assemblage: A. Hale, personal information
12. EUL: CW114/70
13. NTSCHA: A. McDonald's diary, 15.6.1898
14. RCAHMS 1928, 134; RCAHMS 2010; RCAHMS Canmore site NL58SE 1; Branigan and Foster 2000, 126
15. Buxton 2008, 14
16. RCAHMS 1928, 137; Wedderspoon 1912, 331–2; see chapter 15

17. Macquarrie 1989, 8
18. NRS: RH4/23/106. Monro may not be reliable: he said that the tiny islands of Flodday, Lingay, and Greanamul had chapels, but no traces or traditions survive.
19. Buxton 1981; RCAHMS: Canmore site NL58SE 2
20. Buxton 2008, 22
21. Muir 1867, 5; RCAHMS: field notebook 1915; RCAHMS Canmore site NL58SE 1; EUL CW114/52, CW150/34
22. NRS RH4/23/106; NTSCHA: A. McDonald's diary, 15.6.1898
23. Macquarrie 1989, 12
24. Borgstrom 1936; Macquarrie 1989; Stahl 1999; Ian Fraser, Ian MacDonald, Anke-Beate Stahl, Barbara Crawford, personal information
25. Anon 1620 in J.L. Campbell (ed.) 1936, 44
26. Ordnance Survey maps; NRS RH4/23/106; A. McDonald 1903, and unpublished notebook (270 names); RMS: John Finlayson letter, 9.3.1892; SSS PN 1976/9; NRS: RHP 44187; EUL: CW114/38, CW150/32
27. Borgstrom (1936) believed the suffix *sdale* in Barra to be derived from Old Norse *stödhull*, 'milking place', which is a likely use of Skipisdale.
28. A. McDonald 1903, 433. Map NTSCHA CH2/3/52 (partially reproduced in J.L. Campbell 2000, 112) and J.L.C.'s placename list of 1931 (see J.L. Campbell 2000, 108) names the stream in the valley Abhainn Sumhsabaist. For derivation of the various forms of the name I am grateful to Dr A. Stahl and Dr B. Crawford (quoting P. Gameltoft). Carmichael: EUL: CW150/31
29. SSS: SA76/175, translation by Mary Kate MacKinnon
30. RCAHMS 2010; RCAHMS Canmore site NL58SE 143; Branigan and Foster 2002, 124–5. Bowen's 1776 map marks buildings only at Mingulay Bay
31. EUL: CW114/72
32. Branigan and Foster 2000, 99 (MY35); RCAHMS 2010 & Canmore sites NL58SE 21
33. Buxton 1981; RCAHMS Canmore site NL58SE 13
34. Branigan and Foster 2000, 97 (MY5)
35. RCAHMS 2010, RCAHMS Canmore site NL58SE 24
36. RCAHMS Canmore site NL58SE 143

Chapter 3: The People and their Culture

1. J.L. Campbell and Eastwick 1966, 90
2. NRS: AF56/225
3. NRS: 1851 census and Cuithir register; other details from NRS: RH21/50; J.L. Campbell 2000, 115–118

4. *Carmina Gadelica* III, 4
5. McKay 1980, 85
6. MacQueen in J.L. Campbell (ed.) 1936, 69
7. NRS: SC29/75/3 (21.5.1873); Jolly 1883; Murray 1888; the petition of 1896 (NRS: AF56/225), which may have been deliberately exaggerated
8. NRS: AF56/225, AF42/1580
9. NRS: 1891 census; see chapter 15
10. C. MacNeil 1988, 40
11. SSS SA 1960/100 A2
12. SSS SA 1960/95 B7
13. SSS SA 1960/95 B4
14. SSS SA 1960/94 B1
15. SSS SA 1960/95 B6
16. SSS SA 1960/100 A5
17. Johnson 1775 (1924 edition, 115)
18. PP XXV 1867, 43
19. SSS SA 1960/95 B3
20. J.F. Campbell 1862,1, iv
21. NLS Adv. MS 50 2 1, f 226–7
22. NLS Adv. MS 50 4 6, f 120
23. Wiseman 2011
24. *Carmina Gadelica* II, 352
25. EUL: CW114/32; translation by A. Wiseman in Wiseman 2011
26. *Carmina Gadelica* I, xxiv
27. NLS Adv. MS 50 4 6, f 120
28. Storey 2007, 75
29. MacGregor 1934, 79–81 (fairy music given)
30. SSS SA 1960/100 All
31. MacGregor 1929, 235–6
32. SSS SA 1960/96 A6
33. SSS SA 1960/100 A5
34. J.L. Campbell and Collinson 1981, 5
35. SCR: N. MacDonald letter 12.1.1830
36. A. McDonald 1958, 9
37. Christine Johnson, personal information
38. Roberton Publications, personal information; Cooper 1985, 2, 211

Chapter 4: Chiefs, Landlords, Tenants

1. *Tocher* 38,1983, 5
2. EUL: CW114/34
3. Goodrich-Freer 1902, 398
4. NRS: CH3/1428/20 (1868)

5. *Collectanea de Rebus Albanicis* 1839, 4
6. J.L. Campbell 1954, 37
7. J.L. Campbell (ed.) 1936, 43
8. Carmichael 1884, 456
9. McKay 1980, 85
10. EUL: CW114/72
11. Ibid; Storey 2007, 90–92
12. Branigan 2010
13. J.L. Campbell (ed.) 1936, 151–188
14. McKay 1980, 87
15. MacCulloch in J.L. Campbell (ed.) 1936, 108; J.L. Campbell (ed.) 1936,152–3,167; for runrig in Barra see Carmichael 1884 and Branigan and Foster 2002, 124–5
16. Branigan 2010, 76–7, 81
17. Ibid., 91; Branigan 2005, 145; J.L. Campbell (ed.) 1936, 177; J.L. Campbell 2000, 118
18. MacQueen in J.L. Campbell (ed.) 1936, 69
19. NRS: CS44/B446, CS46/4274 (rental 1836–7)
20. *Carmina Gadelica* III, 111. This quote has been erroneously interpreted as evidence of eviction *from* Mingulay; see J. Prebble, *The Highland Clearances,* 1963
21. J.L. Campbell 1990, 73 (SCR: N. MacDonald letter 4.3.1831)
22. Branigan 2005, Appendix 2 (records cover 1772–1851); J.L. Campbell 1990, 72; MacKenzie 1983; S.R. MacNeil 1979
23. SSS: SA 1960/89
24. Branigan 2005, 141ff; Branigan 2010, 84ff ; NRS CS96/4274 (letter 17.11.1836)
25. NLS: 10706/93, 279
26. NRS: NLC2/1/5, 55
27. NLS: 10706/93, 357
28. NLS: 10706/94 (1837 & 1838 reports); NRS CS96/4274 (letter re factory not operating). On 28.6.1835 two children of (separate) Berneray parents were baptised by the priest. Locations of baptisms are not given, but on the same date four children of separate Barra parents were baptised so these must have taken place at the church in Barra (NRS: RH21/50/1). This does not imply that the Berneray families were living in Barra; they could have travelled from Berneray.
29. Branigan 2010, 90
30. Buxton 2008, 36–38
31. EUL: CW150/31. Nan MacKinnon said that Mingulay was re-let to enterprising people from Tangusdale
32. Branigan 2005, 148; Branigan 2010, 104–106
33. PP 1847 LIII, 190–2
34. J.L. Campbell (ed.) 1936, 219–226; Richards 1982, 402–418

35. PP 1847 LIII, 297
36. NRS: RHP 44187
37. NRS NLC2/1/25, 53
38. PP 1895 XXXIX(i), 931
39. J.L. Campbell (ed.) 1936, 231; PP 1884 XXXIII, 655
40. RMS: letter 4.10.1888
41. PP 1884 XXXIII, 695
42. PP 1895 XXXIX(i), 927 (Glen and quote); Storrie 1962 (Garrygall)
43. NRS: AF50/7/5, VR103
44. NRS: LC15/2/13
45. RMS: letter 27.2.1897
46. *Aberdeen Journal* 25.9.1891
47. RMS: letter 27.2.1897
48. PP 1906 CIV, xvii
49. RMS: letter 26.7.1889

Chapter 5: A Living from the Land

1. NRS: LC15/528, partially reproduced in PP 1892 LXIV; conflicts with less detailed figures in NRS: AF50/7/5 and LC15/2/13. No map of individual crofts has been located.
2. NRS: VR103; croft division in Barra: PP 1844 XXI, 363
3. NRS: CS46/4274; PP 1895 XXXIX, 931
4. CEBB: estate document
5. NRS: AF50/7/5
6. NRS: LC15/2/13
7. Hunter 1976
8. SSS SA 1960/99 Al
9. PP 1908 LXXXVIII, 34
10. SSS SA 1960/92 A3
11. J.L. Campbell 2000; see also I.F. Grant 1961
12. SSS SA 1960/99 A6
13. SSS SA 1960/99 A1
14. details of crops, planting, harvesting, in SSS SA 1960/92, /95, /99, /100; see also I.F. Grant 1961
15. many refs, e.g. C. MacNeil 1992, MacGregor 1929
16. E. Sinclair said 'everyone or every other household' (SSS SA 1960/97 A2) had one, M. Campbell said every crofter (SA 1960/99 A2). Only three crofters mentioned having barns in 1887 (NRS: LC15/2/13).
17. details of winnowing and drying in SSS SA 1960/95, /99. C. MacNeil said husks were loosened with a spade before winnowing (SA 1960/95 A4).
18. Mitchell 1880

19. PP 1884, XXXIII, 663
20. SSS SA 1960/99 A2
21. Nan MacKinnon, personal information
22. RCAHMS 2010, and Canmore site no. NL58SE 134; Geddes 2013
23. details in NRS: LCI5/2/13; stock numbers in NRS: AF50/7/5
24. Anon in J.L. Campbell (ed) 1936, 44
25. NRS: RH21/50/4
26. F. Shaw 1980
27. MacQueen in J.L. Campbell (ed.) 1936, 80
28. CEBB: estate document
29. NRS: AF50/7/5
30. SSS SA 1960/95 A1
31. TES: school logbook, e.g. 1905
32. CEBB: estate document
33. NRS: AF50/7/5
34. SSS SA 1960/95, 99
35. SSS SA 1960/99 A1
36. CEBB: estate document
37. NRS: AF50/7/5
38. NRS: LC15/2/13
39. Harman 1997
40. Report on ponies in Highlands and Islands NRS: AF42/3213; J.M. MacDonald 1937, 45–9
41. RMS: letter 24.8.1899
42. peat cutting: SSS SA 1960/97 Al, /99 A5, A8; creels, SA 1960/92 A2, A4
43. Hale 2004; Branigan & Foster 2000, 124–5; RCAHMS: Canmore
44. EUL: CW114/32

Chapter 6: Fishing and the Sea

1. These and other statistical details from NRS: AF17/156, /157; other details from SSS SA 1960/92, /95, /96, /99
2. NRS: AF56/225 (reproduced in Storey 2007, 162–5)
3. PP 1884 XXXIII, 673
4. F. Shaw 1980
5. PP 1847 LI11, 190
6. Wiseman 2014
7. RMS: letter 24.8.1899
8. Tocher 20, 159
9. dogfish oil: John Finlayson letter, undated (RMS)
10. PP 1884 XXXIII, 673
11. Scottish Fishermen's Nautical Almanack 1903

12. NRS: HH62/19 (1900)
13. Buxton 2008, 63–4
14. *Caledonian Mercury* 27.7.1820; NRS: RH21/50/4
15 *Scottish Fishermen's Nautical Almanack* 1903
16. MacGregor 1971, 144
17. *Tocher* 20, 157
18. NRS: register of deaths
19. Carmichael 1884, 458
20. NRS: AF17/157
21. Hunter 1976, 171
22. description of beach landings and launchings in Lewis in D. MacDonald 1978, 94
23. MacGregor 1967, 163
24. B. Buxton l981; Branigan & Foster 2000, 125; RCAHMS Canmore site NL58SE 14
25. NRS: register of births 6.8.1907 (informant); AF67/137 (police report 14.7.1908); NLC3/1/2; see chapter 15
26. SSS SA 1960/95 A2
27. NRS: HH62/14 (1897)
28. PP 1890 XXVII, 14
29. details of derrick in NRS: AF42/146, /833, /1580
30. as his photographs show (SAU nos. 76 & 156)
31. NRS: AF42/5369 (report on Mingulay)
32. PP 1906 CVII

Chapter 7: Catching the 'Feathered Tribes'

1. NRS CH3/1428/20, 1868
2. NRS: RH21/50/4
3. Nicolson in J.L. Campbell (ed.) 1936, 195
4. RMS: letter 27.4.1903
5. Baldwin 1974
6. from SSS SA 1960/99 B8, and personally from Lisa Storey, unless otherwise indicated
7. Harvie-Brown and Buckley 1888, 162
8. RMS: letter 27.2.1897; another Finlayson quote in Storey 2007, 16
9. *Carmina Gadelica* II, 364
10. Gordon 1937, 127
11. names also in Elwes 1869
12. descriptions in Harvie-Brown and Buckley 1888, 163; Bird 1866; Elwes 1869; Walker 1870; SSS SA 1960/96 A5, /99 B6
13. Baldwin 1974
14. Harvie-Brown and Buckley 1888, lxxxiii
15. Ibid., 162

16. SSS SA 1960/92 Al
17. Elwes 1869
18. Harvie-Brown and Buckley 1888, 163; figures also given in EUL: CW150/32
19. Harman 1997
20. SSS SA 1960/99 B8
21. SSS SA 1960/96/B4
22. Gordon 1937, 127
23. RMS: letter 24.8.1899
24. RMS: Harvie-Brown's journal 16.7.1887
25. RMS: letter 27.2.1897
26. Baldwin 1974
27. MacGregor 1967, 162

Chapter 8: The Village: Walls and Work

1. quoted in RCAHMS Canmore site NL58SE 16; see also Buxton 1981; RCAHMS 2010. Buxton called for the scheduling in the first edition of this book
2. NRS: RHP 44187
3. respectively J. MacDonald 1811, 793; PP 1867 XXV 43; Nicolson 1840; descriptions of Barra housing in NRS: HH62/19 (1900), /21 (1901); MacLellan 1961, 207–8
4. roofing details in SSS SA 1960/97 A2. See also EUL: CW114/32
5. from former inhabitants, their descendants and the 1960 tape recordings
6. Historic Scotland 1994, 59
7. NRS: HH62; Sanitary Department of Inverness; Day 1918
8. in 1891: NRS: LC15/2/13
9. Goodrich-Freer 1902, 400; SSS SA 1960/99 A7; Geddes 2013; 1901 census he is living in house with 3 rooms with windows; in 1891, 2
10. NRS: HH62/21 (1901), /33 (1907)
11. details of interior in SSS SA 1960/97
12. SSS SA 1960/97 A7
13. SSS SA 1960/99 A7 (workshop), /95 A3 (clothing)
14. details of food in SSS SA 1960/95, /97
15. MacGregor 1967, 162
16. *Tocher* 38, 19, 21
17. RMS: letter 27.2.1897
18. Weir 1984, quoting Nan MacKinnon
19. SSS SA 1960/97 A9
20. SSS SA 1960/92 B1
21. Buchanan 1942, 156
22. SSS SA 1960/98 A7

23. *Tocher* 38, 7
24. *Carmina Gadelica* IV, 89
25. SSS SA 1960/97 A8
26. Cheape l989
27. *Aberdeen Journal* 6.6.1905

Chapter 9: Sickness and Death

1. NRS: HH62/4 (1892)
2. NRS: HH62/14 (1897)
3. Sanitary Department of Inverness 1893; Day 1918
4. NRS: HH62/19 (1900)
5. NRS: HH62/8 (1894)
6. this and next paragraph: NRS: HH58/6
7. NRS: HH62/14 (1897)
8. NRS: entered in register of births
9. PP 1906 CIV, xix
10. NRS: HH62/19 (1900), 21 (1901)
11. C. MacNeil 1992
12. NRS: HH62/14 (1897)
13. description in Buxton 1981
14. *Aberdeen Journal* 6.6.1905
15. EUL: CW114/54
16. *Tocher* 38, 43–5
17. Ibid., 45

Chapter 10: The Ladies' School

1. for early education in Barra see D. Buchanan 1942, J.L. Campbell (ed.) 1936, J.L. Campbell and Eastwick 1966; Sandray: Buxton 2008, 34–5
2. PP 1867 XXV 46
3. PP 1867 XXV, 90; N. Walker 1895
4. on which much of this chapter is based; dates refer to the reports of those years NRS: CH3/1428/20. The account of the school's origin is confirmed in the NLC records.
5. the most north-easterly building. Muir's sketch shows it to have been on the same site as the Board school in 1878 (OS map), but the map of 1861–3 (NRS: RHP 44187), of uncertain accuracy, shows it as the northernmost building; however, no change of schoolroom is recorded after 1859.
6. EUL: CW114/40
7. Ibid.
8. *Celtic Monthly* 1898. Grandmother: NTSCHA: A. MacDonald's diary 14.6.1897; M. MacDonald 2012c

9. he and his brother Alexander were among students requesting a book of lectures by Rev. J. McLachlan; the certificate issued him for the Board school indicates that he was a non-graduate
10. 'uncle' John Finlayson letter 27.4.1875. Letters of 'uncle' John, who emigrated to Canada in 1832, to Mingulay John's brother Alexander, survive (in private hands)
11. NRS: CH3/1428/20 1871, 32; M. MacDonald 2012a
12. N. Walker 1895
13. *Celtic Monthly* 1898
14. PP 1884 XXXII, 103

Chapter 11: Mingulay Public School

1. PP 1884 XXXII; Day 1918
2. PP 1884 XXXII, 67ff, 96ff; XXXIII, 697; J.L. Campbell in Rea 1964, xivff
3. TES: GB CL IN4/45, the source of most of the information and quotes in this chapter; also NRS: SC29/75/3 and TES: GB CL IN4/1/R.334–5; Powell 2012
4. PP 1884 XXXIII, 697
5. Withers 1984
6. Harden 2011
7. PP 1884 XXVI, 284
8. SUEA: Duplicate Chartulary, 55–61
9. RMS: letter 27.4.1903
10. NTSCHA: A. MacDonald's diary, 14.6.1897; partially quoted in J.L. Campbell 2000 and M. MacDonald 2012c
11. RMS: letter 24.8.1899
12. RMS: letter 3.3.1890
13. RMS: letter 13.8.1904
14. Chaimbeul 1982, 46; translation by Roderick MacNeil
15. J.L. Campbell (ed.) 1960
16. information on Sarah MacShane from Eleanor Hunter
17. SSS SA 1960/98 A5
18. NRS: AF42 8181; Buxton 2008, 157–9
19. *Aberdeen Journal* 6.6.1905
20. SSS SA 1960/100 A10
21. J.L. Campbell (ed.) 1936, 97

Chapter 12: A 'most devout group of Catholics'

1. Giblin 1964, 172–4
2. J.L. Campbell (ed.) 1936, 10
3. Ibid.
4. Blundell 1917, 10

5. Ibid., 18; Macquarrie 1989, 25
6. NRS: RH21/50, various dates in registers of baptisms
7. NRS: RH21/50/2
8. NRS: RH21/50/4
9. *Catholic Directory*
10. Blundell 1917, 21
11. SSS SA 1960/95 B2
12. SSS SA 1960/98 A6
13. Geddes 2012 & 2013; RCAHMS Canmore site NL58SE 7
14. SUEA: Duplicate Chartulary 1
15. R. MacDonald 1978; M. MacDonald 2012
16. Chisholm: Buchanan 1942, 99; Glancy: RMS: John Finlayson letter 24.8.1899. Glancy died in 1898
17. NTSCHA: A. McDonald's diary
18. J.L. Campbell & Hall 1968
19. these stories are not in McDonald's collection
20. *Catholic Directory* 1909, 1910
21. EUL: CW114/54

Chapter 13: The 'Impossible Place'

1. RMS: letter 7.4.1905
2. SSS SA 1960/96 B3
3. PP 1908 LXXXVIII, 34
4. NRS: AF42/146 (Fr J. Chisholm letter)
5. *Tocher* 38, 6
6. Buxton 2008, 41–3
7. PP 1895 XXXVIII, 28; XXXIX(ii), map 58
8. PP 1908 LXXXVIII, 35
9. PP 1895 XXXIX 932
10. Buxton 2008, 77
11. *Glasgow Herald* 19.2.1908
12. NRS: AF67/134 (police report 30.6.1906)
13. SSS SA 1960/92 B1; NRS: AF67/134; Buxton 2008
14. NRS: AF67/134 (police report 26.2.1907)
15. *Glasgow Herald* 21.1.1908
16. Wiseman 2014
17. PP 1908 LXXXVIII, 34
18. NRS: AF67/137 (police reports 2.1.1908 and later); AF67/135; Buxton 2008, 137ff; Branigan 2005, 62–6; *Glasgow Herald* 18.7.1908
19. NRS: AF42/5380
20. NRS: AF42/5369 (list of August 1908): AF42/5494 (list of November 1908)
21. Buxton 2008, 83–4, 99

22. 1.4.1908
23. Buxton 2008, 1ff, 107ff
24. report and photo in *Edinburgh Evening News* 2.6.1908
25. NRS: AF67/136
26. 19.7.1908
27. 20.7.1908
28. 25.7.1908
29. NRS: AF42/5369
30. Ibid. (report on Mingulay)
31. Ibid., see also letter from John Sinclair AF42/5269
32. NRS: AF42/5494
33. Day 1918, 218; Buxton 2008, 124ff
34. NLS: letter 19.6.1909; see also petition in J.L. Campbell (ed.) 1936, 274
35. Buxton 2008, 136
36. NRS: AF42/8287; Buxton 2008, 138
37. SUEA: letters MacDonald to MacShane and MacKinnon, both 9.12.09; fishing: NRS: AF17/156
38. NRS: AF42/8425
39. NRS: AF42/5369 (report on Vatersay farm, 1908)
40. NRS: VR103
41. NRS: AF42/8425; the April 1911 census recorded five families, each in a separate house
42. NLS: letter 14.8.1911
43. NRS: AF42/8509
44. NRS: AF42/8425
45. NRS: AF17/156
46. NRS: AF42/7198
47. SAU: note on negative 1181,1922
48. SSS SA 1960/92 B1
49. SSS SA 1960/99 B7
50. NRS: AF67/134 (police report 24.5.1907)
51. Hunter 1976, 190; Cameron 1996, 109ff
52. Moisley 1966

Chapter 14: The Deserted Island

1. NRS: 1911 census
2. MacLean advertised in the *Scotsman*. Adam: info in negative register (SAU: no. 1151)
3. SUEA: Duplicate Chartulary 2, 392
4. NTSA DA/9/3/3; Sutherland 1940; M Shaw 1993
5. NTSA DA/9/3/1; the *Scotsman* 5.6.36; MacGregor 1971; Pochin-Mould 1953
6. NTSA DA/9/3/1 letter Bishop Martin 18.6.36

7. MacGregor 1971
8. Thomson 2005: Julie Brook: Ward 2007
9. notes on the Chapel House by D E Baird (in private hands); RCAHMS Canmore site NL58SE 7
10. *The Scotsman* 14.4.2000
11. *Guth Bharraigh* 31.7.2009
12. *Scotland in Trust,* Spring 2013
13. Buxton 2008, 177

Chapter 15: Berneray

1. Foster and Krivanek 1993; Branigan and Foster 2000
2. RCAHMS Canmore site NL58SE 32
3. MacPherson 1768, 321; MacQueen, 1794, in J.L. Campbell (ed) 1936, 76; Stevenson, 1830: NLS: 10706/223; Bird 1866, 650; Carmichael, 1867, EUL: CW114/28, CW362; Anderson 1893; RCAHMS 1928, 132–3; Branigan and Foster 2000, 133–4; MacKie 2007; RCAHMS Canmore site NL58SW 4
4. NRS: RH4/23/106
5. RCAHMS Canmore site NL58SW 3; RCAHMS 1928, 133. NRS: RHP 44187; Branigan and Foster 2000, 132–3
6. Foster and Krivanek 1993, 427 (site plan); RCAHMS 1928, 137; NRS: RH4/23/106
7. EUL: CW114/75
8. EUL: CW114/54 and 114/37
9. MacQueen in J.L. Campbell (ed.) 1936, 69
10. RCAHMS Canmore site NL58SW 3
11. EUL: CW114/37
12. Foster and Krivanek 1993
13. RCAHMS: C72316
14. EUL: CW114/56
15. MacNeil: SCR: letter 12.1.1830; emigration: Branigan 2005, Appendix 2
16. NRS: NLC2/1/25, 53
17. NRS: CS46/4274
18. MacNeil family & Canon John: J.L. Campbell 2000, 119–20; Alan: NRS: NLC
19. Geddes 2012, 37; NRS: SC29/44/22; MacKinnon nd
20. *Gloucester Echo* 9 May 1905
21. C. MacNeil 1988, 32
22. EUL: CW114/72
23. NLS: 10706/223, 1828; NRS: AF50/7/5
24. MacGregor 1967, 163; SAU: photographs of 1907 visit
25. Foster and Krivanek 1993; RCAHMS Canmore
26. RMS: John Finlayson letter 9.3.1892

27. NRS: AF17/155; *Scottish Fishermen's Nautical Almanack* 1903
28. Wiseman 2014
29. NLS: 10706/223
30. NRS: RHP 44187, Ordnance Survey 1880
31. NRS: SC29/75/3
32. TES: GB CL IN4/45
33. NRS: NLC2/1/78; SUEA: Duplicate Chartulary 1, 197
34. Rea l964, 24
35. NRS: AF67/137 (police report 18.7.1908); NRS: AF42/5367
36. SUEA: letter to Jonathan MacLean 21.1.1910
37. NRS: AF42/6592, AF42/7629; Buxton 2008, 153
38. NRS: AF42/8425 and 1911 census
39. NLS: Acc. 10688; Buxton 2008, 151
40. SUEA: letter, factor to Sinclair 17.8.1912
41. Munro 1979
42. NRS: NLC2/1/4, letters 20.10.1829 & 8.1.1830
43. sources for the following account are NRS: NLC and NLS: Acc 10706; for buildings, cemetery, etc. RCAHMS Canmore
44. *West Highland Free Press* 21.11.1980

Chapter 16: Pabbay

1. Cheke and Reed 1987, 74
2. Ibid., 71
3. Gilbertson et al 1996, 92, 95
4. Branigan and Foster 2000, 2002; for earlier fieldwork see Edwards 1981, RCAHMS 1928
5. Carmichael 1874 (Pabbay, Barra is specified)
6. by the Ordnance Survey, NRS: RH4/23/106, not seen by the excavators, who believed this happened after 1878; the map (OS 1880) appears to show a complete sub-circular structure with another structure within it
7. *Proceedings of the Society of Antiquaries of Scotland* XXXV, 278
8. Papar project, H4; RCAHMS Canmore site NL68NW 2
9. Gilbertson et al 1996, 92
10. EUL: CW/X.BA25 (item)
11. Papar project, H4
12. Ibid.
13. Anderson 1897
14. EUL: CW/X.BA25 (item); cemeteries also in CW150/22
15. photo on p. 279 of Gordon 1950 shows marran-covered sand
16. RCAHMS 1928, 126
17. Papar project, H4
18. Ibid.

19. EUL: CW/X.BA25 (item); Cheape 2008, 130. This is not the only example of confusion between the two Pabbays
20. McKay 1980, 85; MacQueen in J.L. Campbell (ed.) 1936, 69
21. NRS: CS44/B446
22. NRS: CS46/4274; PP 1895 XXXIX(i), 931
23. *Inverness Courier* 18.5.1847
24. NRS: RH4/23/106
25. *John O'Groat Journal* 20.5.1869
26. NRS: LC15/528
27. NRS: LC15/528
28. CEBB: estate document; NRS: AF50/7/5
29. CEBB: estate document
30. NRS: AF50/7/5
31. NRS: RH21/50/4
32. Branigan and Foster 2000, 85
33. John MacNeil (Iagan an Dollaich), former shepherd, personal information
34. NRS: AF17/155
35. Gordon 1950a; see also *Inverness Courier* 11.5.1897
36. John MacNeil (Iagan an Dollaich), former shepherd, personal information
37. NRS: RH21/50/4
38. Harvie-Brown and Buckley 1888, 163
39. Edwards 1981; Branigan and Foster 2000, 86
40. CEBB: account book of Malcolm MacAulay
41. NRS: RH21/50/4
42. NRS: AF67/137 (police report 18.7.1908); AF42/5369
43. NRS: AF42/7688
44. NRS: AF42/8425
45. SUEA: letter John MacDonald to Thomas Wilson 8.11.1911
46. Earle 2010

Bibliography

Publications, unpublished reports and theses

Anderson, Joseph (1893) 'Notice of Dun Stron Duin, Bernera, Barra Head', *Proceedings of the Society of Antiquaries of Scotland* XXVII, 1892–3, 341–6
—— (1897) 'Notices of some recently discovered inscribed and sculptured stones' *Proceedings of the Society of Antiquaries of Scotland* XXXI, 1896–7, 293–308
Anon, c.1620: description of Barra in A. Mitchell (ed.), 1907: *Walter MacFarlane's Geographical Collections Relating to Scotland,* (reproduced in J.L. Campbell (ed.) 1936)
Baldwin, John (1974) 'Seabird fowling in Scotland and Faroe', *Folklife* 12, 1974, 60–103
Ball, Timothy R. (1976) 'An investigation of the soils and vegetation, including fungi, of Mingulay, Outer Hebrides', unpublished BSc dissertation, University of Aberystwyth
Barron, James (1903) *The Northern Highlands in the Nineteenth Century,* Edinburgh (3 vols) (an index to the *Inverness Courier*)
Bird, Miss (1866) 'Pen and pencil sketches among the Outer Hebrides', *Leisure Hour* XV, 1866, 646–50, 668–9 (Berneray)
Blundell, Odo (1917) *The Catholic Highlands of Scotland,* London
Borgstrom, C.H. (1936) 'The Norse place-names of Barra' in J.L. Campbell (ed.) 1936
Bowen, Thomas, (1776) 'The south part of Long Island from Bara Head to Benbecula' (map, by Murdoch MacKenzie)
Boyd, J. M. and Boyd, I. L. (1990) *The Hebrides, a Natural History,* London
Branigan, Keith (2005) *From Clan to Clearance, History and Archaeology on the Isle of Barra c.850–1850 AD,* Oxford
—— (2010) *The Last of the Clan, General Roderick MacNeil of Barra 41st Chief of the Clan MacNeil* Stroud
—— & Foster, Patrick (2000) *From Barra to Berneray, Archaeological Research and Excavation in the Southern Isles of the Outer Hebrides,* Sheffield

—— & Foster, Patrick (2002) *Barra and the Bishop's Isles, Living on the Margin* Stroud

Buchanan, Donald (1942) *Reflections of the Isle of Barra,* London

Buchanan, G. (1582) 'History of Scotland', in P. Hume Brown (1893) *Scotland Before 1700,* 232–5

Buxton, Ben (1975) 'Blackhouses' (Mingulay), Schools Hebridean Society *Annual Report,* 1975

—— (1981) 'The Archaeology of Mingulay Bay, Mingulay, Outer Hebrides', unpublished BA dissertation, Department of Archaeology, University of Durham

—— (1991) 'Museum Provision in Barra, Western Isles', unpublished MA dissertation, Department of Museum Studies, University of Leicester

—— (2006) 'The decline and fall of Mingulay' in Islands Book Trust, 2006 (also published as Islands Book Trust Island Notes no. 22)

—— (2008) *The Vatersay Raiders* Edinburgh (includes the earlier history of Vatersay, and Sandray)

—— (2009) 'Sandray'*Scottish Islands Explorer* May/June 2009

—— (2012) 'An introduction to Mingulay' in Chambers 2012 (includes illustrations of the schools)

Buxton, N.E. (1987) 'Report on the Vegetation of Mingulay' *Royal Air Force Ornithological Society Journal* 17,1987, 64–77

Cameron, Ewen (1996) *Land for the people? The British Government and the Scottish Highlands, c.1889–1925,* Edinburgh

Campbell, J.F. (1862) *Popular Tales of the West Highlands,* Edinburgh (4 vols)

Campbell, J.L. (1954) 'The MacNeils of Barra and the Irish Franciscans' *Innes Review* V, 1954, 33–38

—— (1975) 'Our Barra Years', *Scots Magazine* 1975, 494–503, 613–623

—— (1990) *Songs Remembered in Exile,* Aberdeen (includes historical background to nineteenth-century emigrations from Barra)

—— (2000) *A Very Civil People,* Edinburgh

—— (ed.) 1936: *The Book of Barra,* London (compilation of contemporary accounts, letters etc., with editorials, and chapters on various subjects)

—— (ed) 1960: *Tales from Barra Told by The Coddy,* Edinburgh

—— and Collinson, F. (1981) *Hebridean Folksongs* vol III, Oxford

—— and Eastwick, C. (1966) The MacNeils of Barra in the Forty-five', *Innes Review* XVII 1966, 82–90

—— and Hall, T.H. (1968) *Strange Things,* London

Carmichael, Alexander (1874) 'On a Hypogeum at Valaquie, Island of Uist' *Journal of the Anthropological Institute* III, 1874

—— (1884) 'Grazing and Agrestic Customs of the Outer Hebrides', PP 1884 XXXII, 451–473 (Barra sections partially reproduced in J.L. Campbell (ed.) 1936)

Carmina Gadelica, edited by Alexander Carmichael and others, 1900–1971, Edinburgh (6 vols)

Catholic Directory, dates indicated in references

Celtic Monthly VI, 1898, 225: 'Dr Alexander Finlayson, Munlochy'

Chaimbeul, Ealasaid (1982) *Air Mo Chuairt,* Stornoway

Chambers, Bob and Shirley (eds), 2012: *A window into life on Mingulay, extracts from the school log book 1875–1910,* Islands Book Trust

Chambers, William (1866) 'My Holiday', *Chambers's Journal* 1866, 632–3 (Berneray)

Cheape, Hugh (1989) 'Shawls and plaids in the Outer Hebrides', *Costume* 23, 1989, 114–9

—— (2008) '"Every treasure you chanced on": Alexander Carmichael and material culture', in D.U. Stiùbhart (ed.) (2008)

Cheke, A.S. and Reed, T.M. (1987) 'The flora of Berneray, Mingulay and Pabbay, Outer Hebrides, in 1964', *Scottish Naturalist* 99, 1987, 63–106

Clark, W.A. (1938) 'The flora of the islands of Mingulay and Berneray', *Proceedings of the University of Durham Philosophical Society* X, 1938, 56–70

Collectanea de Rebus Albanicis, Iona Club 1839

Comunn Eachdraidh Bharraigh agus Bhatarsaigh (CEBB) (Barra and Vatersay Historical Society) (1994) *Mingulay, an Island Guide,* Castlebay

—— (1993) *Tales, Songs, Tradition, from Barra and Vatersay* (recorded from Nan MacKinnon), Castlebay

Congested Districts Board *Annual Reports* 1899–1912 (published in *Parliamentary Papers*)

Cooper, Derek (1985) *The Road to Mingulay: a View of the Western Isles,* London

County Medical Officers *Annual Reports for Inverness-shire,* 1892–, Inverness (see NRS)

Crawford, Barbara E. (1987) *Scandinavian Scotland,* Leicester

Day, J.P. (1918) *Public Administration in the Highlands and Islands of Scotland,* London

DEFRA http://jncc.defra.gov.uk/protectedsites/sacselection/sac.asp? EUcode=UK0030364 (East Mingulay SAC)

de l'Hoste Ranking, D.F. (1904) 'The Island of Barra, past and present', *Celtic Monthly* 12, 1904, 175–7, 202–4

Diamond, A.W. (1965) 'Notes on the birds of Berneray, Mingulay and Pabbay', *Scottish Birds* 3, 1965, 397–404

Dunn, Rob and Grant, Jonathan (2015) 'Mingulay and Pabbay seabird monitoring report 2015' unpublished report, National Trust for Scotland

Earle, Ferdia (2010) 'Climbing on Pabbay' *Scottish Islands Explorer*, September/October 2010

Edinburgh Evening News, 'The Vatersay Squatters in Court Today', 2.6.1908

Edwards, Marion (1981) 'An Archaeological Survey of Pabbay, Barra', unpublished BA dissertation, Department of Archaeology, University of Durham

Elwes, H.J. (1869) 'The bird stations of the Outer Hebrides', *The Ibis* 1869, 20–37 (Mingulay and Berneray)

Foster, Patrick, and Krivanek, R. (1993) The Anglo-Czech survey of the island of Berneray in the Outer Hebrides, Scotland', *Archeologickce rozhledy* XLV, 1993, 418–27

Gaelic Schools Society: *Annual Reports* 1811–1845, Edinburgh (Barra sections reproduced in J.L. Campbell (ed.) 1936)

Geddes, George (2012) St Columba's Roman Catholic Chapel and presbytery, Miùghlaigh. Unpublished report for the National Trust for Scotland. RCAHMS WP003814

—— (2013) St Columba's Roman Catholic Chapel and Presbytery, Miùghlaigh, Report 2, Survey. Unpublished report for the National Trust for Scotland. RCAHMS WP003813 (includes John MacKinnon's house and mill)

Geikie, Archibald (1865) *The Scenery of Scotland*, Edinburgh

Giblin, C. (1964) *The Irish Franciscan Mission to Scotland*, Dublin

Gilbertson, David, Kent, M. and Grattan, J. (1996) *The Outer Hebrides, the last 14,000 years*, Sheffield

Glasgow Herald, details given in references

Goodrich-Freer, A. (1902) *Outer Isles*, London (Mingulay pp. 394–404)

Gordon, Seton (1937) *Afoot in Wild Places*, Edinburgh

—— (1950a) 'A half-forgotten tragedy of the sea' *Country Life*, 30 June 1950 (Pabbay)

—— (1950) *Afoot in The Hebrides*, Edinburgh

Grant, I.F. (1961) *Highland Folk Ways*, London

Hale, Alex (2004) 'An archaeological survey of the island of Mingulay', *Scottish Archaeological News* Spring 2004, 16

Hall, James (1807) *Travels in Scotland*, London

Harden, Jill (2011) 'Mingulay School & Schoolhouse: a conservation statement' Unpublished report for the National Trust for Scotland

Harman, Mary (1997) *An isle called Hirte, history and culture of the St Kildans to 1930* Maclean Press

Harvie-Brown, J. A. and Buckley, T.E. (1888) *A Vertebrate Fauna of the Outer Hebrides*, Edinburgh (Mingulay and Berneray lxxvii–lxxxiii, and under individual species)

Historic Scotland (1994) *The Ancient Monuments of the Western Isles*, Edinburgh

Hunter, James (1976) *The Making of the Crofting Community*, Edinburgh

Inverness Courier, details given in references

Islands Book Trust (2006) *The decline and fall of St Kilda, proceedings of an international conference to mark the 75th anniversary of the evacuation of St Kilda*, Port of Ness

Jehu, T.J. and Craig, R.M. (1925) 'Geology of the Outer Hebrides part 1: the Barra Isles', *Transactions of the Royal Society of Edinburgh* 53, 1925, 419–441

John O'Groat Journal details given in references

Johnson, Samuel (1775) *A Journey to the Western Islands of Scotland*, London (1924 edition, Oxford)

Jolly, William (1883) 'The Nearer St Kilda: Impressions of the Island of Minglay', *Good Words* 1883, 716–720

MacCulloch, John (1824) *The Highlands and Western Isles of Scotland*, London (4 vols) (Barra sections reproduced in J.L. Campbell (ed.) 1936)

McDonald, Allan (1903) 'The Norsemen in Uist Folklore', *Saga Book of the Viking Club*, III, 1901–1903, 413–433 (includes Mingulay place names)

——(1958) *Gaelic Words and Expressions from South Uist and Eriskay*, Dublin (edited by J.L. Campbell)

MacDonald, Donald (1978) *Lewis: a History of the Island*, Edinburgh

MacDonald, James (1811) *General View of the Agriculture of the Hebrides*, Edinburgh

MacDonald, J.M. (1937) *Highland Ponies and some Reminiscences of Highland Men*, Stirling

MacDonald, Michael (2012a): 'Recalling the church and school on Mingulay' *Scottish Islands Explorer* Nov/Dec 2012, 46-8

——(2012b) *The church and Mingulay* Island Note 37, Islands Book Trust

——(2012c) 'Church Life on Mingulay' http://www.rcdai.org.uk/

MacDonald, R. (1978) 'The Catholic Gaidhealtachd' in D MacRoberts, 1978: *Modern Scottish Catholicism*, Edinburgh

MacGillivray, William (1830) 'On the birds of the Outer Hebrides', *Edinburgh Journal of Natural and Geographical Science*, 1830 II

MacGregor, Alasdair A. (1929) *Summer Days among the Western Isles*, Edinburgh

——(1934) *The Haunted Isles*, Edinburgh

——(1967) *The Enchanted Isles*, London

—— (1971) *Islands by the Score*, London (Mingulay pp. 126–153; illustrations)

McKay, Margaret M. (ed.)(1980) *The Rev. Dr. John Walker's Report on the Hebrides of 1764 and 1771*, Edinburgh

MacKenzie, Archibald (1983) The MacKenzies' *History of Christmas Island*, Ontario

MacKie, E.W. (2007) *The Roundhouses, Brochs and Wheelhouses of Atlantic Scotland c.700 BC–AD 500*, BAR British series 444(II), 444(1), 2 V. Oxford

MacKinnon, Mairi Ceit, 'The Church of Our Lady, Star of the Sea' www.barracatholic.co.uk

MacLellan, Angus,(1961) *Stories from South Uist*, London (translated and edited by J.L. Campbell)

MacNeil, Calum (2008) 'Carmichael in Barra' in D.U. Stiùbhart (2008)

MacNeil, Catriona (1988) *Only the Sunny Days: Memories of a Barra Childhood*, Glasgow

—— (1992) *Mo Bhrogan Ura*, Glasgow

MacNeil, S.R. (1979) *All Call Iona Home*, Antigonish, Nova Scotia

MacPherson, John (1768) *Critical Dissertations on the Origin, Antiquities . . .of the Ancient Caledonians*, London

Macquarrie, Alan (1989) *Cille Bharra, The Church of St Finbarr*, Droitwich (covers Early Christian, Norse, and later medieval periods in Barra)

MacQueen, Edward (1794) 'Parish of Barray', *Statistical Account of Scotland*, vol XIII, 326–342 (reproduced in J.L. Campbell (ed.) 1936)

MacRury, John (1894) 'The birds of the Island of Barra', *Annals of Scottish Natural History* 1894, 140–145, 203–214

Mair, Craig (1978) *A Star for Seamen: the Stevenson Family of Engineers*, London

Martin, Martin (1703) *A Description of the Western Islands of Scotland*, London (Barra section reproduced in J.L. Campbell (ed.) 1936)

Mitchell, Arthur, 1880: *The Past in the Present*, Edinburgh

Moisley, H.A. (1966) 'The Deserted Hebrides', *Scottish Studies* 10, 1966

Monro, Donald (1774) *A Description of the Western Isles of Scotland called Hybrides* (c.1549), Edinburgh (Barra section reproduced in J.L. Campbell (ed.) 1936)

Munro, R.W. (1979) *Scottish Lighthouses*, Stornoway

Muir, T.S. (1867) *Barra Head, a Sketch*, Leith (Mingulay and Bemeray; drawings in the 15 copies printed were by hand and details are not consistent)

—— (1885) *Ecclesiological Notes on some of the Islands of Scotland etc*, Edinburgh (reproduces text but not drawings of above)

Murray, Mrs (1888) 'Yachting in the Hebrides', reprinted from *Helensburgh and Gareloch Times,* November 1888 (Mingulay)
Newby, Andrew (2000) 'Emigration and clearance from the Island of Barra, c.1770–1858' *Transactions of the Gaelic Society of Inverness* 61, 2000, 116–148
Nicolson, Alexander (1845) 'Parish of Barray', *New Statistical Account of Scotland,* Edinburgh (reproduced in J.L. Campbell (ed.) 1936)
Oban Times, details given in references
O Lochlainn, Colm (1948) *Deoch-Slàinte nan Gillean,* Dublin
Ordnance Survey: 1:10,560 map sheets LXIX (Pabbay), LXX (Mingulay and Berneray); 1st edition 1880 (surveyed 1878), 2nd edition 1904 (surveyed 1901)
Pankhurst, R.J., and Mullin, J.M. (1991) *The Flora of the Outer Hebrides,* London
Papar Project: http://www.paparproject.org.uk/
Parliamentary Papers (PP); (1844) XXI: 'Minutes of Evidence Taken Before the Poor Law Inquiry Commission for Scotland'
—— (1847) LIII: 'Correspondence . . . related to measures adopted for the relief of the distress in Scotland'
—— (1847–8) XXXIII: 'Second Annual Report of the Board of Supervision for Relief of the Poor (Scotland)' (Appendix B)
—— (1851) XXVI: 'Report to the Board of Supervision by Sir John McNeill on the Western Highlands and Islands'
—— (1867) XXV: 'Report on the State of Education in the Hebrides'
—— (1867) XXVI: 'Statistics Relative to Schools in Scotland'
—— (1867) LXIV: 'Wrecking in the Hebrides'
—— (1884) XXVI: 'Report of the Committee of Council on Education in Scotland 1883–4'
—— (1884) XXXII–XXXVI: 'Report of Her Majesty's Commissioners of Inquiry into the Condition of the Crofters and Cottars in the Highlands and Islands of Scotland'
—— (1890) XXVII: 'Report of the Commission Appointed to Inquire into Certain Matters Affecting the Interests of the Population of the Western Highlands and Islands of Scotland'
—— (1892) LXIV: 'Report of the Crofters Commission for 1891'
—— (1895) XXXVII, XXXIX: 'Royal Commission (Highlands and Islands, 1892)'
—— (1906) CIV: 'Reports . . . on the Burden of the Existing Rates and the General Financial Position of the Outer Hebrides'
—— (1906) CVII: 'Eighth Annual Report of the Congested Districts Board'
—— 1908 LXXXVIII: 'Return of Correspondence . . . with Reference to the Seizure and Occupation of the Island of Vatersay'
—— (1908) LXXXVIII: 'Report . . . of the County Council of

Inverness upon Applications for Allotments in North Uist and
Barra in 1897'

Pochin-Mould, D.D. (1953) *West-Over-Sea*, Edinburgh

Powell, David (2012) 'More than the history of a school: the
Mingulay school log book in context' in Chambers 2012

Proceedings of the Society of Antiquaries of Scotland XXXV, 1900–
1901: 'Proceedings of the Society, May 13, 1901', 276–280

Ratcliffe, D.A. (1977) *A Nature Conservation Review*, Cambridge
(2 vols)

Rea, F.G. (1964) *A School in South Uist: Reminiscences of a
Hebridean Schoolmaster 1890–1913*, London (edited by J.L.
Campbell)

Richards, Eric (1982) *A History of the Highland Clearances*, London

Robertson, J.F. (1964) 'The Glasgow University Exploration Society
Expedition to Mingulay', *Nature* 4953, 1964, 25

RCAHMS (1928) *Inventory of Monuments and Constructions in the
Outer Hebrides, Skye, and the Small Isles*, Edinburgh

——(2010) *Mingulay Archaeology and Architecture* Edinburgh
(broadsheet)

——CANMORE http://www.rcahms.gov.uk/canmore.html

Sanitary Department of the County of Inverness: *Annual Reports*
1891– , Inverness (held by Inverness Public Library)

Scottish Fishermen's Nautical Almanack (1903)

Scottish Natural Heritage (1993) *Information sheet, Mingulay and
Bemeray*

Sergeant, D.E. and Whidbourne, R.F. (1951) 'Birds on Mingulay in
the summer of 1949', *Scottish Naturalist* 63, 1951, 18–25

Shaw, Frances (1980) *The Northern and Western Isles of Scotland:
their Economy and Society in the 17th Century*, Edinburgh

Shaw, Margaret Fay (1993) *From the Alleghenies to the Hebrides: an
Autobiography*, Edinburgh (Mingulay pp. 100–103, illustrations)

Stahl, Anke-Beate (1999) *Place-names of Barra in the Outer Hebrides*
(unpublished PhD thesis, University of Edinburgh)

Stiùbhart, Domhnall Uilleam (ed.) (2008) *The life & legacy of
Alexander Carmichael*, Port of Ness

Storey, Lisa (2007) *Muinntir Mhiughalaigh, Clàr*, Glasgow

Storrie, Margaret C. (1962) Two early resettlement schemes in
Barra', *Scottish Studies* VI, 1962, 71–84

Thomson, Iain R. (2005) *The endless tide*, Edinburgh

Tocher 20 (1975) 'Hook, line, and sickle', 146–164

——38, 1983: 'Nan MacKinnon', 1–48

Walker, John (1764), see McKay 1980

Walker, N. (1895) *Chapters from the History of the Free Church of
Scotland*, Edinburgh

Walker, Theodore (1870) 'Bird-haunts of the Outer Hebrides',

The Zoologist V, 1870, 2073–7, 2113–9, 2163–71; VI, 1871, 2423–9 (Mingulay and Berneray)
Ward, Stephen (2007) 'Living on the edge, an artist on Mingulay', *Scottish Islands Explorer*, May/June 2007
Warwick, T. (1939) 'Animal Life on Mingulay', *Scottish Naturalist* 1939, 127
Wedderspoon, J. (1912) The shell middens of the Outer Hebrides', *Transactions of the Inverness Scientific Society and Field Club*, VII, 1906–1912, 326–335 (paper read 1912)
Weir, Tom (1984) The Curse of St Kilda', *Scots Magazine* 1984, 630–635
West Highland Free Press, details given in references
Wiseman, Andrew (2011) 'Folklore on Mingulay', *Scottish Islands Explorer* May/June 2011, 19–21
——2014: An oral account of the Vatersay raiders http://calumi-maclean.blogspot.co.uk/2014/03/an-oral-account-of-vatersay-raiders_27.html
Withers, C.W.J. (1984) *Gaelic in Scotland 1698–1981*, Edinburgh

Unpublished sources (listed under institution in which they are housed)

Comunn Eachdraidh Bharraigh agus Bhatarsaigh (CEBB) (Barra and Vatersay Historical Society):
Estate document, 1856, giving details of crofters and their stock;
photograph of Mingulay men in Vatersay, R.M.R. Milne, August 1909
Admissions register of Mingulay Public School, 1889–94

Edinburgh University Library (EUL)
Carmichael Watson Archive (also online http://www.carmichaelwatson.lib.ed.ac.uk/)

National Library of Scotland (NLS)
J.F. Campbell collection:
letter H. MacLean to J.F. Campbell, 30.9.1860 (Adv.MS.50.2.1, ff 226–7);
Rory Rum portrait (Adv.MS.50.4.6, f.H9v)

Letterbook of Neil MacPhee of Vatersay, 1909–12 (microfilm copy, Acc. 10688; access restricted)

Business records of Robert Stevenson & Sons ACC 10706:
10706/93: Reports on Northern Lighthouses 1830–37
10706/223: travelling journal of David Stevenson

National Records of Scotland (NRS)

AF 17: Fishery Board records. AF17/156, /157, Stornoway Fisheries Office records, from 1888

AF 42: Congested Districts Board records, relating to the derrick (AF42/146,7833, /1580), and to the settlement of Vatersay (numerous files, given in references)

AF 50: Royal Commission on the Highlands and Islands, 1883. AF50/7/5, details of crofts and stock

AF 56: Scottish Office Fishery Files; AF56/225, petition for landing facilities in Mingulay, 1896

AF 67: Scottish Office Crofting Files. AF67/134, /135, /136, /137, relating to raiding and settlement of Vatersay

CH3/1428/20: Ladies' Highland Association Annual Reports 1854–1877

CS44/B446: Estate of Barra rental 1810–11

CS46/4274: Roderick MacNeil of Barra . . . Sederunt Books 1836–7. Includes Estate of Barra rental 1836–7, letter Mr Shaw to Mr Barstow, 17.11.1836

HH 58: Scottish Home and Health Department, infectious diseases. HH58/6 includes typhoid on Mingulay, 1894

HH 62: Scottish Home and Health Department, County Medical Officers reports from 1892

LC 15: Scottish Land Court records. LC15/2/13, applications for rent reductions, details of croft improvements, 1887

LC15/528, details of crofts and arrears, 1891

NLC: Records of the Commissioners of Northern Lighthouses (Northern Lighthouse Board), minute books, reports

RH4/23/106: Ordnance Survey Object Name Book, Barra Parish, 1878

RH 21: Roman Catholic Diocese of Argyll and the Isles records. RH21/50/1, /2, /3, registers of baptisms, marriages and deaths (Craigstone), 1805 onwards

RH21/50/4, account book of Fr Angus MacDonald, Craigstone, 1818–22

RHP 44187: plan of Barra Parish, 1861–3, by Otter and Edye, scale approx. 1:15,000 (Admiralty Chart)

SC29/44/22: will of Neil MacNeil, 1885

SC29/75/3: School Board of Barra Minute Book 1873-84

VR 103: valuation rolls, Inverness-shire, 1855 onwards

Former General Register Office for Scotland:
Census enumerators' returns, 1841–1911
Registers of births, marriages and deaths, 1855 onwards
Church of Scotland register of baptisms, Barra Parish, 1836–54

National Trust for Scotland Archives (NTSA)
Mingulay documents:
DA/9/3/1: copies of legal documents 1929-38
DA/9/3/2: 'Life on Mingulay' a biography of J.H. Russell by Mr
    Lambie
R.M.R. Milne album of photographs 1909

National Trust for Scotland Canna House Archives (NTSCHA)
CH2/3/52: Map of Mingulay with placenames (partly reproduced in
    J.L. Campbell 2000
Fr Allan McDonald's diary 1897–8 (library no. 519) (partly repro-
    duced in M. MacDonald 2012
MF Shaw photographs 1932

**Royal Commission on the Ancient and Historical Monuments of
    Scotland (RCAHMS)**
Plan of Bara-Head or the Island of Bernera . . .1829 C72316
Field notebook, Barra Parish, 1915

Royal Museum of Scotland (RMS)
Harvie-Brown Collection:
letters of John Finlayson to Harvie-Brown: 4.10.1888, 26.7.1889,
    9.3.1892, 17.10.1892, 27.2.1897, 24.8.1899, 27.4.1903, one
    undated
letters of Morag Campbell Finlayson to Harvie-Brown, 13.8.1904,
    7.4.1905 (both box 20, file 329)
letter of William Norrie to Harvie-Brown, 25.2.1889 (box 37, file
    628)
Harvie Brown's journal, 16.7.1887.

Scottish Ethnological Archive (SEA)
Alasdair A. MacGregor collection of photographs: Mingulay,
    1948–9 (C15083–15104)

St Andrews University (SAU)
Robert M. Adam collection of photographs: Mingulay, June 1905,
    July 1922: Berneray June 1905, July 1907

School of Scottish Studies (SSS)
Tape recordings of Mingulay people made in 1960: SA 1960/89,192,
    /93, /94,795, /96, /97, /98,/99,/100, /101; SA76/175 (Nan
    MacKinnon)
Place name tape PN 1976/9
Robert Atkinson collection of photographs: Mingulay 1950

Scots College, Rome (SCR)
Letters of Fr Neil MacDonald to Fr Angus MacDonald, 13.7.1828,
12.1.1830, 4.3.1831 (reproduced in part in J.L. Campbell 1990)

South Uist Estate Archives (SUEA)
Gordon Cathcart Estate Archive:
Duplicate Chartulary 1 Barra & South Uist 1876–97
Estate factors' letterbooks, 1901–5,1909–12

Tasglann nan Eilean Siar (TES) (Western Isles Archives)
GB CL IN4/45: logbook of Mingulay Public School, 1875–1910
    (held in Castlebay Public Library; also available online)
GB CL IN4/1/R.334–5 minute book of Barra School Board,
    1888–1918

In private hands:

School library lending register 1907 onwards
Letters of 'uncle' John Finlayson to Mingulay John's brother,
    Alexander
Notes on the Chapel House, D.E. Baird, 28.8.1960

Appendix 1

Population table for the southern islands and Barra

	Mingulay	Berneray*	Pabbay	Sandray	Vatersay	Barra**
1764	52	20	16	40	104	1,097
1794	8	3	3	9	–	–
(families)						
1841	113	21 (30)	25	14	84	1,977
1851	114	28 (44)	10	10	64	1,624
1861	145	20 (33)	14	9	32	1,569
1871	144	20 (38)	24	7	17	1,751
1881	150	21 (56)	16	10	19	1,854
1891	141	17 (36)	13	4	32	2,125
1901	135	10 (17)	11	3	32	2,417
1911	11	0 (5)	5	0	288	2,311

— not recorded (1794)

Figures include persons recorded as 'temporarily absent', and exclude those 'temporarily present' between 1861 and 1901; but see * below (applies to Mingulay and Barra only). Numbers present on census night in Mingulay, if different, were: 1861: 139; 1871:141; 1891:142.

* Figures in the first column are residents; those in brackets are totals including lighthouse keepers, and fishermen staying temporarily (the latter not regarded as 'temporarily present' there, or 'temporarily absent', in the case of Mingulay men, from Mingulay).

** Figures for Barra Parish as a whole between 1801 and 1831: 1801: 1,925; 1811: 2,114; 1821: 2,303; 1831: 2,097

Appendix 2

'Song to the Isle of Mingulay'

This song was composed by Neil MacPhee of Mingulay (Niall Chaluim Dhòmhnaill, 1874–1927) many years after the desertion of the island. The emotions contrast starkly with those he expressed in his letters at the time of the desertion, though of course the circumstances and purpose of these were quite different. Still, one feels that time has healed the wounds of the suffering the people endured in Mingulay in their last years there.

'Oran do Dh'eilean Mhiulaidh'	'Song to the Isle of Mingulay'
Bidh m' aigne fhèin a' gabhail reug	My mind takes a trip,
Air siubhail sgèith mo smaointinnean,	Travelling on the wings of my thoughts,
Ag aiseag spèis o ghrunnd mo chlèibh	Conveying esteem from the bottom of my heart
Gu sgeireag èidich aonaraich	To a stormy lonely rock
Far an tug mo mhàthair ghràidh	Where my beloved mother
A dh' àireamh chlann nan daoine mi,	Brought me into the circle of humankind
Is far an iarrainn fois a' bhàis	And where I would desire the tranquillity of death,
Nam biodh e 'n dàn dhomh fhaotainn ann.	If it were my fate to receive it there.
Chunnaic mise 'n càbhlach èisg	I have seen the fishing fleet
A falbh 's am brèidean sgaoilt' orra,	Proceeding with sails spread,
A tolladh slige ghorm nan speur –	Piercing the blue shell of the sky –
Cha bhreug tha sin ged shaoilear e:	No lie that though it may seem so:
Cha robh san àm mo fhradharc fann,	My eyesight then was not faint,
'S cha sealladh meallta draoidheachd e	And no deceiving bewitched sight was it
Ach rud a bh' ann 's a bhitheas ann,	But something that was and shall be,
Is chì a' chlann dhiubh daonnan e.	And the children shall always see it.

280

'S tric a dh'èisd mi gàir nan
   tonn
Ri cladach lom nan caolasan,
Is m' aigne fhèin cho rèidh ri phong
'S mo chridhe trom a' smaointinn air
A liuthad car a chaidh den t-sruth
On chruthaicheadh an saoghal seo
Air ais 's air aghaidh gus an-diugh,
Is fuaim a ghuth gun chaochladh air.

'S tric air feasgar Chèitein chiùin,
'S gun leam ach speil de dh'fhaoileagan,
A shuidh mi greis gun mòran suim
Air binneag druim na h-aoineige;
An àm don ghrèin bhith dol sa chuan,
Bu mhaiseach snuadh a h-aodainn
   leam,
'S ged rinn i mìle mìle cuairt,
Cha tainig tuar na h-aois' oirre.

Leam bu mhiann bhith 'g amharc uam
Air madainn fhuaraidh Fhaoilleachail,
A gabhail beachd air neart nan stuadh
Bu ghreannach, gruamach, caoir-ghealach,
A' cur nan car dhiubh, tè mu seach,
Len cìrein geal 'nan laomannan,
A' nighe cas nan creagan glas
'S a' froiscadh as a' mhaoraichc,

Bhiodh druim a' chuain bu cholgach stuadh
Gu sgolbach duaichnidh braois-thonnach,
A sròlachadh suas on aigeal chruaidh
Gu colbhach, cruachach, craobh-steallach;
Gu molach, borb, dubh-ghlas is gorm,
Gu bronnach, bolgach, craos-ghealach,
Le luasgadh dian nam mìltean
   sian
O linntean cian an t-saoghail seo.

An siud bidh dùbhlan borb na h-iarmailt
Gun chuibhreach, srian no taod oirre,
Ag iomairt neart 's a' marcrachd sian
Air sgiathan fuar nan gaothannan;

Often have I listened to the roar of the
   waves
On the bare shores of the sounds,
And my thoughts so attuned to its note,
And my heart heavy thinking of it –
How many turns the tidal stream has made
Since the world was created,
backwards and forward to this day,
And the sound of its voice never changing.

Often on a calm evening in May,
Alone but for a flock of seagulls,
Have I sat without any thoughts
On the peak of the moorland ridge;
At the time of the sun dipping into the ocean,
Beautiful was the appearance of her face to
   me,
And despite her thousands of rounds,
She does not appear aged.

Great my desire to look afar;
On a cold January morning
Noting the power of the waves,
So forbidding, gloomy and white-tipped,
Rolling one after the other
With their white crests in great groups,
Washing the base of the grey rocks
And shaking off the shellfish.

The open ocean with raging waves,
Divided, fearsome, wide-open waves,
Flowing up from the sea bottom,
Streaming, peaked, spouting;
Stormy, fierce, dark-grey and dark blue,
Bellied, pressing out, white at opening,
With the intense movement of thousands
   of aeons
Since the early centuries of this earth.

There the fierce challenge of the elements
Without chain, bridle or halter on it,
Conveying strength and riding the elements
On the cold wings of the winds;

An dealan lùb-chlischritheach geur
A' lasadh speur nan craoslaichean,
'S an tàrneanach a' tighinn 'na dhèidh,
Toirt Mòrachd Dhè gum
 smaointinnean.

The sudden bending shiver of the lightning
Setting the skies aglow in belts
And the thunder following,
Bringing the Majesty of God to my
 thoughts.

Den teachlach ghreadhnach shuidh gach
 oidch'
Mun chagailt cruinn – bha naoinear
 ann –
Chan eil an-diugh air lom an tuinn
Ach mise caoidh' nam aonaran.
Tha 'n tràthach gorm mun teinntean
 fuar,
Gun beò mun cuairt ach caoraich air,
Is luchd mo ghràidh 'nan seòmar
 suain
Is glasan buan an aoig orra.

Of the joyful family who sat each
 night
Round the hearth – there were nine of
 them –
There are not today alive
But I alone lamenting;
The green grass is about their fireplaces
 cold,
With sheep alone alive around them,
And my beloved folk in their chamber of
 slumber,
The eternal fetters of death on them.

Tha chreagan corrach, sgorach, ciar,
Is trusgan liath na h-aois orra,
Ag èirigh suas mar bhalla-dìon
An aghaidh sian nam Faoillichean.
Ged thug gailleann gart
 is greann
Air barr nam meall 's nam maolaidhean,
Tha cluaintean fasgach 'n
 achlais bheann
Is dreach an t-samhraidh daonnan orr'.

Its rocks unstable and with clefts dark grey,
The grey garment of age on them,
Rise up like a protecting wall
Against the elements of winter.
Though storm has wrought bareness and
 surly scowl
On the peaks and brows,
There are sheltered meadows within the
 arms of the bens
With the bloom of summer even on them.

San luchar Shamhraidh bhiodh am bàrr
Le cinneas fàs air raonaidhean,
'Na bhanndail uaine dualach àrd
Le cuisle làn gu laomadh air;
Bhiodh eòrna 's coirc' na curachd thràth
Gudiasach, grànach, craobhagach,
Is duilleag ghorm air a' bhuntàt'
'S am flùr bàn air sgaoileadh air.

In the heat of summer the crops
Would be growing in the fields
In green clumps with high strands
And veins full to overflowing;
Barley and oats of the early sowing
Eared, grained, spreading,
With green leaf on the potato
And the white flower spreading on it.

Translation into English
by Roderick MacNeil

Appendix 3

'Neil's Trip to Mingulay' *('Turas Nèill a Mhiùghlaigh')*

This song concerns the adventure of Niall Mòr Mac Nèill 'Ic Iain Bhain' ('Big Neil son of Neil son of Fair John') of Mingulay. He was in Castlebay while on his way home after working at the barley harvest in the Lowlands. He had been drinking with some other Mingulay people with whom he was to return to the island, but he left early in the morning without them, and in no state to control a boat. The boat drifted south and, luckily for Neil, landed on Sgeir Leehinish, a rocky islet off the south coast of Sandray. By a further stroke of fortune, he was spotted by some fishermen working out of Castlebay, who rescued him and put him ashore at Sandray. The boat drifted away, with 'Hector's jacket that he had only worn for part of a Sunday', and Neil was concerned about earning the money to repay the boat's owner, ?Donald Campbell. None of the characters in the song are definitely identified.

The song was composed by Father Allan MacLean, known locally as *Sagart Beag no Spàinne,* 'the Curate of Spain', as he had been at the Scots College at Valladolid. He was priest or curate at Craigstone, Barra, from 1837 to 1840, and known to be a composer of songs. He may have composed it at this period, but there are clues suggesting it may have been later. MacLean was subsequently a curate in South Uist until 1850, and later emigrated to Cape Breton, Nova Scotia, where he died in 1872.

The song was put in the mouth of the person involved in the event, a common practice in Gaelic, and the tune is a well-known one. This version was recorded from Ealasaid Sinclair of Mingulay (SSS SA 1960/97 B4; the song, with the title used here, was also recorded from John Johnston and published by Colm Ò Lochlainn in 1948). The song is still known in Barra today.

Turas Nèill a Mhiùghlaigh

(Is) Och mar tha mi, is mi nam aonar,
Dol throimh na caolais far robh mi
    eòlach:
Cho moch 's a dh'fhalbh mi gun bhiadh
    gun ùrnaigh –
'S e thug mo thur asam sugh an
    eòrna.

A-null aig Sanntraigh bha 'ghaoth an
    ceann oirnn:
Gun do leum an crann a-mach a broinn
    na bròige.
Mur a biodh Sgeir Lìthinnis gu robh mi
    millte;
Ged a fhuair mi innte bha
    m'inntinn brònach.

Bha Eòghain Stiùbhart e fhèin fo chùram ...
Gu robh e 'n duil gur e bh'unnam bòcan,
'S mi cho dùrachdach air mo ghlùinean
'S mi gabhail m'ùnaigh, 's ann dhomh bu
    chòir e.

Bha Iain Caimbeul na dhuine làidir:
Cha robh e sgrathail [sgàthail], bu bheag
    a chòir ris.

Neil's Trip to Mingulay

Alas for my state, my solitary state,
Sailing through the narrows I knew so
    well:
I left so early without breakfast
    or prayers –
And what deprived me of my wits was
    John Barleycorn.[1]

Across by Sandray the wind was
    against us:
The mast leapt out of its place in
    the step.
But for Sgeir Lìthinnis I would have been
    destroyed;
Though I got ashore there my mind was
    full of misery.

Hugh Stewart himself got agitated,
Because he took me for an evil spirit,
While I was so devoutly on my knees
Saying my prayers, as well I
    might.

John Campbell was a mighty man:
He had no fear, it was hardly
    his way.

'S e thuirt e: 'Stiùiribh i null ga
  h-ionnsaigh,
'S e th'ann ball-bùrta rinn Mac
  an Tòisich.'

What he said was: "Steer her over towards
  it:
What's there is someone whisky has made
  a fool of."

Nuair a thug iad mi null a Shanntraigh,
Bha mi cho fann 's gum bu ghann bu bheò
  mi:
Na daoine ciatach a bh'ann thug biadh
  dhomh –
Nar fhaiceadh Dia iad am pian no 'n
  dòrainn.

When they brought me across to Sandray,
I was so weak I was scarcely
  alive:
The fine people there gave me
  food –
May God never see them in pain or
  sorrow.

Tha na Caimbeulaich orm-sa 'n diombadh:
Chan eil sin leam-sa na ghnothach neònach.
Móran euchdan ac' innt' le chèile:
Mam pàidh mi 'n éirig gu dè nì m'eòrna?

The Campbells are angry with me:
This is not something that surprises me.
They had done great deeds in her [the boat]:
By the time I pay her ransom what good
  will my barley [money] do?

Nuair a thig a' samhradh théid mi gu
  Galldachd
A thoirt na calldachd a ceann gach
  ròpa:
Ged a b'ann sa Ghearmailt a gheibhinn-s'
  airgead,
Cha lig mi 'm meanbh-chrodh air falbh le
  Dòmhnall.

When summer comes I'll go to the
  Lowlands
To pay the damages due on every rope
  [of her];
Even if I have to earn my money in
  Germany,
I won't let my sheep be taken away by
  Donald.

Tha mac Iain Mhìcheil na ghille sìobhalt':
'S math cho dileas 's a bha e dhòmh-sa.
'S ann a gheibh sinn bàta ni feum na h-àite:
A chaoidh cha phàigh thu bonn fàrdainn
  dhòmh-sa.

Iain Mhìcheil's son is a well-behaved lad:
I'm glad he has been so loyal to me.
We'll find a serviceable boat in her place:
You'll never have to pay me a farthing.

1. Literally 'the juice of the barley.'

Transcribed and translated into English by
Alan Bruford and Donald Archie MacDonald.

Appendix 4

The following are those Mingulay people recorded on tape by the School of Scottish Studies in 1960, who are referred to in the text:

Mary Campbell (maiden surname MacNeil; Màiri Aonghais Nèill Bhig), born 1887, family moved to Castlebay sometime after her mother's death in 1898, and to Vatersay about 1908 (SSS SA 1960/89, /98, /99, /100). (Her father appears in plate 24.)

Catherine MacNeil (maiden surname MacLean; Catrìona Iain Chaluim; plate 6), born 1892, moved to Vatersay in 1910 (SSS SA 1960/94, /95).

Roderick MacNeil (Ruairidh Iain Sheumais), born 1882, moved to Sandray in 1908, then to Vatersay in 1909 (SSS SA 1960/94, /96).

Michael MacPhee (Mìcheal Dhòmhnaill Dhòmhnaill), born 1885, moved to Vatersay in 1907 (SSS SA 1960/92, /96).

Ealasaid Sinclair (Ealasaid Iain Dhunnchaidh), born 1885, moved to Vatersay in 1907–8 (SSS SA 1960/93, /97, /98, /101).

Appendix 5

Plan of Mingulay Village

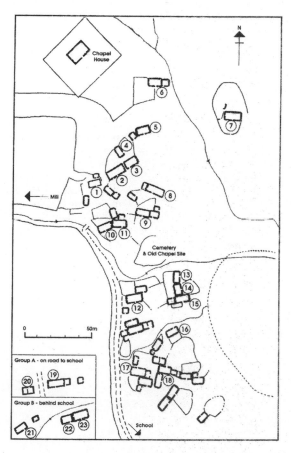

The numbers refer to the list of names, in English and Gaelic, of the last occupants of the houses, where known. (Reproduced from *Mingulay, an island guide Comunn Eachdraidh Bharraidh 1994. Names researched by Mary Kate MacKinnon and John Alan MacNeil; map surveyed by Ben Buxton*)

1. John MacKinnon — Iagan Dhòmhnaill Nèill
2. John MacNeil — Iain Sheumais
3. Anne MacNeil — Anna Ruairidh, John MacNeil's widowed mother
4. Hector MacNeil — Eachann Ruairidh
5. Donald MacNeil — Dòmhnall Mòr a' Bhocain
6. John Finlayson — schoolmaster 1859–1897
7. Original school (later a house)
8. Michael MacNeil — An Rìgh
9. Effie & Catherine MacNeil — Rìgh's aunts
10. John MacLean — Barnaidh
11. Calum MacLean — Cadaidh, John MacLean's father
12. John Gillies — Iain Nèill
13. John Campbell — Iain Ruairidh
14. Angus MacNeil — Aonghus Beag
15. Angus MacNeil — Aonghus Nèill Bhig
16. Michael MacLean — Am Beanachan
17. Calum MacPhee — Mac Dhòmhnuill Mhoir
18. Donald MacPhee — Mac Dhòmhnuill Mhoir
19. John Sinclair — Iain Dhunnchaidh
20. Donald MacPhee — Dòmhnall Bàn
21. Donald MacDonald — Dòmhnall Nèill Chaluim
22. Donald MacNeil — Dòmhnall Aonghuis
23. Angus MacNeil — Aonghus Dhòmhnaill, Donald MacNeil's father

Appendix 6

Notable dates, 1549–2000

1549 first mention of Mingulay

1636 Franciscan missionaries begin working in the islands

1807–28 emigrations to Canada

[1833 Barra Head lighthouse built]

1835 the people are evicted for up to a year

1859–71 The Ladies' School

1875 Barra School Board school opens

1881 new schoolroom built

1896 petition for boat landing facilities

[1897 Pabbay boat disaster]

1898 Chapel House built

1901 derrick for landing supplies is installed

1907 raiding of Vatersay begins

1912 last people leave for Vatersay

1912–2000 Mingulay is used for grazing

2000 National Trust for Scotland buys Mingulay, Berneray and Pabbay

Index

Subject headings in the main index exclude Berneray and Pabbay, for which see the separate indexes at the end, but the names of people, organisations and other places mentioned in chapters 15 and 16 are included in the main index.

BERNERAY

St Mary's Chapel 208
school 221–2
seabirds 7–8, 15, 203, 214, 225, 227
sheep 211, 213, 219, 232
Site of Special Scientific Interest 15, 198
Sloc na Beiste 247
Sotan 203
Special Protection Area 15

tallow, sale of 91–2

visitors' accounts 18, 214–20

wind, violence of 12, 224, 225–6

other references to Berneray: 13, 128, 172, 189, 194, 195, 196, 197, 199–200
see also Barra Isles

PABBAY

boat disaster 58–9, 105, 177, 246–8
boats 236, 246–8

cattle 236, 243, 246
chapel, medieval 234, 241, 243
cliffs 233, 248, 250
court cases 77, 244
crofts 244–5, 246
cross-incised slabs 238–9, 241

desertion 244, 249–50
Dunan Ruadh 234, 235–7

Early Christian occupation 32–3, 241–2
education (in Mingulay) 249
emigration 244
evictions 72–5, 244; threatened 78, 188–9
excavations 234–7

families 243–5
feathers, sale of 248
fishing 236, 244–5, 246, 247, 248, 249
font stone 242–3
fowling (on Mingulay) 248

geology 12–13, 233
graveyard 234, 237–8, 240, 241

houses 248–9, 250

landing places 246

marriages, to Mingulay people 48–9

Norse occupation 33, 242

Pabbay, meaning of name 33, 241
peat 240, 246
peat bog 234
Pictish occupation 236–7
Pictish symbol stone 32–3, 239–40
pins, bronze 32, 237, 238, 240, 241
ponies 246
population 243–4, 249–50, 279
prehistoric building 234–5

rent 243–4, 245, 250
rock climbers 199, 200, 250
roofing material from 121
Rosinish 233, 235

sand, development of 16, 234, 240–1
seabirds 233, 236
sheep 235, 236, 241, 243, 246, 248, 250
Sloc Glansich 245
South Uist families 244–5
Steir 246

tailor 244
tallow, sale of 91–2, 246

whisky distilling 129, 245, 248

other references to Pabbay; 18, 77, 189, 194, 195, 196, 197, 199–200
see also Barra Isles